Attitude,
Ego-Involvement,
and
Change

Attitude,
Ego-Involvement,
and
Change

Edited by

Carolyn W. Sherif

Muzafer Sherif

Psychosocial Studies Program
The Pennsylvania State University

John Wiley & Sons, Inc.
New York • London • Sydney

FIRST CORRECTED PRINTING, MAY, 1968

Contributors

Wendell Bell
Professor and Chairman, Sociology Department, Yale University

James Bieri
Professor of Psychology, The University of Texas

John D. Campbell
Research Social Psychologist. Laboratory of Socio-Environmental Studies, National Institute of Mental Health

Lutfy N. Diab
Chairman, Department of Psychology, American University of Beirut, Lebanon

Eugene L. Hartley
Professor of Psychology, City University of New York

O. J. Harvey
Professor of Psychology, University of Colorado

Joseph T. Klapper
Director of Social Research, Columbia Broadcasting System

Bertram L. Koslin
Assistant Professor of Psychology, Princeton University

Charles W. Moskos, Jr.
Associate Professor of Sociology, Northwestern University

Morris Rosenberg
Research Sociologist, Laboratory of Socio-Environmental Studies, National Institute of Mental Health

Carolyn W. Sherif
Associate Professor of Psychology, The Pennsylvania State University

Muzafer Sherif
Professor of Sociology, The Pennsylvania State University

Harry C. Triandis
Associate Professor of Psychology, University of Illinois

Karl E. Weick
Director of Laboratory for Research on Social Relations, University of Minnesota

James O. Whittaker
Professor and Chairman, Psychology Department, North Dakota State University

Preface

This book is the product of generous and expert efforts by many individuals, notably the authors of its several chapters. Most of the chapters were originally presented by the authors at the symposium held at The Pennsylvania State University, May 19–21, 1966, on this problem area. The tasks of the symposium were stated in the following words:

> In a world of rapid social change, problems of attitude and attitude change have come to the foreground. The Symposium is primarily a stock-taking of some of the significant problems and trends in theory and research.

In response to that call, each author was free to focus upon the particular aspect of attitude problems and their study to which he had devoted his theoretical acumen, his research skills, and his energies. After the symposium, Lutfy Diab (of The American University, Beirut) and O. J. Harvey (of the University of Colorado) gave their summaries of extensive research on attitude problems, which are included in this volume as Chapters 8 and 11.

The primary debt incurred by the editors and the readers of this volume is to its contributors, who wrote in the highest spirit of scholarship and dedication to scientific inquiry.

The symposium was made possible by the support of the Administration of The Pennsylvania State University. The insight and effective backing of Kenneth D. Roose, Dean of The College of The Liberal Arts, were responsible for its materialization.

Donald P. Kent, Head of the Department of Sociology, which sponsored the symposium, was helpful from its very inception in contributing to the manifold tasks of its planning and arrangements. Although we regret that his busy professional schedule prevented his participation in the editorial tasks of preparing this volume, we are happy to acknowledge his important part in the actualization of the symposium and, consequently, of this volume.

These individuals participated with distinction as chairmen of the various sessions of the symposium: Estella Scott Johnson of Cheyney State College; S. E. Asch and Dean Peabody of Swarthmore College; Robert C. Williamson of Lehigh University; and Robert E. Clark, George M. Guthrie, Dale B. Harris, Bernard C. Hennessy, Charles M. Lanphier, Richard M. Lundy and George A. Theodorson of The Pennsylvania State University.

For helping with the chores of conducting the symposium and for reading the manuscript and printer's proof, we are indebted to these graduate students at The Pennsylvania State University: John Fleming, Donald Granberg, James Harper, Merrilea Kelly, Michael LaParte, Larry Rogers, and Gian Sarup.

The careful typing of the various chapters of the manuscript was expertly done by Mrs. Doris Sands of State College, Pennsylvania, and Mrs. Betty Frensley of Norman, Oklahoma.

Carolyn W. Sherif
Muzafer Sherif

University Park, Pennsylvania
February 1967

Contents

Part IV

Attitude,
Ego-Involvement,
and
Change

1. Introduction

Muzafer Sherif

Today we are more keenly aware than ever before of the differing beliefs, values, ways of life, and ideologies of various human groups and societies. These differences are reflected in the *attitudes* of individuals belonging to the various groups. Because the differences are frequently revealed in actual and potential conflict, problems of attitude and attitude change are among the most vital and timely in this world of rapid change.

Today, differences in attitudes among various peoples are not issues to be treated with detachment or with the aloofness that represented academic orthodoxy in the past. Diverse groups and cultures have traffic with one another inevitably, whether they like it or not. The modern achievements in communication, transportation, industry, and commerce as well as the instrumentalities of destruction have created mutual dependence among human groups for their livelihood and for their survival.

Therefore, in a very practical way, it does matter how various groups of people conceive *their* ways of life, *their* ways of doing things, *their* stands on the family and on social, religious, economic, and political issues and how they conceive the ways and stands of others. When we talk of these things we are, at the same time, also talking about *attitudes*.

What kind of events are we talking about when we speak of attitudes? We are talking about events in which individuals are influenced by more or less lasting assumptions about their world. We are talking about people who have *premises* and enduring *expectations* about the way the world operates; about people who hold their family in high esteem; about people who view other groups from

1

different *perspectives;* about people who *value* their religion and their country; who have *beliefs* that strengthen their adherence to a political party; who have *convictions* about what is right and what is wrong; about people whose *sentiments* bend them toward this or that person and this or that group, instead of others. When we deal with lasting assumptions, lasting premises, lasting beliefs, lasting convictions, and lasting sentiments, we are dealing with attitudes. All these different terms are within the generic domain of attitude study.

It is clear that these are vital matters to individuals. Today, they are vital topics for everyone. A person's attitudes define for him what *he is,* and what he is *not,* that is, what is included within and what is excluded from his *self-image.* They define what family, what groups, what schools, what political party, what ideology, what religion are his and which ones are not. These are not *momentary* or *transitory* affairs for the human individual. In fact, we find there is a tendency for attitudes to endure even when the problems of the world around us change. I refer, of course, to the general problem of the cultural lag, which is revealed in the area of attitude problems when individuals maintain premises and perspectives for a world that is no longer there, because it has changed while their attitudes have not.

Many terms have been used to refer to what we shall be discussing in this volume. Already, I have spoken of sentiments, perspectives, premises, values, stands, and goals. Perhaps it is well to inquire more specifically into what we mean when we talk about an attitude or about its change.

When we talk about attitudes, we are talking about what a person has *learned* in the process of becoming a member of a family, a member of a group, and of society that makes him react to his social world in a *consistent* and *characteristic* way, instead of a transitory and haphazard way. We are talking about the fact that he is no longer neutral in sizing up the world around him: he is *attracted* or *repelled, for* or *against, favorable* or *unfavorable.* We are talking about the fact that his behavior toward other persons, groups, institutions, and nations takes on a *consistent* and *characteristic* pattern as he becomes socialized. We are talking about his ties, stands, and sentiments regarding the family and toward various social, religious, political, and economic issues. We are talking about the fact that what we see and listen to are selectively chosen from a mass of potential stimulation surrounding the individual. We refer to *how* we see ourselves and others after we have attended to some aspect of the multifaceted world about us.

As all of these examples have implied, a person's attitudes are always inferred from some comparison, some choice or some decision that he makes among alternatives. Such comparisons, choices, or decisions imply a judgment process. That is why there is discussion of the judgment process in various chapters of this book.

But the examples of attitude I have cited show something else. Specifically, when a person's attitudes are involved in an issue, the judgment process is no longer neutral. It is highly charged affectively, emotionally, and motivationally. It is not neutral because it relates to matters touching his cherished relatedness, his stand, his commitment, in short, the stuff of which his very self-identity is composed. This is why the term "ego-involvement" is included in the title of the book and why several of its authors focus their discussions around the concept of self (ego) and the varying importance of its constituent attitudes. When a person reacts to matters related to his attitude, he is not only making a neutral discrimination but an *evaluation* at the same time.

Attitudes relate the individual to aspects of his world as intimate as those pertaining to his friend and family as well as those of the less immediate but nevertheless deeply cherished matters concerning self and other groups, religious issues, economic, political, and other social issues. Attitudes and attitude change are thus problems in several academic disciplines, for example, in psychology, sociology, anthropology, and political science. The area of attitude studies is the central meeting ground where psychology, sociology, political science, and anthropology can discover that they are approaching similar problems. As such it is an ideal problem area in which to develop integrative concepts, theories, and appropriate measurement techniques, utilizing the lessons that each discipline has to contribute to the huge task. The task is too big to be grappled with single handedly by any of these disciplines. Therefore, the most fruitful results of interdisciplinary cooperation may be foreseen in the domain of problems on attitude, ego-involvement, and their change.

Yet, it cannot be said today that the nature of human attitudes is fully understood. It cannot be said that we are agreed on many principles or even on the fundamental topics to be studied. There are still rival theories, and in some quarters attitude problems are scarcely accorded the importance they deserve.

For the reasons briefly mentioned, problems of attitude and attitude change forged themselves to the foreground as an area of concentration for a good many social scientists. Particularly outside the genteel academic surroundings, there is an urgency today about discovering the nature of human attitudes and the principles that govern their

operation. Each day we become more keenly conscious of how far
the social sciences lag behind, while man's knowledge of physical
nature has reached the point that he can destroy the human race.
This danger shall be with us until man also gains the knowledge
for prediction and control over his relationships with his fellow men,
especially in intergroup and international relations. The danger shall
be with us until man develops his evaluative processes, manifested
in his attitudes, so that they are in phase with the actualities of
the world of today, instead of regulating his behavior by attitudes
that reflect the closed systems and blinders of the past.

So, there is an urgency today for breakthroughs in the frontiers
of knowledge about human relationships and attitudes related to
them. Perhaps the stock-taking in this volume will expose some reasons why there is such a fearsome lag in this and other significant
topics of human relations, particularly as these concern the problems
of group-to-group and nation-to-nation relationships.

I may suggest that one reason, among others, for the lag, is the
terrifying insulation that we in each of the different disciplines build
to shut out the sight and sound of the others. In its most extreme
form, we have, on the one hand, the rigor of laboratory experiments
applied to piddling little problems that cannot be considered significant even by the greatest stretch of the imagination. On the other
hand, we have masses of data from surveys of professional pollsters
that are concerned only with a dated business of the day and not
with the underlying processes of attitude formation and attitude
change.

The objective of the symposium where the chapters of this book
were presented and discussed was a stock-taking of the state of theory,
method, and research on attitude and attitude change. In some respects the scope is modest and limited. No claim is made that all
of the major topics of attitude and attitude change are covered. De-
liberately, no effort was made to represent all the rival theories dealing
with problems of attitude and attitude change. The goal did not
include an effort to be an encyclopedic compendium.

The objectives of this book will be conveyed best by reading its
various chapters, written by distinguished and active participants in
the study of attitude, ego-involvement, and attitude change. Thanks
to the high quality of their contributions, the volume is bound to
have an impact on future developments in theory and research.

A brief introductory statement to a volume such as this can easily
have the effect of suggesting a definite set toward each chapter, a
set that may not always be congruent with the author's intentions.

Therefore, this statement closes with a challenge to the reader to look for continuities and for inconsistencies in order to appraise for himself the ragged lines of progress and the gaps of ignorance that characterize our current efforts in attitude theory and research. By such active participation, hopefully some readers of this book may contribute themselves to solving the enormous problems posed by attitudes and their change.

Part I

2. Studies in Attitude Formation: The Development of Health Orientations

John D. Campbell

As a child grows up those around him direct their efforts both intentionally and unintentionally toward the task of shaping him to conform to a particular social mold. At the same time, the child expends part of his energy in smoothing his rough edges that do not fit society's model. But he also chips away at certain portions of the mold that, when tried on for size, prove particularly chafing to the edges of his own individuality. Thus, socialization and personality development move side by side in a fashion far from perfect, yet reasonably effective.

During his social growth, the child naturally learns about many different substantive areas of life, including institutions, events, people, and even the states that he and other individuals experience. In so doing he develops certain underlying predispositions that serve as potentials for his actions. For each such area, the child forms evaluative judgments and acquires standards that define *appropriate* functioning in relation to it. As a result he acts in a particular way when relevant circumstances arise. Together, such underlying predispositions and their consequences for action constitute an individual's *orientations*. These orientations represent clusters of phenomenally related social attitudes with their component beliefs, feelings, values, standards, and performances.

One strategic way to examine personality formation and socialization is, then, to ask the question, "How are these orientations formed?" This is the general issue upon which this chapter is focused. Of course, I cannot deal with all the classes of phenomena toward which the child develops social attitudes. I shall explore facets of just one such area, that concerned with illness and health. The examination of health orientations may, nevertheless, serve as an illustrative review of some general processes in the formation of social attitudes.

To gain an understanding of the development of *any* orientation, we must accomplish several necessary tasks. Three tasks that I view as central are (1) phenomenological assessment, (2) examination of changes that take place in the orientation, and (3) appraisal of factors that may be critical in the development of the orientation. Here I shall give major emphasis to the last of these, namely the influences at work in shaping broad social attitudes. Still the other two warrant our attention initially to provide a necessary perspective. After all, the various facets of an orientation and the changes that take place, either within an orientation or among several, constitute the resultants of various influences associated with their development, the process under scrutiny here. Certainly, consideration of a framework for specifying these complex resultants may avoid an oversimplified view of processes and end products alike.

THE PHENOMENOLOGICAL TASK

Systematic description of the diverse facets of an individual's orientation is a central but sometimes neglected requirement. MacLeod's admonition to the social psychologist has been heeded too infrequently, namely, he should ". . . seek to determine, without regard to conventional attitudinal categories, exactly what there is for the person, what structures with what properties and related in what ways" (1947, p. 202). Such an emphasis on a phenomenological perspective is not, of course, a post-Second World War innovation. It made its appearance earlier in the work of Sherif (1935) and Heider (1944) among others. A still earlier statement of the issue that is appealing to me is Walter Lippmann's (1922). He noted that we as individuals have to act in a complex environment; but in order to manage this we must and do reconstruct the world on a simpler model. "To traverse the world men must have maps of the world. Their persistent difficulty is to secure maps on which their own need, or someone else's need, has not sketched in the coast of Bohemia" (p. 11).

The social scientist must recognize what Lippmann refers to as "the triangular relationship between the scene of action, the human picture of that scene, and the human response to that picture working itself out upon the scene of action" (p. 11). MacLeod has stated the phenomenological question simply as "What is there?" However, the researcher interested in characterizing the social world of the individual can rarely approach the issue from such a broad perspective.

No matter what his intent, at the outset the researcher superimposes some structure on the nature of the world as the subject experiences it. Suppose we wish to study a particular cluster of related social attitudes. If for no other reasons, the need to economize on time and effort leads us almost automatically to restrict the nature of the data to be obtained from each subject. A consideration of the components of an orientation can serve to avoid restrictions that, by definition, prevent satisfactory coverage of the area in question.

Any orientation has cognitive, affective, normative, and behavioral components. These can be illustrated very briefly by examples of such components in children's health orientations, as follows:

(a) The child acquires certain *beliefs and opinions* about health, illness, and health related matters. For example, he develops certain working definitions of illness. He gains information concerning therapeutic processes, hygienic measures, and the like. He formulates his own views or adopts those of others concerning the extent to which the individual is responsible for illness.

(b) In addition, an *affective component* is a part of any individual's health orientation. The child *likes* or *dislikes* aspects of the sick role, *accepts* or *rejects* certain persons in their role as caretakers, has certain feelings about others who are ill or disabled, and so forth.

(c) He acquires standards that constitute the *normative components* of his health orientation. He has views of how he should act when he is ill, of how readily he should accept the sick role, of the extent to which heightened emotionality is appropriate. He also develops notions about the appropriate ways for others to function as patients or as caretakers. He acquires various standards concerned with health maintenance.

(d) In specific situations an orientation is manifested in action, its *behavioral components*. We may note whether the child readily adopts the sick role at the onset of symptoms. We may observe the extent to which he stoically accepts the pain and discomfort of illness and of therapeutic procedures. We may determine the extent to which he carries out certain standards of cleanliness, and so on.

The person's *orientation* toward health necessarily includes the several factors illustrated briefly above. Two qualifying comments are needed. First, the identification of components is by no means new. Second, the aspects of an orientation here described are not neatly isolated one from another; they are inextricably intertwined.

The components of orientations given here are basically similar to classifications of attitudinal components that are frequently used (for example, see Harding, Kutner, Proshansky, and Chein, 1954). One point of difference is worth noting. When attitudes are considered, often that datum representing the individual's performance in a given situation (behavioral component) is not viewed as an integral aspect of the attitude. Indeed a perennially popular research question is "How well do attitudes and behavior fit?" (for example, see Deutscher's recent statement, 1966). This is a perfectly legitimate question, but it is vastly oversimplified. The issue at hand gains deeper perspective when examined within the context of the interrelation between the several components of an orientation.[1] This interrelation is a subject for study and appraisal, not premature simplification.

Although I have mentioned different *aspects* of orientations, these aspects are not separate or even distinct *entities*. There is practical utility in treating them as if they were. This is one strategy for appropriately describing the phenomena that are of central concern. It is as if we were dealing with several maps of the same region. One map presents only elevations, thereby providing one important type of information. Another yields data on the road network, clearly another important type of information. It is evident that there is a relation between these two maps. But it is convenient to have each of these aspects abstracted for scrutiny. The viewer, however, must bear in mind that the elements abstracted are not independent of one another. (Woe be to the traveler who neglects to consider the elevations when plotting his trip by the map of roads.)

EXAMINATION OF CHANGES IN ORIENTATIONS

Once an orientation has been described adequately, the study of the development of an orientation must consider the *changes* in orientations during the course of the child's growth. Two issues of change warrant our attention.

[1] The issue of the degree of correspondence between behavioral and other components of health orientations falls beyond the purview of this chapter. In passing, we may note that the degree of such correspondence is a function of a variety of factors, including attitudinal salience and the nature of the constraints presented by the immediate situation. (See Hartley and Hartley, 1952, pp. 548–552.)

First, there is the need to examine the developmental changes that take place *within a given component* of an orientation. Let us take as an example one of the areas of attitude development that has been studied intensively. In the area of ethnic relations and prejudice in particular, a body of data has accumulated that permits a plotting of the development of a single dimension, awareness of race. The data indicate that such awareness can be detected about the third or fourth year. By the age of five racial awareness is generally well established (Goodman, 1952; Radke and Trager, 1950). When studying health orientations, it would be pertinent to inquire in similar fashion about the nature of the child's developing concept of illness and age trends in children's views of various behaviors relevant to health.

Second, there is a need to explore an aspect of developmental changes in orientations that is studied much less frequently. We need to examine the *nature* and *extent* of change in the *patterning of interrelationships* among the components of orientations. A landmark study on the formation of "racial" attitudes provides an illustration. Horowitz (1936) measured the affective components of such attitudes by having white boys indicate their liking of white and Negro children depicted in photographs. Two other tests yielded reports of behavioral dispositions: the boys selected white or Negro companions and indicated whether they would participate in various activities if a Negro child were present. The three tests yielded *three* different developmental curves, suggesting that the course of development was not uniform from one component to another. Further, the intercorrelations among the tests were greater for *older* subjects than for younger. These data demonstrate both developmental changes in single facets of a social attitude (from the separate examination of each growth curve) and the changing interrelationships of orientational components examined over time.

In the development of health orientations there is a comparable need to examine the changing nature of the organization of the components. As yet such an examination has not been made.

ASSESSMENT OF FACTORS SHAPING ORIENTATIONS

At the outset the assessment of variables that may influence the development of an attitudinal orientation was listed as one of three major tasks to gain understanding of the process. The bulk of this chapter on health orientations is directed to this problem. Such influences may be classified usefully along a dimension, the proximity or distance through which a given influence impinges directly on the individual. This proximal-distal dimension is determined relative to the individual and therefore includes both immediate sources of stimulation and intervening sources through which more remote events are channeled.

In dealing with the development of health orientations, I examine three general classes of determinants on this dimension:

(a) At the distal end of the continuum, broad sociocultural factors and pervasive environmental influences.

(b) In the intermediate range, factors concerned chiefly with the nature of social relationships and interpersonal communication.

(c) Proximal factors that may be viewed at a given time as resident in the individual himself.

As prelude to the discussion, let us set the qualifying boundaries. It is difficult (if not impossible) to draw sharp boundaries between proximal and distal influences. The distinctions are a matter of *degree* rather than of kind. Further, let it be clear that no influence functions in isolation from the others. (There is clear consensus that the determinants of social attitudes interact with one another. See Allport, 1961, pp. 180–181; Hartley and Hartley, 1952, p. 714; Krech and Crutchfield, 1948, pp. 182–183; Sherif, Sherif, and Nebergall, 1965, p. 223.) Finally, let me repeat that personal orientations are *resultants* of various influences and that the impact of the various forces at work need not be unidirectional. These various influences and orientations constitute an interactive process. The changed orientations of persons may serve as the causal agents at a given time, leading to modifications of the social world in which these persons function.

In the discussion that follows I examine the impact of single influences viewed to a considerable extent as if in isolation. Such a view risks the danger of oversimplification. Yet, two reasons incline me in this direction, each of them sound. Such a procedure mirrors the approach adopted in many inquiries where investigators have been concerned with the impact of a single independent variable on a single dependent variable. Insofar as the effort has been to strip the phenomenon to its essentials in order to appraise a specific hypothesis, this approach has proven tactically sound. Needless to say, viewing one type of influence at a time serves as a simple way of organizing an array of information about the determinants of health orientations that would otherwise prove cumbersome.

Distal Influences

In noting the influence of factors more distal for the individual on the development of health orientations, my natural inclination as a social psychologist is to concentrate primarily on sociocultural factors, largely ignoring those pervasive nonsocial characteristics of the environment that might make their presence felt. However, logic requires that at least passing attention be paid to the latter, although evidence is scant.

It is true that man may alter much of his physical environment, including many aspects responsible for the occurrence of disease. Yet it is also true that many diseases, though controllable by man's actions, are not themselves *caused* by his actions. The existence of disease-producing vectors, the frequency and the nature of diseases in any society constitute objective elements that people experience and react to. Such attributes of the environment may then be viewed as relevant in shaping opinions and attitudes about illness.

For example, in some parts of South America infant mortality is more than 200 per thousand (Blumberg, 1961). Such a high incidence of infant mortality may well help to determine the outlook on illness of persons living in those regions.

One cannot make a sharp delineation of social and nonsocial factors operating at this level. This is apparent if we reflect on the progress of scientific medicine during the twentieth century. Advances in therapeutic procedures have been widespread. Similarly, there have been major developments in controlling many characteristics of the physical environment that were responsible for illnesses. Thus social processes have changed the nonsocial world.

The changes in the nonsocial world are reflected in attitude changes as well. For example, within the past generation advances in medical science in this country have modified the objective circumstances concerning illness, its frequency, its severity, and its duration. There should, therefore, be a concomitant change in the extent to which illness constitutes a salient attitudinal area, particularly the extent to which it is a major source of anxiety or concern. One evidence of such a change is the information presented by Harris (1959), who compared the attitudes of a sample of American adolescents toward fifteen life problems with the views expressed twenty-two years earlier by a similar group of young people. In 1935, problems of health were rated *second* in importance by the adolescents. Not quite a generation later the appraisal of this issue had changed more than that of any other. It dropped to twelfth place among the fifteen issues considered. Changing times and circumstances brought about marked changes in salience of this area as a problem for young Americans.

There is clear research evidence demonstrating the relationship between sociocultural factors and the various aspects of health orientations. For example, the relation of sociocultural factors to *cognitive* components appears in evidence obtained on over a thousand U.S. Army inductees who responded to the Cornell Medical Index, a health questionnaire to secure reports of the presence of symptoms in a variety of areas. Ethnic background was significantly related to the frequency with which the men indicated the presence of symptoms (Croog, 1961). The differential reports can hardly be attributed to objective differences in symptomatology. All the men in the sample had recently passed both preinduction and induction physical examinations, thus it is reasonable to consider them a population with a generally high health level.

Children's liking or disliking persons with different types of physical handicaps reveals the impact of sociocultural factors on the *affective* component of their health orientations. Across the various geographic regions of this country, there is considerable uniformity in the way children rank a standard set of drawings of children who differ only with respect to physical disability (Richardson, Hastorf, Goodman, and Dornbusch, 1961). However, when the rankings made by Jewish and Italian children were examined, it was clear that they did not hold the same values related to physical appearance as a control group (Goodman, Dornbusch, Richardson, and Hastorf, 1963).

The impact of sociocultural factors on both *normative* and *behavioral* components of health orientations showed up in research concerned with socioeconomic status differences in reported reactions to various symptoms (Koos, 1954). Persons in higher social classes were markedly more likely than those at a lower socioeconomic level to say that the presence of a given symptom should be called to the attention of a doctor. Unfortunately the normative and the behavioral components cannot be considered separately in this instance. In fact, this is generally the case when data derive exclusively from the verbal reports of the subject. Nevertheless, it is highly probable in this case that there would be a strong positive association between what these individuals said they *should* do and what they actually *would* do in such circumstances.

Such terms as *culture, ethnicity,* and *social class* are boxcar concepts. They carry a lot of explanatory freight, but we must look inside to determine the exact nature of the contents. Sizable relations between broad sociocultural factors and the health orientations of individuals are evident in the information I have just reviewed. But there is an accountability gap, a difference between the simple knowledge that such relationships exist and our ability to *describe* the operation of mechanisms that lead to their establishment. The gap is consider-

able. It will not be closed if we fail to ask what variations in basic
conditions of life encountered by persons in different cultures or subcultures might lead to such differences in health orientations as those
reported.

One effort in the direction of closing the gap is research on beliefs
and feelings about tuberculosis. Jenkins (1966) found that Negroes
and whites clearly did not share a common perspective on TB. To
account for the differences in orientation, he offered the central explanatory hypothesis that ". . . the history of a group's experience
with a disease might be a potent determinant of its current perceptions of that disease" (p. 427). Using mortality rates as an index
of the perceptual impact of a disease on social groups, he indicated
that death rates from tuberculosis in Florida over the past generation
have been from two to four times higher among Negroes than among
whites. It is this that may explain the dread and emotional as well
as cognitive involvement that Jenkins found in Negroes' views of
tuberculosis. Perhaps relatively few Negroes have had any personal
experience with TB themselves. The incidence of that illness has de-
clined dramatically since 1940, especially among Negroes. But in view
of past rates and the continuing Negro-white differential, it is not
surprising that Negroes held beliefs and feelings about tuberculosis
differing markedly from those of white Floridians. Jenkins concludes:
"A specific past event need not have happened to a given individual
to mold his perception into a replica of his group's common perception. Thus the collective experience of the previous generation could
influence the perception of the next" (p. 428).

Influences in the Intermediate Range

Jenkins' discussion of the role of general life conditions encountered
by different ethnic groups may serve as a first step forward in consideration of less distal influences, since it represents an effort to
consider intervening links in accounting for the effect of broad social-
structural characteristics upon health orientations. Yet the impact of
general life conditions on a particular member of a given culture
or subculture can be quite indirect. Let us turn now to variations
in social organization and in parental functioning, which are encountered by the individual even more directly. Here we consider such
factors as residing in the intermediate range of the proximal-distal
dimension.

The role played by differences in social organization is the subject
of Suchman's intriguing and satisfying effort (1964) to dig beneath
surface relationships between health orientations and ethnicity. First,

he established the existence of associations between ethnicity and three major areas of medical concern, namely knowledge of disease and its prevention, attitudes toward medical care, and responses to illness. Then he proceeded to demonstrate that the observed relationships were, at least in part, a function of an intermediate-range factor, that is, differences in social organization. The more ethnocentric and cohesive the social group is (the greater the degree of "in-group" identification), the lower was the level of knowledge about disease, the higher the degree of skepticism toward medical care, and the greater the reported dependency when ill. These data show that the form of social organization clarifies differences in the health orientation that might be attributed glibly to ethnic-group membership. Of course, ethnicity, like social class, serves as a factor contributing to parochial or cosmopolitan social organization. However, as Suchman has stated, ". . . it is this latter variable which continues to show the highest and most consistent relationships to health orientation" (p. 328). Thus these research results tend to support a model of a causal sequence that can in this instance best be described as one in which ethnicity leads to differences in social organization, and these in turn lead to differences in health orientation.

Certainly among the most pertinent factors influencing social attitudes are the various specific relationships in which the individual finds himself. During the child's early years, the figures most central for him are undoubtedly his parents. They affect the nature of the child's developing orientations in several ways.

The parent as well as other adults define a perspective on the nature of the social world even though they may not actively intervene with that purpose. Hartley and Hartley made the point as follows: "In early childhood the individual must look to parents and other adults to define objects and situations. Because these adults are likely to be right in many instances, the individual then expects this to be so in all situations, and accepts their way of looking at the social world" (1952, p. 249). Parental attitudes, beliefs, and values are themselves often shaped by sociocultural and general environmental factors. But parents may transmit them, as it were, osmotically without specific intent or conscious attempts at instruction.

Even the general quality of parent-child relationships may be one of the factors contributing to the child's reaction to illness. For example, Prugh and others (1953) have suggested that this is one of the most important variables determining children's reactions to hospitalization. Although I think such an association is plausible, the generalization needs additional hard data to support it.

In serving as role models for the child, parents make a further contribution to the development of his social attitudes. Data from both field studies and laboratory experiments point to the general relevance of such modeling for the acquisition of behavior (Bandura and Walters, 1963). Although little research has been directed to the *ways* in which parents serve as role models in forming children's health orientations, it is likely that they do indeed function as models. As the child grows up he has ample opportunity to note his parents' views and feelings concerning illness, to learn of their health-relevant standards, and to observe his mother and father in both patient and caretaker roles. It is highly probable that some such parental functioning does "rub off" to influence the various components of the child's health orientation.

Certainly the most obvious way that the parent serves to inculcate orientations in the child is along a much more straightforward path. The parent communicates directly his beliefs, attitudes, and standards to the child. The parent reinforces what he deems to be desired behavior in the child. Data from my own current research on the development of health orientations in children are illustrative. The extent to which a child feels that his own actions might have contributed to his ill health, that is the degree to which the child attributes to himself responsibility for illness, is related to his mother's reports of scolding the child for doing things that contributed to his becoming ill.[2] The child's own outlook on this aspect of his health orientation has apparently been subjected to the modifying influence of parental suasion. This is, of course, what one would expect in terms of one of the predominant theories of child development held by many parents and even by some other experts in the field.

Although parents may in fact be entitled to receive much of the credit as well as much of the blame for the broad social attitudes of their children, social science must not be transmuted to social science fiction. This can happen easily if we assume either that broad and general parental training is necessarily a determining factor in the child's response to a particular situation or that parental influences operate independently of forces exerted by other social agents and other situations that may affect the child's developing beliefs, evaluative judgments, standards, and actions.

---

[2] Here and in subsequent portions of this Chapter where I report findings from my study of children's health orientations, the research results derive from preliminary analyses of reports of 80 mother-child pairs, which constitute part of a larger sample of 6-to-12-year-old children and their mothers.

Indeed, Levy (1959), examining children's reactions to hospitalization, found that the extent to which parents trained their children
to respond to *general* stress situations was *not* closely related to their
children's reactions to hospitalization. At the same time, parental training directed at the *specific* stress of hospitalization *did* have a significant impact on the nature of the child's reactions. Another investigator exploring the relation between children's health attitudes and
those of their mothers reached the conclusion based on generally
sound data that ". . . the degree of variance in children's responses
that can be explained by the mothers' responses is *extremely small*"
(Mechanic, 1964, p. 447).

The child selectively responds to the social forces impinging on
him as indeed an adult does too. If parental orientations are consonant
with those of *other* significant reference persons (as is frequently
the case), the probability of the child's adopting parental orientations
is enhanced. Young children may be more receptive to parental influence than older children in part because the parental role is so pervasive in the early years, blanketing nearly every aspect of the child's
life. In addition, life for the young child is full of more perplexing
ambiguities and uncertainties than it is for older children, who have
a greater stockpile of experience from which to draw.

As time passes, the child's social horizons broaden. He has an opportunity to test in the company of his peers certain alternatives to
the views held by his parents. His social attitudes may change accordingly. Surely it is no accident that in my own work on the development of health orientations a comparison of mothers' reported
norms concerning whether it is all right for a child to drink from
a cup used by another or to lick off a friend's ice cream cone with
the children's own reports of whether they actually *do* these things
shows that older children are significantly more likely than the
younger to describe their behavior in a fashion that falls short of
the mothers' expressed standards. The child may have *learned* parental standards in this area, but in the company of his peers he
may also have learned to emancipate himself from them.

The Proximal Determinant: The Self

The nature of the social world in which the child functions—its
stability and change, its consistencies and inconsistencies—has much
to do with the development of his orientations. But the child does
not merely respond passively to external stimulation. He is not simply
a connecting link between extrapersonal factors and behavior. In a
very real sense he is an important and active agent in the development

of his social attitudes as well as in their expression. Allport has stated it as follows: "Whatever tendencies exist reside in a person, for a person is the sole possessor of the energy that leads to action" (1966, p. 2). If this is the case, we must consider the continuing contribution of the self to the individual's orientations.

In a lithograph, "Hand with Reflecting Globe," the contemporary Dutch artist, Maurits Escher, has skillfully depicted the way in which the individual is the center of his own personal world. Gardner has aptly described this picture as follows:

> Escher is seen staring at his own reflection in the sphere. The glass mirrors his surroundings, compressing them inside one perfect circle. No matter how he moves or twists his head, the point midway between his eyes remains exactly at the center of the circle. "He cannot get away from that central point," says Escher. "The ego remains immovably the focus of his world" (1966, p. 121).

This depiction may represent for the philosopher the "egocentric *predicament*," but for the social psychologist I believe it must be viewed as the "egocentric determinant." Whatever the nature of the world, each of us is at the center of his own social space. It is our own apprehension of the world that is incorporated and translated into beliefs, values, and actions. Extrapersonal stimuli impinge on the individual and are rightly viewed as important causal antecedents. But these stimuli operate after they have been subjected to selective and modifying processes within the individual. The self serves as the final screen channeling the course of development of social attitudes.

The notion that we select and interpret the stimuli that we encounter is not a novel one. Even so we often neglect the part that the self as perceiver plays in determining our orientations. If we examine the bulk of contemporary research concerned with the role of the parent in the course of the child's social development, it is obvious that the basic causal assumption being made is this: "What the parent does shapes the child's development." This view is limited by its failure to recognize that the child's own perceptions of his parent constitute a critical selecting and interpreting element in this causal chain.[3]

[3] A recently expressed view comparable to my own is the following: "Only a handful of studies have focused attention on children's perceptions of parental behavior or on children's feelings about and reactions to parents' childrearing methods. There has been widespread failure even to realize that it is not only parental behavior to which the child responds but also to his perception of parental behavior" (Dubin and Dubin, 1965, p. 809).

My own research illustrates the importance of the child's own perspective on parental action as a critical factor in shaping some aspects of his health orientation. Consider the nature of the link between the child's acceptance of responsibility for illness and the possibility of parents' scolding the child for becoming ill. The data indicate that there *is* an association between the mother's report of such scolding and the child's attribution of illness responsibility to himself. However, there is a still stronger relationship between the child's *own* report of having been scolded and his saying that he at times has been to blame for becoming ill. Indeed, the association between the child's report of scolding and his acceptance of personal responsibility for illness remains clear even when one controls for mothers' self reports on whether or not they scolded the child in such circumstances. In a natural social learning situation the rewards and punishments meted out by parents are not entirely free of ambiguity. Under some circumstances, a mother's frown of concern might be interpreted by the child as an indication of disapproval. Shakespeare, naturally enough, put it more felicitously:

> Look how we can, or sad or merrily,
> Interpretation will misquote our looks . . . .
> *King Henry IV*, Part I, V, ii

To reckon without this important function of the self as an interpreter of the events is to neglect one of the most critical determinants of thought and action.

Given the notion of the self as the center of social space for the individual, there are two propositions that can prove helpful in understanding the development of social attitudes in general and health orientations in particular. First, an integral aspect of the development of the self is the individual's development of a relationship to the world about him that is generally consistent and enduring, including the concurrent development of a generally consistent and stable set of social attitudes. Second, with the developing sense of self, the individual is influenced by a tendency to maintain an adequate self-picture in his perception of and response to the social world. The self, perceived as a valued object, is protected and enhanced.

Perhaps much of the stability of the self derives from the generally predictable nature of the world in which the individual functions. However, for the young child every new situation he encounters has considerable ambiguity about it. With the passage of time and increased experience, the growing individual learns the patterned regularities of his physical and social environment. He achieves a stabilized impression of his social world, and concomitantly he achieves a considerable degree of stability in his self-identity.

One aspect of this stability of the self is reflected in the evidence of increased consistency in children's attitudes with age (Horowitz, 1936; Stevenson and Stewart, 1958; Vaughan, 1964; Wilson, 1963). This increased consistency has predictive utility. One can look at certain enduring general values and dispositions of the individual as intervening variables that will aid in interpreting specific aspects of health orientations. For example, even though in our society we typically attach considerable value to self-reliance, there is, nevertheless, variation in the extent to which this attribute is highly prized by particular individuals. Given an emphasis on self-reliance as a stable characteristic of a person and an assumption of intrapersonal consistency, one would expect that such an individual would not be inclined to accept readily the dependent status that illness implies. Such is indeed the case. Research findings indicate that those who value self-reliance highly are the least likely to express a willingness to adopt the sick role (Phillips, 1965). Thus general personal values may influence the expression of more specific orientations.

In the process of socialization we not only achieve a considerable degree of stability of the self-image, we also come to prize that stability. Events that cause a person to lose his bearings in physical or social space can, then, be highly disruptive. Feelings of anxiety, uncertainty, and distress may result when anchorages in one's surroundings are lost, as Sherif and Harvey's (1952) experimental evidence demonstrates.

Placed in the context of illness and health, the onset of illness can be viewed as a departure from a normal stable and valued state. For adult and child alike such a departure is disruptive. In fact, it may be especially disturbing for the younger child, since he lacks information that would provide some degree of clarification and some of the defenses that older children and adults have erected to cope with such circumstances.[4]

Since the self is a generally valued object, a threat to one's health is a threat to personal equilibrium. This general view of the self as a valued object may be one of the factors affecting appraisal of physical symptoms by the individual and what they mean to him. This can be illustrated by one aspect of my own current research

---

[4] Illustrative of this disruptive effect is Barraclough's (1937) observation that younger children often display considerable fear on a first admission to the hospital, a fear that might be attributed to the heightened ambiguity of the circumstances.

on health orientations. As part of our effort to get at definitions of illness, we have asked children to indicate for each of thirteen different symptoms whether, if they themselves had that symptom, they would be ill. We have also asked each child whether his mother would be ill if she had these symptoms. A count of the number of symptoms reported as indicative of illness in the child can be compared with a similar count of the number for which the mother is seen as ill. Such a comparison reveals that the children were significantly more apt to attribute illness to the mother, given these symptoms, than they were to say they themselves were sick. The same pattern, greater attribution of illness to the *other* than to the self, is even more apparent in mothers' responses than in their children's. And, predictably, the trend is markedly more pronounced in *older* than in younger children.

Given the ambiguity of illness onset, it may be both easy and important to deny illness, to preserve the image of health as a valued attribute of the self. To see illness in another person may not be quite as threatening. Obviously this interpretation does not fully explain the responses described, but it does emphasize once again that the concept of the self enters importantly into the shaping of health orientations.

CONCLUDING REMARKS

The issues in the formation of health orientations have been explored only partially here. Yet some guidelines are suggested from the discussion. Let me briefly consider just two such guidelines, emphasizing in some way the complexity of the process with which we are concerned.

There is a continuing need for us to recognize that *any* social attitude has many determinants. This recognition must be reflected both in our conceptualizations and in our research strategies. We must probe beneath the surface of simple relationships to uncover the manner in which several determinants of social attitudes may *interact* with one another. Suchman's (1964) demonstration that, in general, social organization proved a more important determinant of sociomedical responses than mere knowledge of ethnicity or social class is illustrative of one possible approach. Methodological and technological strides in recent years have opened still further a variety of multivariate procedures that should prove helpful in our pursuit of the question, "Why?" Although complexity of design should not be equated with soundness of research approach, we need perhaps to consider whether we have reached a point where continued efforts to verify hypotheses concerning the relation of a single independent to a single dependent variable may no longer be an economical way to advance our knowledge.

Just as we recognize the complexity of causality in formation of social attitudes, we should also note the complexity of the orientations individuals hold. Often research designs with a developmental orientation reflect a single-minded pursuit of causal antecedents of a single specific dependent variable. For example, a series of experiments in social learning might attempt to account for dependent behavior by examining the effects of systematic variations in social stimuli or methods of disciplining or role models. Studies in attitude formation often proceed on much the same lines. For example, an investigator might say in effect: "I'm interested in authoritarian attitudes. Are these influenced by the social structure? Or are they influenced by parental functioning?" In both these examples the focus is on *one* specific dependent variable. The "side effects" of the social learning process are often left out and are not considered.

Yet the logic of considering such side effects is reasonable enough. To the extent that the components of social attitudes constitute an interrelated system, it is possible that modifying one part of that system may modify other components of that system as well whether one wishes it or not. This can be illustrated with further information from my own study of health orientations.

Consider the possible impact of parental scolding on two aspects of the child's orientation. When mother and child agree that the mother has scolded the child for becoming sick, the child is much more likely to attribute to himself some degree of responsibility for illness than when child and mother agree that there has been no such parental scolding. Thus, if a parent's main aim is to persuade the child that to avoid illness he should guard against infection, eat correctly, and so forth, this parent may feel our findings provide evidence that a little judicious scolding when next the child is ill may produce the desired results. However, before anyone adopts this guide to action, it might be well to note the following: the proportion of children who say that when they are ill, they *worry* about it, is twice as great among the "scolded" group as among the "not scolded." It is unlikely that many parents would intentionally encourage the sick child to worry about his illness. However, if the pattern just described is at all representative of what takes place, such a side effect may indeed be the consequence of some parental efforts at inculcating health responsibility in the child.

In this examination of the development of health orientations, I have ended with an emphasis on complexity. Perhaps this is a necessary conclusion. Intricacy is the rule for any social attitude, rather than the exception. The present characterization of the components of such orientations and of the processes at work in their formation and change may be an incomplete approximation. Yet it provides a perspective to point to gaps in our knowledge with the aim of encouraging further formulations to guide fruitful research.

REFERENCES

Allport, G. W., 1961. *Pattern and growth in personality.* New York: Holt, Rinehart and Winston.
Allport, G. W., 1966. Traits revisited. *Amer. Psychologist.,* 21, 1–10.
Bandura, A., and Walters, R. H., 1963. *Social learning and personality development.* New York: Holt, Rinehart and Winston.
Barraclough, W. W., 1937. Mental reactions of normal children to physical illness. *Amer. J. Psychiat.,* 93, 865–877.
Blumberg, B. S., 1961. The bearing of genetics and epidemiology on social and cultural aspects of arthritis. *Publ. Health News,* 42 (10), 302–305.
Croog, S. H., 1961. Ethnic origins, educational level, and responses to a health questionnaire. *Human Organization,* 20, 65–69.
Deutscher, I., 1966. Words and deeds: social science and social policy, *Social Problems,* 13, 235–254.
Dubin, R., and Dubin, Elisabeth R., 1965. Children's social perceptions: a review of research. *Child Develpm.,* 36, 809–838.
Gardner, M., 1966. The eerie mathematical art of Maurits C. Escher. *Scientific American,* 214, 110–121.
Goodman, Mary E., 1952. Race awareness in young children. Reading, Mass.: Addison-Wesley.
Goodman, N., Dornbusch, S. M., Richardson, S. A., and Hastorf, A. H., 1963. Variant reactions to physical disabilities. *Amer. sociol. Rev.,* 28, 429–435.
Harding, J., Kutner, B., Proshansky, H., and Chein, I., 1954. Prejudice and ethnic relations. In G. Lindzey (Ed.), *Handbook of social psychology.* Vol. 2. *Special fields and applications.* Reading, Mass.: Addison-Wesley, pp. 1021–1061.
Harris, D. B., 1959. Sex differences in the life problems and interests of adolescents, 1935 and 1957. *Child Develpm.,* 30, 453–459.
Hartley, E. L., and Hartley, Ruth, 1952. *Fundamentals of social psychology.* New York: Knopf.
Heider, F., 1944. Social perception and phenomenal causality. *Psychol. Rev.,* 51, 358–374.
Horowitz, E. L., 1936. The development of attitudes toward the Negro. *Arch. Psychol., N.Y.,* 28, No. 194.

Jenkins, C. D., 1966. Group differences in perception: a study of community beliefs and feelings about tuberculosis. *Amer. J. Sociol.*, **71**, 417–429.

Koos, E. L., 1954. *The health of Regionville*. New York: Columbia Univ. Press.

Krech, D., and Crutchfield, R. S., 1948. *Theory and problems of social psychology*. New York: McGraw-Hill.

Levy, E., 1959. Children's behavior under stress and its relation to training by parents to respond to stress situations. *Child Develpm.*, **30**, 307–324.

Lipmann, W., 1922. *Public opinion*. New York: The Macmillan Co., reprinted by Pelican Books, 1946.

MacLeod, R. B., 1947. The phenomenological approach to social psychology. *Psychol. Rev.*, **54**, 193–210.

Mechanic, D., 1964. The influence of mothers on their children's health attitudes and behavior. *Pediatrics*, **33**, 444–453.

Phillips, D. L., 1965. Self-reliance and the inclination to adopt the sick role. *Social Forces*, **43**, 555–563.

Prugh, D. G., Staub, Elizabeth M., Sands, Harriet H., Kirschbaum, Ruth M., and Lenihan, Ellenora A., 1953. A study of emotional reactions of children and families to hospitalizations and illness. *Amer. J. Orthopsychiat.*, **23**, 70–106.

Radke, Marian J., and Trager, Helen G., 1950. Children's perception of the social roles of Negroes and whites. *J. Psychol.*, **29**, 3–33.

Richardson, S. A., Hastorf, A. H., Goodman, N., and Dornbusch, S. M., 1961. Cultural uniformity in reaction to physical disabilities. *Amer. sociol. Rev.*, **26**, 241–247.

Sherif, Carolyn W., Sherif, M., and Nebergall, R. E., 1965. *Attitude and attitude change: the social judgment-involvement approach*. Philadelphia: Saunders.

Sherif, M., 1935. A study of some social factors in perception. *Arch. Psychol.*, *N.Y.*, No. 187.

Sherif, M., and Harvey, O. J., 1952. A study in ego functioning: elimination of stable anchorages in individual and group situations. *Sociometry*, **15**, 272–305.

Stevenson, H. W., and Stewart, E. C., 1958. A developmental study of racial awareness in young children. *Child Develpm.*, **29**, 399–409.

Suchman, E. A., 1964. Sociomedical variations among ethnic groups. *Amer. J. Sociol.*, **70**, 319–331.

Vaughan, G. M., 1964. The development of ethnic attitudes in New Zealand school children. *Genet. Psychol. Monogr.*, **70**, 135–175.

Wilson, W. C., 1963. Development of ethnic attitudes in adolescence. *Child Develpm.*, **34**, 247–256.

3.   Psychological Selectivity in Self-Esteem Formation

Morris Rosenberg

My chief object is to call attention to a psychological principle involved in attitude formation that affects the formation of self-esteem.
The objective may seem puzzling, since attitude theory, on the one
hand, and self-theory, on the other, are frequently viewed as having
but a remote connection. In large measure, this is surely attributable
to the varied meanings which have been assigned to the term "self."
In a scientific field generally undistinguished by the precision of its
terminology, the "self" stands as a concept foremost in the ranks of
confusion. The substitution of related terms—the ego (Sherif and
Cantril, 1947), the proprium (Allport, 1955), identity (Erikson,
1956)—has not dispersed the clouds, mist, and vapors.

The terms "self" or "ego" have been used to refer to the "inner
nature" or "essential nature" of man (Fromm, 1941, 1947; Maslow,
1954; Moustakas, 1956); to the experience and content of self-aware-
ness (Chein, 1944); to the center of the psychophysical field (Koffka,
1935); to inner or subjective being, or psychological faculties or dispositions, taken concretely (James, 1950); to the individual as known
to the individual (Hilgard, 1949; Murphy, 1947; Raimy, 1948; Rogers,
1951; Wiley, 1961); to a constellation of attitudes having reference
to "I," "me," or "mine" experiences (James, 1950; Sherif and Cantril,
1947); to individual identity and continuity of personal character
(Erikson, 1956); to a set of mental processes operating in the interest
of satisfying inner drives (Freud, 1933; Symonds, 1951); and, most
simply, to the person.[1]

[1] Useful clarifications and elaborations of these terms appear in Allport (1943);
Brownfain (1952); Combs and Soper (1957); Hall and Lindzey (1957); and
Symonds (1951).

Without attempting to resolve the insoluble problem of what the self "really" is, we shall focus on one definition of the self that corresponds to our immediate interest and that has a relatively clear and unequivocal meaning. This is Gardner Murphy's definition of the self as "the individual as known to the individual" (1947, p. 996). *So conceived, the self is squarely located in the realm of attitudes.* The self is simply an attitude or a cluster of attitudes toward an object. Just as we have attitudes toward an endless number of objects in the world—indivduals, groups, institutions, material objects, and artistic and cultural products—so we have attitudes toward ourselves. Attitudes toward soups, soaps, and selves are in the same realm of discourse.

If this is so, then one may suggest that all the dimensions which have been elaborated to characterize attitudes in general are completely appropriate to attitudes toward the self. For example, attitude theory and research have shown that attitudes can be described in terms of direction, intensity, salience, importance, clarity, stability, consistency, content, and verifiability. Thus, one may like or dislike oneself just as one may like or dislike the Republican party or modern art (the dimension of *direction*); one's liking of oneself may be strong or mild, which could be equally true of one's feelings toward Brahms (the dimension of *intensity*); considerations of the self may be at the top of one's mind, intruding into a wide variety of situations, as might also be the case with Vietnam (the dimension of *salience*); one's self-attitudes may make a major difference in one's life, just as may one's attitude toward democracy (the dimension of *importance*); one's self-picture may be clear and sharp or vague and hazy, which might equally be true of one's picture of the Soviet Union or the Supreme Court (the dimension of *clarity*); and so on.[2] Thus, all the dimensions suitable for the study of attitudes toward any object in the world are completely appropriate for the study of attitudes toward the self.

To say that self-attitudes are like all other attitudes, however, is not to deny that they have certain distinctive qualities. Five of these have special relevance in the present context.

First, it may be noted that the self is reflexive. The person holding the attitude and the object toward whom the attitude is held are encased within the same skin. Such statements as "I hit myself" or "I hate myself" express the point that the self is both subject and

[2] Detailed discussions of the range of attitude dimensions appear in Krech and Crutchfield (1948) and Newcomb (1950).

object. It is immediately apparent that this fact will influence the perspective brought to bear upon the object; one can scarcely perceive the self with complete objectivity and detachment.

A second distinctive quality is this: In studies of self-attitudes, as differentiated from studies of other objects, people are perceiving *different* things. For example, if one man thinks Picasso is superb whereas another considers him abysmal, then these men disagree. But if one man considers himself intelligent and another considers himself stupid, these men do not disagree. They are looking at different objects. A study of self-attitudes thus deals with precisely as many different objects as there are members of the sample.

Third, there are certain differences in the kinds of influences that have a bearing upon self-attitudes and attitudes toward many other objects. Our attitudes toward Vietnam, the President, the Democratic party, and the Soviet Union are heavily influenced by newspapers, radio, magazines, and television, whereas mass communications rarely have direct bearing upon our self-images. We shall see the special relevance of this fact in another context.

Fourth, although there is wide variation in the importance attached to various objects in the world by different people, the self is important to everyone. Attitudes toward Vietnam, toward modern art, toward Pennsylvania State University will vary in importance from person to person, but it is hard to think of someone who is totally indifferent to himself. As Murphy observes: "Whatever the self is, it becomes a center, an anchorage point, a standard of comparison, an ultimate real. Inevitably, it takes its place as a supreme value" (1947, p. 498). Lecky (1945) has expressed the point vividly in the statement that the self is the basic axiom of the individual's life theory.

This observation leads logically to the fifth distinctive characteristic of self-attitudes, namely that everyone is motivated to hold the *same* attitude toward the object—a favorable one. This is what is meant by self-esteem. "Self-love and pride are universal in human nature, even though in mature personalities they are not necessarily sovereign," said Gordon Allport (1961, p. 155). Of the many sentiments stipulated by McDougall (1932), the sentiment of self-regard was not merely one additional sentiment on a long list but was the master sentiment, the sentiment to which the remainder of values were subordinated. And Murphy (1947) told us that the one thing of which we can be certain from culture to culture is the phenomenon of self-love.

Plainly, people do not suffer low self-esteem with equanimity, contentment, and good cheer. The results of our study (Rosenberg, 1965) of 5000 high school students were strikingly consistent with these conclusions. In this sample, only 1 out of 25 of those adolescents with the highest self-esteem were characterized as "highly depressed" compared with 20 out of 25 of those with the lowest self-esteem. Similarly, the latter were eight times as likely as the former to manifest a large number of psychosomatic symptoms that had been shown to be closely associated with neuroticism (Star, 1950). Clinical observation also reveals that low self-esteem and depressive affect are consistently associated. This, then, is one of the most important distinctive qualities of self-attitudes: that almost everyone would *prefer* that this attitude be a positive or favorable one.

Although Freud almost totally disregarded the self-image in his theoretical work, his famous defense mechanisms, as both Murphy (1947) and Allport (1961) observed, are primarily designed to maintain a favorable self-attitude. Concepts such as repression, denial, rationalization, projection, regression, sublimation, compensation—"these concepts," Allport observed, "are of value in understanding our strategies for guarding our own self-esteem (1961, p. 163)." In this discussion we wish to illustrate just one principle that is peculiarly relevant to the defense and enhancement of the self, namely, the principle of psychological selectivity. How does selectivity enable a person to defend, maintain, and enhance his ego or self?

Before examining the operation of the principle in the maintenance of favorable self-attitudes, it is useful to recall how selectivity operates in the maintenance of attitudes generally and the role it plays in resistance to attitude change.

SELECTIVITY IN ATTITUDE STUDIES

Let us consider how three types of selectivity—selective memory, selective exposure, and selective interpretation—have been shown to render an individual's attitudes relatively impervious to communications.

The phenomenon of selective memory and retention has been demonstrated in a number of studies (Edwards, 1941; Levine and Murphy, 1943; Wallen, 1942). The classic Levine and Murphy (1943) experiment on the remembering and forgetting of controversial material is the archetypal illustration of selective memory. In this study, pro-Communist and anti-Communist students were asked to read pro-Communist and anti-Communist writings. The pro-Communists were more likely to remember the facts and arguments in the pro-Communist materials and to forget the others, whereas the anti-Communist memories operated in the reverse direction.

Selective *exposure* represents one of the most consistent principles in the entire field of mass communications (Lazarsfeld, 1940; Lazarsfeld and Merton, 1943; Lazarsfeld, Berelson, and Gaudet, 1948). In the 1940 Erie County election study (Lazarsfeld, *et al.*, 1948), for example, the local press was Republican whereas the radio was relatively impartial; however, the Democrats were thought to gain an advantage by virtue of Roosevelt's masterful radio presence. In exposing themselves to election materials, Republicans were more likely to select the newspapers, Democrats the radio.

One can scarcely doubt the generality of the principle of selective exposure. Is there any question that the great bulk of the readers of the *Daily Worker* are Communists and that the vast majority of *National Review* readers are conservatives? Who listens to the speeches at mass civil rights meetings but those who already favor civil rights? Probably most readers of Barry Goldwater's *Conscience of a Conservative* favored Goldwater before they read the book.

As a general principle, it is plain that people tend to expose themselves to impersonal and interpersonal communications with which they agree and to avoid those with which they disagree. The result is to reinforce and harden their initial attitudes.

Perhaps the most interesting mechanism rendering attitudes impervious to communications is *selective interpretation*. The studies by Cooper and Jahoda (1947) and Kendall and Wolf (1949) strikingly demonstrate this mechanism. An agency intent on fighting prejudice considered lampooning prejudiced people by using cartoons to cast prejudiced people in a ludicrous light. A number of cartoons was developed, focusing upon a cantankerous and disagreeable-looking character, "Mr. Biggott," who, in a variety of situations, made prejudiced remarks that were presumably humorous by virtue of their absurdity. (Example: Mr. Biggott, interviewing an American Indian for a job, says: "I'm sorry, Mr. Eaglefeather, but our company's policy is to employ 100 percent Americans only.")

The sample consisted of working men. The interviewers, by engaging the respondents in conversation, ascertained their prejudice toward minority groups. The respondents were then shown the cartoons. By and large, the unprejudiced respondents got the joke whereas the prejudiced respondents did not get the point of the cartoons; they did not see that the cartoons were attempting to ridicule prejudice. There was a selective understanding of the cartoons that generally enabled each group to maintain its original attitudes intact.

Selectivity may thus be viewed as one type of psychological mechanism operating in the interests of certain needs. One problem in many discussions of psychological mechanisms is that it is difficult to stipulate the *conditions* under which they will find expression. This is much less true of the mechanism of selectivity. Selectivity, we suggest, is particularly free to operate under two conditions: (1) where the situation is unstructured or ambiguous, and (2) where the range of options is wide. These conditions will vary with the particular attitude under consideration. With regard to self-attitudes, we suggest, ambiguity is particularly great and the range of options unusually wide. For these reasons, the principle of selectivity operates with particular force in regard to self-evaluation. Without claiming to be exhaustive, we wish to point to five types of selectivity that may influence self-attitudes, namely, selectivity of values, of interpretation, of standards, of interpersonal relations, and of situations.

SELECTIVITY OF SELF-VALUES

Just as a man may hold political, religious, and other social values, so he may hold values regarding himself. Although widely overlooked in self-esteem studies, it is fairly obvious that a man's global self-esteem is not based solely on his assessment of his constituent qualities. His self-esteem is based on his self-assessments of qualities that *count*. This point was emphasized with characteristic felicity by William James as far back as 1890. He observed:

> I, who for the time have staked my all on being a psychologist, am mortified if others know much more psychology than I. But I am contented to wallow in the grossest ignorance of Greek. My deficiencies there give me no sense of personal humiliation at all. Had I "pretensions" to be a linguist, it would have been just the reverse. . . .
>
> Yonder puny fellow, . . . whom everyone can beat, suffers no chagrin about it, for he has long ago abandoned the attempt to "carry that line," as the merchants say, of self at all. With no attempt, there can be no failure; with no failure no humiliation. So our self-feeling in this world depends entirely on what we *back* ourselves to be or do (1950, p. 310).

The relevance of self-values is easily demonstrated from our adolescent study. Consider the quality "likeable." Some students think they are very likeable whereas others think they are not. As we would anticipate, those who consider themselves likeable are more likely to think well of themselves in general, to have high global self-esteem. *But the strength of this relationship depends upon the importance attached to being likeable* (Rosenberg, 1965).

As Table 3.1 shows, among those who *care* about being likeable, the relationship of the self-estimate to global self-esteem is very strong, whereas among those who to whom this quality matters little, the relationship is much weaker.

Table 3.1 *Self-Estimate as "Likeable" and Global Self-Esteem According to Value Attached to Being "Likeable"*

Global Self-Esteem	Care about Being "Likeable" (Self-Value)					
	Care a Great Deal			Care Somewhat, Little, or Not at All		
	Actually Consider Oneself Likeable (Self-Estimate)					
	Very	Fairly	Little or Not at All	Very	Fairly	Little or Not at All
High	54%	45%	17%	46%	49%	31%
Medium	39	42	33	39	43	50
Low	7	13	50	15	8	19
Total percent	100	100	100	100	100	100
N	(345)	(569)	(52)	(41)	(133)	(34)

It is especially interesting to consider those students who said they were "little" or "not at all" likeable. Among those who did *not* care about whether they were likeable, only 19 per cent had low global self-esteem, whereas among those who cared a great deal, fully 50 percent had low self-esteem.

Lest one assume that this result is unusual, we have chosen the 16 qualities out of the 44 in our study which were most highly valued. Consider just those people who feel they are *poor* with regard to these qualities, that is, they do *not* consider themselves likeable, or dependable, or intelligent, or conscientious. How many of these people have global low self-esteem? The answer is that it depends on how important each of these qualities is to the individual. Table 3.2 shows that with regard to 15 of these 16 qualities, those who *cared* about the quality had lower self-esteem than those who considered the quality unimportant. Yet these people ranked themselves the same way with respect to their possession of the qualities in question. To know that someone considers himself deficient with regard to a particular quality is plainly an inadequate indication of what he thinks of himself. We must also know how much he *values* this quality.

Table 3.2 *Low Self-Estimates and Low Self-Esteem According to the Importance of Qualities Rated*

Rate Self *Poor* on Qualities below	*Care* about Qualities Listed	
	Great Deal	Little or Not at All
	Percent with Low Self-Esteem	
Good student in school	32	18
Likeable	50	19
Dependable and reliable	36	23
Intelligent, good mind	34	26
Clear-thinking, clever	34	22
Hard-working, conscientious	28	17
Easy to get along with	38	23
Realistic, able to face facts	30	17
Friendly, sociable, pleasant	29	24
Honest, law-abiding	42	21
Mature, not childish	29	31
Good sense, sound judgment	33	26
Kind and considerate	28	22
Get along well	39	21
Well-liked by many different people	35	23
Stand up for rights	27	26
Moral and ethical	32	25

Now, with regard to self-values, the principle of selectivity is free to operate because the range of options is so inordinately wide. Many years ago, Allport and Odbert (1936) compiled a list of over 17,000 adjectives by which objects could be characterized. Not all of them, to be sure, are applicable to individuals, but an enormous number are. There scarcely seems to be any limit to the types of qualities an individual may consider important in evaluating himself. He may consider it important to be generous, good at working with his hands, a third generation American, popular, nonconformist, hip, daring, moral, thoughtful, good at dancing, cute, ruthless, imaginative, and so forth.

Given this enormous range of options, which values will the individual tend to select as important? One obvious hypothesis is that he will be disposed to value *those things at which he considers himself good and to devalue those qualities at which he considers himself poor.* As one illustration, consider the quality "good at working with your hands." Table 3.3 shows that among those who felt they possessed this skill, 68 percent valued the quality highly, whereas among those who believed they lacked this quality, only 6 percent attached

Table 3.3 *Self-Estimate and Self-Value for Quality "Good at Working with Your Hands"*

Self-Value: Care about Working with Hands	Self-Estimate: Actually Consider Self "Good at Working with Hands"		
	Very	Fairly	Little or Not at All
Care a great deal	68%	27%	6%
Care somewhat or little	32	73	94
Total percent	100	100	100
N	(224)	(392)	(533)

that much importance to it. Indeed if we consider the same 16 qualities mentioned above, we find, *without exception,* those who considered themselves good in terms of these qualities were more likely to value the qualities than those who considered themselves poor. Self-values, we see, tend to be selected in such a way as to enable the individual to maintain a congenial self-picture.

If people are reasonably free to choose their own values, then we are led to an interesting paradox of social life, namely, that almost everyone can consider himself superior to almost everyone else as long as he can choose *his own* basis for judgment. For instance, take four boys. One is a good scholar, the second a good athlete, the third very handsome, and the fourth is a good musician. So long as each focuses upon the quality at which he excels, each is superior to the rest. At the same time each person may blithely acknowledge the superiority of the others with regard to qualities to which he himself is relatively indifferent.

The freedom to select one's values in a fashion congenial to one's self-image is not, of course, without limit; we shall consider some of these limits later. The selection of self-values does, however, have wide latitude because of the enormous range of alternatives available and the private nature of self-values. Under these circumstances, psychological selectivity will play its anticipated role.

SELECTIVE INTERPRETATION

Let us now consider how the principle of selectivity may operate to influence the interpretation of evidence about the self. Our contention is that, since the meaning of the evidence regarding the self is generally so ambiguous, the likelihood will be considerable that the interpretation of the evidence will be selective in the interests of psychological comfort.

In judging oneself, one must take account of the "facts." But "facts," as everyone knows, are amenable to highly varying interpretations. Take a soldier who, in the heat of battle, rushes into the enemy stronghold; taking them by surprise, he destroys or captures them. What he has done is an objective fact. But how shall his act be interpreted? Does it prove that he is a man of utmost courage, fearless to the core? Or does it mean that he is simply too stupid to recognize obvious danger when it stares him in the face? The man's act is clear, but whether the act reflects the quality of "courage" or of "foolhardiness" is a matter of interpretation.

Now let us consider an example closer to the high school student's experience—his grade average. Grades are an objective measure of performance. But what do grades mean? This, to a substantial extent, is up to the individual to decide. Consider a number of characteristics that reflect intellectual qualities: good student in school; intelligent, a person with a good mind; clear-thinking and clever; imaginative and original; knowing quite a bit about many different things; a person with good sense and sound judgment; a logical, reasonable type of person. Table 3.4 reveals striking differences in the *degree* of association between grade average and self-estimations on these qualities. The association of objective grades to the belief that one is a good student in school is .52, but the association of grades to the conviction that one is clear-thinking and clever is only .16, and the association of grades to the belief that one is imaginative and original is only .08.

Table 3.4 *Association between School Grades and Self-Estimates with Regard to Various Aspects of Intellectual Competence*

Relationship between School Average and Estimate of Oneself as . . .	Coefficient of Contingency (C)
A good student in school	.52
Intelligent	.40
Clear-thinking and clever	.16
Logical and reasonable	.16
Know quite a bit about many different things	.15
A person with good sense and sound judgment	.14
Imaginative and original	.08

In other words, most people agree that grades are a good indication of whether they are good students, but they are by no means convinced that grades tell much about whether they are "clear-thinking and clever" or "imaginative and original." Table 3.5 shows that nearly three fourths of the students with D or F averages consider themselves as very or fairly likely to be imaginative and original, and the same is true with regard to having good sense and sound judgment.

Table 3.5 *Grade Average and Self-Estimate as "Imaginative and Original"*

Self-Estimate: Consider Self "Imaginative and Original"	Grade Average in School			
	A	B	C	D-F
Very	26%	26%	25%	32%
Fairly	56	49	49	41
A little	17	23	22	24
Not at all	1	2	3	3
Total percent	100	100	100	100
N	(77)	(438)	(485)	(148)

This need not reflect a denial of reality. A student averaging D or F knows that he has poor grades. But there are many aspects of intelligence, and there is nothing in the objective situation to compel the student to interpret his poor grades as relevant to these aspects of intelligence.

If the relevance of grades to intellectual abilities is so vague, how much more ambiguous must be the relevance of evidence regarding such characteristics as "moral," "interesting," "easy to get along with," and the like. Here there are no report cards, no test scores, no class percentile ranks. There are no General College Entrance Examination scores for tact, consideration, or independence. Under these circumstances, the inflation of the self-estimates (reflected in extremely skewed distributions of the estimates) is to be anticipated.

Another factor introducing ambiguity into the interpretation of evidence is the nature of trait language. Traits are the main dimensions by which individuals are characterized (Murphy, 1947, p. 506). Yet the language of traits is simply permeated with evaluative overtones. Even a superficial glance at a list of adjectives shows that the vast majority are not simply descriptions but imply negative or positive judgments. To call a person kind is not a description; it is an accolade. To call him cruel is not to describe him, but to condemn him.

The nature of trait language, therefore, permits the anomaly that *opposite* linguistic patterns are entirely appropriate to the description of the *same* behavior. For example, if one man calls us clever and thoughtful whereas another calls us shrewd and calculating, are they really describing anything different? If a friend says we are kind, warm, and generous and an enemy says we are maudlin, sirupy, and prodigal, is there really any disagreement about what we are like? Indeed both I and my critic may agree that I am Bohemian and nonconformist, a term he employs to condemn a quality in which I take the utmost pride. Even though people may agree on the evidence, then, they assuredly do not agree on its evaluation.

The fact that this process is so extreme and yet so common highlights the nature of self-evaluation more sharply than perhaps any other single thing. *There is scarcely any behavior which cannot be interpreted as admirable in some way* (the last resort is to say that "at least" one is not the opposite appalling extreme). Furthermore, the individual who engages in "reverse interpretation" cannot clearly be proved wrong.

We can go on playing this game endlessly, and the wonder of it is that everyone comes out a winner. It is a game that nations, as well as individuals, play most adeptly, so adeptly, in fact, that disputes and conflicts rend the world while every nation considers itself absolutely right. Both the Americans and the North Vietnamese agree on the fact that we bomb them. But, to us, this act means that we are strong, technologically advanced, lovers of freedom, true to our word and commitment, solicitous over the fate of the potentially helpless captives of communism, and admirably realistic in our appraisal of events. To the North Vietnamese this behavior proves that we are killers, cannibals, oppressors, imperialists, bloodthirsty monsters, and the rest of the verbal weaponry that stocks the vast arsenal of vilification.

The evidence with regard to the self is less dependent on consensual validation than international affairs evidence. In the silence of our minds, generally unimpeded by the intrusion of alternative interpretations, we are free to review and evaluate the evidence as our biases dictate, to shift perspectives until a congenial one emerges, and to emerge with a comfortable conclusion.

Just as selectivity holds sway with regard to interpreting the meaning of evidence pertaining to the self, so it has free rein when it comes to the choice of evidence in the first place. The type of evidence relevant to a given characteristic is widely varied. On what basis shall a man judge his generosity—whether he has contributed to the Community Chest, whether he has recently given money to a beggar, whether he bought his wife or child a birthday present, whether he loaned money to a friend, whether he picked up the check at a restaurant for a party, or what? He is not obliged to consider all these criteria; he can choose one—any one he wants, any one that fits. And he is right at least in one respect: the situation is so unstructured that *there is no way to prove him wrong*. The same is obviously true of the vast range of qualities that characterize a man.

Thus from the mass of experiences or communications available to the individual, he will tend to select those best suited to providing a congenial interpretation. To the outside observer these interpretations may appear bizarre or ludicrous. They are not, however, necessarily pathological. Selective interpretation of evidence is easy in this area, both because there is actually little clear objective evidence about the self and because there are so few generally accepted criteria of evaluation.

A high level of ambiguity and wide range of options thus makes possible selectivity of interpretation, linguistic selectivity, and selectivity of evidence. That these mechanisms are effective is suggested by the data from our adolescent study. In this investigation the students were asked to rate themselves on 48 qualities that are generally considered desirable and that are not sex-linked. With regard to every quality but one, the subjects were more likely to rank themselves favorably than unfavorably. This result is clearly consistent with people's preferences for positive self-attitudes.

SELECTIVITY OF STANDARDS

In his trailblazing discussion of the self in 1890, William James (1950, p. 310) devised a most ingenious formula: Self-esteem equals success over pretensions. It was but a small step for him to point out that it may be as blessed a relief for the individual to reduce the denominator as to increase the numerator.

The truth of this observation is apparent from the fact that it is not simply how good a person thinks he is with regard to some quality but how good he *wants to be* that counts. In the realm of standards, too, the range of options is wide, and the situation is extremely unstructured.

How good is "good enough"? Assume that people are satisfied to be fairly good students in school, a choice they can make unhindered. By this criterion, as Table 3.6 shows, all of the A students, almost all of the B students, seven tenths of the C students, and even nearly half of the D or F students qualify as fairly or very good students. Using this moderate standard, most people meet it very well.

Table 3.6 *Grade Average and Self-Estimate as Student in School*

Self-Estimate: Consider Self "a Good Student in School"	Grade Average in School			
	A	B	C	D–F
Very	82%	31%	6%	9%
Fairly	18	63	64	36
A little	—	5	24	38
Not at all	—	1	5	17
Total percent	100	100	100	100
N	(73)	(439)	(498)	(154)

This is all the more true of standards with regard to more ambiguous qualities. A man may want to be "considerate" or "dependable and reliable," but he is under no pressure to be *extremely* considerate or dependable. It is perfectly satisfactory if he is reasonably so. In view of the ease with which evidence can be selected and interpreted in a congenial way, we can reasonably assume that most people can meet the moderate standards they select for themselves.

People have a wide range of options in setting standards for themselves. One can aspire to the pinnacle of achievement, to a good level of performance, to moderate accomplishment, or even to modest success. A man may aim to be a dominant figure in the world of business or politics or to be a competent plumber or carpenter. This principle is all the more true of nonoccupational goals. One person may aspire to be the ultimate in sweetness, goodness, and kindness, whereas another is content just to be a decent fellow. One person may set a goal of being absolutely punctual and of never making an error, whereas another may be satisfied to be reasonably reliable. There is thus a great choice available in the setting of standards of performance in the great sweep of areas pertaining to the self.

Given these options, what standards do people select for themselves? If any single conclusion is suggested by the great body of literature concerning level of aspiration appearing in the forties, it is that most people tend to set goals that they interpret as falling within a reasonable range of their potential accomplishments. When college students were told that WPA workers, college students, and authors and literary critics had made certain scores on a test of literary acquaintance and were asked how well they expected to do, their estimates centered about the hypothetical college students' average (Chapman and Volkmann, 1939). Similarly, when individual students were "graded" on a task and then asked how well they expected to do next time, their estimates changed to conform to a new realistic assessment.

Gordon Allport has summarized the level of aspiration studies in a sentence. He commented: "The history of ten years' research on the Lewinian problem is too intricate to trace here, but, unless I am mistaken, every investigation has directly or indirectly confirmed Hoppe's initial claim that the subject behaves in such a manner as to maintain his self-esteem at the highest possible level" (1943, pp. 470–471).

More recent surveys of occupational aspirations tend to confirm the laboratory findings. In a study of college students' values (Rosenberg, 1957), a sample of respondents was asked: "What business or profession would you *most like* to go into?" and "What business or profession do you realistically think you are most apt to go into?" Although in an abstract sense each student might ideally like to be a surgeon, corporation lawyer, or millionnaire, these young people did not choose these aspirations. Seventy-six percent said they realistically expected to enter the occupation they most desired, and the course of time had the effect of bringing occupational aspirations and expectations still closer together. Most of the students had scaled down their aspirations to correspond to what they considered within the range of realistic fulfillment. The individual thus tends to select goals (standards and levels of performance) in accord with his assessment of his qualities. This selectivity enables him to achieve his personal goals, to consider himself "good enough," and to maintain a favorable opinion of himself.

It may be noted that many standards are normatively determined and that the principle of selectivity of standards characterizes groups as well as individuals. One might call these "societal coping mechanisms." Such standards, it should be noted, are not always high.

For example, the occupational achievements of people of working class origins are considerably lower than those raised in a middle-class environment. Does their lower success result in lower self-esteem? Not necessarily, because their aspirations (or "pretensions") are much lower. It is not necessary to repeat here Hyman's (1953) ample documentation of this fact. It is sufficient to observe that a working-class boy who wants to become a plumber is as likely to achieve his goal as a middle-class boy who wants to become a doctor.

It is thus both apparent and important that groups have normative aspirations that are internalized by individuals as their private standards. These normative aspirations tend to be within realistic range of fulfillment.

INTERPERSONAL SELECTIVITY

One of the most consistent findings in mass communications research, as noted earlier, is that people elect to expose themselves to communications with which they agree. With regard to self-esteem, of course, the mass media are largely irrelevant. What is most important is the communications we get from other people. But selectivity operates in interpersonal communications as well as impersonal communications. We may advance as a fundamental principle of social life that people, when given the choice, will tend to associate with those who think well of them and to avoid those who dislike or despise them, thereby biasing the communications about themselves to which they are exposed in a favorable direction.

The outstanding case in point is *friendship*. Friendship is the purest illustration of picking ones propaganda. It is characteristic of a friend that not only do we like him but that he also likes us. To some extent, at least, it is probable that we like him *because* he likes us.

Indeed, it is well-nigh impossible to be friends with someone who hates us, not only because we would have no taste for such a friendship but because *he* would not allow the friendship to exist. The upshot of friendship selection is thus to expose people to implicit and explicit interpersonal communications that reflect well on themselves. They hear much less from people who dislike them.

All friendship, then, is at least to some extent a "mutual admiration society," whereby each partner helps to sustain the desired self-image of the other. If Mead (1934) and Cooley (1912) were correct in assuming that our self-evaluations are largely dependent upon the evaluations others have of us, then the principle of selectivity involved in friendship helps to explain why people are more likely to hold favorable than unfavorable attitudes toward themselves.

Perhaps one of the most important appeals of *romantic love* is the great intensity with which the mutual admiration is held. To be sure, love may be unrequited, but where it is mutually held, it is surely a great prop to self-esteem. To find that someone considers us the most beautiful girl in the world or the most wonderful boy is to find a source for the kind of communication that we select to hear over others.

What is true of friends and lovers is equally true of *groups*. The avid search for social acceptance is one of the prime enterprises of youth. Young people are constantly in quest of environments where they will be accepted, whether it be the peer group, the beatnik group, Greenwich Village, or whatever. They rebel against their parents, who disapprove of their behavior, characteristics, or qualities—a disapproval offensive to self-esteem—and gravitate toward groups that accept and approve of them, thereby enhancing their self-esteem.

In addition to the individual's selection of interpersonal communications, a social selection with a normative character holds sway. We might say there exists a world-wide social conspiracy designed to elevate the general level of self-esteem. We are all part of that conspiracy. The secret, of course, is *tact*. "Tact is everything, talent nothing," it has been said. One of Webster's definitions of tact is a "peculiar ability to deal with others without giving offense." A person devoid of tact is rejected as a boor or a clod.

Men living in society are thus under pressure to protect one another's self-esteem. To imply that someone is stupid, immoral, or disagreeable is to give offense. This behavior is not only punished by the object of attack, but by everyone else as well, since it threatens a social norm that protects the self-esteem of all. Under certain social conditions, such as in the search for scientific truth, it is functionally indispensable to violate the norm. In ordinary social relations, however, it is acceptable to express our admiration and regard for another (although even this must be done in a normatively acceptable way) but not to express our disdain and disrespect. To censor our disdain for another person is also the better part of valor, for we can be assured that the expression of such sentiments will stimulate their object to make observations ill-designed to enhance our own self-esteem.

There is one further point about interpersonal communication that merits attention, namely, that its ambiguity permits the principle of selective interpretation to operate with great freedom. Cooley expressed most vividly the point that our attitudes toward ourselves are importantly influenced by the views others hold of us. "Each to each a looking glass, Reflects the other that doth pass" (1912, p. 152). But Cooley was careful to stress that it was not what others *actually* thought of us but our *imagination* of their thought that was decisive. When we read a newspaper or book, we can usually read the lines; but when we read the mind of another human being, particularly his attitudes toward us, we must usually read between the lines. In this great blank white space it is relatively easy to see a message that is congenial.

The communications about ourselves are thus either biased in a generally favorable direction or are sufficiently ambiguous that our own biases are free to operate. That this is the case is suggested by the responses of our adolescent subjects to the question: "What do most people think of you?" Nearly 97 percent said that most people thought very well or fairly well of them, and only three percent said fairly poorly or very poorly. Even two thirds of those with low self-esteem attributed such benevolent attitudes to others. They may, of course, be right. It is possible that a vast wave of mutual love and good will engulfs the world. One cannot, however, evade at least the suspicion that with the ambiguity inherent in appraising another's attitudes toward us, a great many people are giving themselves the benefit of the doubt.

We cannot, of course, completely control our interpersonal environments. The limitations are considered below. However, to the extent that we have the option, and the latitude is fairly wide, we tend to expose ourselves and to be exposed to interpersonal communications of a favorable sort. The communications we thereby receive are heavily biased in a favorable direction.

SITUATIONAL SELECTIVITY

Finally, we may briefly consider the phenomenon of situational selectivity. In a complex, multifaceted society, men are not always able to *make* their environments, but they are often able to *select* their environments. A major motivation in such selectivity, we would suggest, is the desire to maintain a congenial self-image. In other words, the individual will be disposed to expose himself to situations in which he excels rather than to those in which he is found wanting.

For example, if a person is good at dancing but poor at bowling, he will usually prefer to go to a dance where his skill is appreciated rather than to a bowling alley where his ineptitude is deprecated. If he is witty rather than deep, he will tend to go to parties or social gatherings rather than to lectures and discussions. Similarly, it is well known that college students tend to elect subjects in which they are good and avoid those in which they are weak.

Occupational choice is a prime example of situational selectivity. In their study of *Occupational Choice,* Ginzberg, Ginsburg, Axelrad, and Herma (1951) accept it as axiomatic that a student will not select an occupation unless he expects to be good at it. When given the choice, then, men gravitate toward situations in which their skills will find expression and their talents elicit appreciation.

In speaking of this issue of selectivity, we have at the same time been illustrating the pervasiveness and centrality of the self-esteem drive. It directs thought and action in a wide variety of areas. To an important extent it determines our selection of our values, our memory processes, our perspectives and interpretations of facts, our standards of evaluation and reference points, our goals, our choice of friends, marital partners, groups, associations, occupations, or environments generally. As a pervasive influence, there are few factors that can match self-esteem. The maintenance of self-esteem is thus a continuing and omnipresent aspect of our daily lives as well as of our longer-range aims.

LIMITATIONS ON SELECTIVITY

We have seen that, owing to the unstructuredness of the situation and the wide range of options, the principle of selectivity is quite free to operate toward forming one's self-attitudes in accord with one's desires. Perhaps the wonder, then, is that people do not all have favorable self-attitudes. Yet we know that many people have mild or moderate doubts about themselves, others serious doubts, and still others have grave doubts or are, in fact, firmly convinced of their unworthiness.

Such evidence does not mean that the principle of selectivity is wrong but that there are certain aspects of human experience in which selectivity is not free to operate without limit. Under conditions of firm structure or a narrow range of options, we would expect selectivity to be inoperative.

The most obvious limitation, of course, is that there are a certain number of objective facts about the self which cannot be evaded. Thus, it is clearly the case that students with low grades are less likely to consider themselves good students than those with high averages. Similarly, there is no way for a short man to think of himself as tall, a poor man as rich, a female as a male, or a lower-class person as an upper-class person, as long as he is in contact with reality.

A much more important limitation on the principle of selectivity is found in the realm of self-values. Self-values are malleable but not infinitely malleable or subservient to the needs of psychological comfort.

Consider the quality "good student." We find that those who think they are good students tend to value this quality and those who think they are not good students tend to disvalue it. But it is interesting to note that among those respondents who considered themselves relatively poor students, over one third nevertheless said that they cared a great deal about this quality. (This is the very group, incidentally, with the lowest self-esteem.)

Still more striking results appear when we consider the quality "good sense and sound judgment." Among those who felt they did *not* possess this quality, nearly two thirds (65 percent) said they *cared a great deal* about it. Similarly among students who felt they actually were not "well liked by many different people," over half (53 percent) said they valued this quality highly. These results are not unusual. With regard to many of these qualities, substantial proportions of those who actually consider themselves poor in these respects nevertheless say they care a great deal about them.

There are several reasons why self-values and self-estimates may be discordant. For one thing, many self-values are acquired long before the opportunity is at hand to test them adequately. Thus, a child from a musical family may learn early to value musical skill, but it only becomes compellingly apparent that he has insufficient talent as time goes by. Self-values, particularly if established early and reinforced by "significant others," may be quite difficult to change even if at a later time it is in the individual's interest to do so.

The second point is that in many cases *traits are to goals as means are to ends*. We cannot conveniently abandon the importance of a particular quality without at the same time abandoning the goal for which this quality is required. Take for an example the son of a doctor who wants to follow in his father's footsteps. This young man will consider the question of whether he has the qualities necessary for academic success as very important. It would be absurd to assume that he can dismiss this value and raise to top priority the value of being a good dancer, a skill at which he excels. So long as he maintains the goal of becoming a doctor, he must be concerned with academic competence; he cannot waltz his way into medical school. Similarly, a girl who wishes to marry and have a family cannot dismiss the importance of physical or social attractiveness and simply replace it with the value of being "dependable and reliable." In other words, certain traits are relevant means for the attainment of certain goals. Their importance to the individual, as long as the goals are maintained, cannot be easily dismissed.

The third, and probably major, reason why self-values do not accord with self-estimates is that self-values often derive from social role definitions and group norms (Kluckhohn, 1952; Rosenberg, 1965; Williams, 1951). As long as men live in society they cannot completely evade the values stemming from these roles and groups. At an early age the child learns what is right or wrong, important or unimportant for him, and these are internalized in his value system. In addition, as he grows up he finds himself judged by these criteria. He finds that if he desires the approval of his group, he must seek to excel in terms of *their* values, not his own. True, he may momentarily enhance his self-esteem by abandoning their values; but this is likely to call down upon him the disapproval or contempt of significant others, which will probably diminish his self-esteem all the more. Self-values thus cannot casually be manipulated to suit the individual's psychological convenience.

Thus, the chief restriction on the operation of the principle of selectivity is to be found in the interpersonal realm. It is in this area of paramount significance for self-esteem that the range of options is most limited. While we are *relatively* free to choose whom we wish as friends, the same is not true of parents, teachers, or children, and far less of neighbors, employers or employees, colleagues, or clients. If our parents scold us, our teachers greet our remarks with sarcasm, our fellow workers laugh at us, or our employer berates us, we are largely deprived of the option of avoiding their company or their criticism. As Cooley (1912) and Mead (1934) stressed, our opinions of ourselves are heavily influenced by what other people think of us (or what we assume they think), and therefore, the absence of option in this area has special significance.

Powerful social norms surrounding family stability also severely restrict options in the marital realm. In American society, people are more or less free to choose their spouses; but having made that choice, they have no assurance that the early mutual admiration will be sustained. It is no secret that the husband and wife who berate one another roundly, soundly detesting one another's intolerable habits, did not feel that way when they approached the altar.

The breakdown in interpersonal selectivity is illustrated by the recent joke: "A man can be one hundred percent stupid and never know it. A single man, that is." The communications passing between marital partners are not always those they would select to hear, were the option available.

Probably the most significant limit on interpersonal selectivity, however, is this: at the time of life especially important for self-esteem formation (say, from about the age of four) the range of interpersonal and situational options is the most severely restricted. The main interpersonal communications about the self at this period come from one's parents, and the child is stuck with them, for better or for worse. If they love him, then he has a decisive basis for thinking well of himself. If they do not, if they disparage or reject him, then it is difficult to evade the conclusion that he is unworthy. As noted earlier, with no options there can be no selectivity.

The work of Hovland, Lumsdaine, and Sheffield (1949) as well as that of Sherif and Sherif (1956) and Berelson (1950) clearly shows that the attitudes that are easiest to change, shape, or form are those that are least structured. Sherif and Cantril (1947) have shown that once attitudes are formed they tend to maintain themselves. Now it is precisely in childhood that the self-image is most unformed and unstructured. The child emerging into the stage of self-consciousness has nothing upon which to base a self-estimate. Hence, with parents holding a virtual monopoly on communications, their attitudes have particularly powerful significance at this time of life.

The relative absence of interpersonal options for the child is matched by restrictions on situational selectivity. The child's environment is largely fixed. A child with musical skill in a lower-class family, where this quality is of no interest, cannot choose to move into an upper-middle-class family, where this talent is valued. Similarly, there is no assurance that one's characteristics will fit in with the norms of the neighborhood peer group. One gains no applause for talents disdained in the group, and one is powerless to select a different school or neighborhood.

In sum, there are important limits to the principle of selectivity, and several of these obtain precisely at the stage of life when the communications are most decisive for self-esteem formation, namely, in childhood.

Despite the generality and power of the principle of selectivity, then, it is easy to see why many people *do* have low or moderate self-esteem. These observations also highlight the central significance of childhood in self-esteem formation and the powerful role played by parents in self-esteem formation.

Although it would exceed the scope of this chapter to document the contention, the evidence is consistent in suggesting that, overall, people are more likely to hold favorable rather than unfavorable opinions of themselves. Such a result would suggest that family environments are generally more benign than malignant and that the mechanism of psychological selectivity, whose various expressions have formed the core of this discussion, is highly effective in enabling people to hold desired self-attitudes. We would suggest that the forms of selectivity bearing upon self-attitudes may also be of value in understanding attitude formation and resistance to attitude change in other areas as well.

REFERENCES

Allport, G. W., 1943. The ego in contemporary psychology. *Psychol. Rev.*, **50**, 451–478.

Allport, G. W., 1955. *Becoming.* New Haven: Yale Univ. Press.

Allport, G. W., 1961. *Pattern and growth in personality.* New York: Holt, Rinehart and Winston.

Allport, G. W., and Odbert, H. S., 1936. Trait-names: a psycholexical study. *Psychol. Monogr.*, No. 211.

Berelson, B., 1950. Communications and public opinion. In B. Berelson and M. Janowitz (Eds.), *Public opinion and communication.* Glencoe, Ill.: Free Press, pp. 448–462.

Brownfain, J. D., 1952. Stability of the self-concept as a dimension of personality. *J. abnorm. soc. Psychol.*, **47**, 597–606.

Chapman, D. W., and Volkmann, J., 1939. A social determinant of the level of aspiration. *J. abnorm. soc. Psychol.*, **34**, 225–238.

Chein, I., 1944. The awareness of self and the structure of the ego. *Psychol. Rev.*, **51**, 304–314.

Combs, A. W., and Soper, D. F., 1957. The self, its derivate terms, and research. *J. ind. Psychol.*, **13**, 134–145.

Cooley, C. H., 1912. *Human nature and the social order*. New York: Scribner's.

Cooper, E., and Jahoda, M., 1947. The evasion of propaganda: how prejudiced people respond to anti-prejudice propaganda. *J. Psychol.*, **23**, 15–25.

Edwards, A. L., 1941. Political frames of reference as a factor influencing recognition. *J. abnorm. soc. Psychol.*, **36**, 34–61.

Erickson, E. H., 1956. The problem of ego-identity. *J. Amer. Psychoanal. Assn.*, **4**, No. 1, 58–121.

Freud, S., 1933. *A new series of introductory lectures on psycho-analysis*. New York: Norton.

Fromm, E., 1941. *Escape from freedom*. New York: Holt, Rinehart and Winston.

Fromm, E., 1947. *Man for himself*. New York: Holt, Rinehart and Winston.

Ginzberg, E., Ginsburg, S. W., Axelrad, S., and Herma, J. L., 1951. *Occupational choice*. New York: Columbia Univ. Press.

Hall, C. S., and Lindzey, G., 1957. *Theories of personality*. New York: Wiley.

Hilgard, E. R., 1949. Human motives and the concept of the self. *Amer. Psychologist*, **4**, 374–382.

Hovland, C. I., Lumsdaine, A. A., and Sheffield, F. D., 1949. *Experiments on mass communication*. Princeton: Princeton Univ. Press.

Hyman, H. H., 1953. The value systems of different classes: a social psychological contribution to the analysis of stratification. In R. Bendix and S. M. Lipset (Eds.), *Class, status and power*. Glencoe, Ill.: Free Press, pp. 426–442.

James, W., 1950. *The principles of psychology*. New York: Dover.

Kendall, P. L., and Wolfe, K. M., 1949. The analysis of deviant cases in communications research. In P. F. Lazarsfeld and F. N. Stanton (Eds.), *Communications research: 1948–49*. New York: Harper, pp. 152–179.

Kluckhohn, C., 1952. Values and value-orientations in the theory of action. In T. Parsons and E. A. Shils (Eds.), *Toward a general theory of action*. Cambridge, Mass.: Harvard Univ. Press, pp. 388–433.

Koffka, K., 1935. *Principles of gestalt psychology*. New York: Harcourt, Brace.

Krech, D., and Crutchfield, R. S., 1948. *Theory and problems of social psychology*. New York: McGraw-Hill.

Lazarsfeld, P. F., 1940. *Radio and the printed page*. New York: Duell, Sloan and Pearce.

Lazarsfeld, P. F., Berelson, B., and Gaudet, H., 1948. *The people's choice*. New York: Columbia Univ. Press.

Lazarsfeld, P. F., and Merton, R. K., 1943. Studies in radio and film propaganda. *Trans. N. Y. Acad. Sci.*, **6**, 58–79.

Lecky, P., 1945. *Self-consistency.* New York: Island Press.

Levine, J. M., and Murphy, G., 1943. The learning and forgetting of controversial material. *J. abnorm. soc. Psychol.,* **38,** 507–517.

McDougall, W., 1932. *The energies of men.* London: Methuen.

Maslow, A. H., 1954. *Motivation and personality.* New York: Harper.

Mead, G. H., 1934. *Mind, self and society.* Chicago: The Univ. of Chicago Press.

Moustakas, C. E. (Ed.), 1956. *The self: explorations in personal growth.* New York: Harper.

Murphy, G., 1947. *Personality.* New York: Harper.

Newcomb, T., 1950. *Social psychology.* New York: Dryden.

Raimy, V. C., 1948. Self-reference in counseling interviews. *J. consult. Psychol.,* **12,** 153–163.

Rogers, C. R., 1951. *Client-centered therapy: its current practice, implications, and theory.* Boston: Houghton Mifflin.

Rosenberg, M., 1957. *Occupations and values.* Glencoe, Ill.: Free Press.

Rosenberg, M., 1965. *Society and the adolescent self-image.* Princeton: Princeton Univ. Press.

Sherif, M., and Cantril, H., 1947. *The psychology of ego-involvements.* New York: Wiley.

Sherif, M., and Sherif, C. W., 1956. *An outline of social psychology.* (Rev. ed.) New York: Harper.

Star, S. A., 1950. The screening of psychoneurotics in the army: technical development of tests. In S. A. Stouffer, *et al. Measurement and prediction.* Princeton: Princeton Univ. Press, pp. 486–547.

Symonds, P. M., 1951. *The ego and the self.* New York: Appleton-Century-Crofts.

Wallen, R., 1942. Ego-involvement as a determinant of selective forgetting. *J. abnorm. soc. Psychol.,* **37,** 20–39.

Wiley, Ruth C., 1961. *The self concept.* Lincoln, Nebr.: Univ. of Nebraska Press.

Williams, R. M., Jr., 1951. *American society.* New York: Knopf.

Part II

4. Promise and Limitations of Laboratory Experiments in the Development of Attitude Change Theory*

Karl E. Weick

Trying to write on an overworked topic such as laboratory experiments can be a disquieting experience. In an effort to say something new, fantasy is often unloosed, and it sometimes leads to strange places. And so it was in the early stages of this chapter.

In thinking about laboratory experiments, my attention became fixated on the letter "D." For example, much of the focus in recent attitudinal research has been on *dissonance, discrepancy,* and *divergence.* Furthermore, if we look at the current batch of criticisms concerning the laboratory, a surprising number of them follow a pattern traced in "D's." For example, laboratory experimenters are now haunted by thoughts of *deception, debriefing, demands, disclosure, discretion, dishonesty, deutero-problems, discomfort,* and *dissembling.* If we go on to look closely at the *responses* to these criticisms, we find disillusionment, defection, dabbling, defiance, or defense. Unfortunately what we do not find is a healthy amount of determination, discipline, deliberation, digging, or daring.

* Preparation of this chapter was facilitated by the National Science Foundation through Grants GS-955 and GS-1042 administered by the author.

It is important to look closely at potential limitations of the laboratory because most investigators are eager to document, demonstrate, describe, delineate, detect, discover, duplicate, and disprove. For many of these activities the laboratory is essential. The purpose of this chapter is to suggest that some of the criticisms of the laboratory have been diversionary; they have centered on pseudo-issues. Once these issues are pinpointed, we can accurately dissect experiments and examine their place in the development of attitude change theory.

It is probably apparent by now how my discussion will end. Most discussions of the laboratory conclude by acknowledging that there are limitations to field research and limitations to laboratory research, and, therefore, science will progress if both methods are used. I take a somewhat more controversial position. My conclusion, stated in advance, is that there are *NO* limitations to experiments. The limitations instead involve laboratory *experimenters,* their decisions and their concerns. Laboratory experiments themselves are not inherently limiting. Instead the limitations arise from the ways in which experiments have been implemented and the conception of what a laboratory is. Given this perspective, it should be apparent that there is hope for change and improvement if we can just get to the experimenters.

The remainder of the chapter will be divided into two main sections. Since I have stated rather blatantly that there are no limitations to experiments, I shall first deal with several ways in which laboratory experiments do, in fact, limit and constrain attitude research. The second main section dwells on promises of laboratory experiments and suggests some solutions to the limitations that are uncovered.

LIMITATIONS OF THE LABORATORY

Fault can be found with laboratory experimenters at many points for their preoccupations, oversights, and naïveté. It is not our intent to absolve them from responsibility for these errors. But, many criticisms of experiments have not been helpful because they have produced labels that are more evaluative than descriptive, more global than specific. As a result, the impression has emerged that several problems in the conduct of laboratory experiments are intractable. It is concluded that experiments are most useful for a selected and relatively narrow range of questions in attitude research. The latter conclusion seems both questionable and premature.

The following discussion enumerates seven properties of laboratory experiments that have blinded experimenters to crucial issues in attitude change. These properties, however, are not immutable. They can be modified by changes in research conceptions and procedure. There is the further possibility that those properties of the laboratory that resist changes can be exploited more fully to provide answers about significant issues in attitude change. The first property contains one example.

The Compliant Laboratory

One crucial drawback of the laboratory for attitude change research is that many laboratory settings produce acquiescence rather than independence (Orne, 1962). The phrase "obedient subject" used to refer to a person who was loyal to a ruler in some mythical kingdom. Lately the phrase has become an onerous threat to the experimenter who tries to demonstrate that he knows something about attitude change.

The aura of compliance in the laboratory stems from several sources: the presumed credibility of the experimenter, his role as an expert, the uncertainty with which subjects approach experiments, their desire to help science, the fact that experiments are tied closely to classroom work because of requirements for credit, and so forth. Because compliance is pervasive, a distorted view of attitude change often emerges from the laboratory.

The experimenter is salient as a powerful person who controls rewards and punishment. Therefore, he is apt to induce some change, but the change is usually fleeting. Even if the experimenter intends that manipulations in an experiment produce enduring change, it is probable that pressures toward compliance would swamp his manipulations. For example, if we adopt Kelman's (1958) terminology, it is conceivable that attitude change could be produced in the laboratory because the subject finds something attractive about the communicator that he would like to emulate (identification). The point is that the subject probably never gets the chance to entertain this possibility. Compliance is more salient, and any changes that are produced reflect the pressures of the immediate experimenter-subject relationship.

One solution to this problem is simply to turn a vice into a virtue. If compliance is a prominent component of the laboratory, if it is expected and therefore has high ecological validity in this setting, why not exploit the laboratory to learn more about compliance? Our knowledge concerning this topic is still scant.

This solution is not very elegant to researchers who are fascinated by other processes. Researchers are also unwilling to have their interests legislated by a shortcoming of laboratory procedures. To many, it seems important instead to discover ways in which pressures toward compliance can be reduced. This is a difficult problem to solve, but it clearly deserves attention.

Pressures toward compliance might be reduced by having accomplices of the experimenter who were noncompliant (accomplices who essentially show that noncompliance is acceptable); by disengaging experiments from classes; by greater usage of hired subjects or subjects in natural settings; by conveying the impression to students that science is fallible; or by using laymen to administer experimental treatments. Admittedly, these are weak suggestions that probably create more problems than they solve. The point is that careful attention directed toward this rather specific issue might go a long way toward increasing the relevance of laboratory experiments for attitude change research.

The Confrontive Laboratory

Numerous issues in attitude change research have been bypassed in the typical experiment simply because once the subject arrives at the laboratory, he is confronted by an attempt to persuade him and he must do something about the attempt before he leaves, even if this means ignoring it. Hovland (1959) noted that laboratory experiments are somewhat unique because subjects have little opportunity to expose themselves selectively to issues. Sherif, Sherif, and Nebergall (1965) make the important point that "the laboratory . . . [omits] the first and crucial phase of most communication situations: the communicator must secure and hold an audience for his message" (p. 171).

The fact of confrontation has many drawbacks other than the omission of the first stage in communication. Dissonance theorists have studied largely postdecisional phenomena. Since their research situations confront subjects with decisions that *must* be made, they have essentially overlooked the fact that persons often *avoid* (*e.g.*, Braden and Walster, 1964) or postpone decisions.

The confrontive nature of the laboratory probably may have persuaded researchers that persons hold beliefs that are highly interrelated. While it may be true that persons *do* strive to maximize consistent linkages among their beliefs, it is also true that the nature of most experimental situations makes it very difficult for a subject to compartmentalize his beliefs and to restrict their linkages. Furthermore, many measurement procedures used in the laboratory actually *suggest* linkages to the subject. Before experimenters conclude that persons try to maximize linkages in consistent directions, they would be wise to reexamine whether this impression might not be an artifact of laboratory procedures.

Still another problem posed by confrontation is that it is difficult for subjects to delay tension reduction. Most laboratory situations compel the subject to deal with discomfort immediately. There is little chance for the subject to maintain discomfort in order to gain more information about an issue. Yet there seem to be many occasions when persons will tolerate inconsistency in order to reexamine their beliefs and decisions and to profit from their mistakes. The impression that persons make immediate and large shifts in their beliefs merely to restore balance may be less a commentary on people than a commentary on the unique pressures that operate in the laboratory.

These problems are serious but not insolvable. Having pinpointed them, we are now in a better position to take corrective action. One implication is that a theory of attitude change built largely on laboratory experiments will have some obvious gaps. These gaps may center on issues of selective exposure, tolerance of momentary discomfort, and number of linkages. But one remedy is to study just these questions. Freedman and Sears (1965), for example, have recently shown that selective exposure can be studied in the laboratory.

Perhaps even more basic is a reconsideration of the issue of change. Hovland (1959) noted that change is demonstrated much more frequently in the laboratory than it is in the field. Presumably, this greater incidence of change is partly due to confrontations. The crucial question, however, seems to be not so much whether the *amount* of change differs in the two settings but whether the form and structure of change differ in the two settings. Latitudes of noncommitment (Sherif, Sherif, and Nebergall, 1965) may be more extensive in the laboratory than they are in the field. If so, change may be demonstrated more readily in the laboratory. But does this mean that there is discontinuity between change processes observed in the laboratory and change processes observed in the field?

Problems of confrontation may also be minimized by embedding an attitude change manipulation in other events, permitting the subject some options concerning exposure. Relevant data would be provided both by those who choose to be exposed and those who do not.

Finally, it seems reasonable to suggest that the laboratory setting, in all its confrontiveness, may provide opportunities to study persuasible moments (Watson, 1966). There are occasions when persons are easily persuaded, for example, after a series of failures (Mausner,

1954). Although these moments may be fleeting, they are certainly not rare in everyday life. They may produce as much impact as more concentrated attempts at persuasion. If laboratory experiments were directed less at trying to simulate the impacts produced by mass media and more at trying to capture fleeting instances when confrontation is plausible and persons are susceptible, they might be better able to supplement existing knowledge.

The Rational Laboratory

Experiments seem to have an uncommonly rational and logical flavor. Literate, knowledgeable college students, whose classroom experience has probably alerted them to gaps in their thinking, are brought into a setting where they are on display before a presumably rational, incisive, sophisticated psychologist. Is it any wonder that these subjects feel some pressures to appear consistent?

The flavor of rationality is often enhanced because large amounts of information are presented that must be read and evaluated. Information is easy to manipulate in an experiment. But its presentation in a single concentrated message can easily prod persons to look for flaws, inconsistencies and gaps. Since there are few distractions in the laboratory while the information is being presented, these flaws may be especially visible. We should not overlook the additional fact that the typical attitude change experiment bears a marked resemblance to the classroom situation where pressures do indeed exist for coherence and consistency of thought.

Remedies for the rational flavor of experiments are difficult to suggest. Remedies may not be necessary if we consider the laboratory as a good setting in which to study the *rational* side of attitude change. Obvious as this point may be, experimenters seem to miss it on occasion. Many theories of attitude change turn out to be hypotheses that should be considered special cases within more general theories of cognition. Failure to grasp this point has meant that experimenters use more complex procedures than would otherwise be necessary. Their time might more profitably be spent examining conditions that cause attention to narrow, conditions that inhibit discrimination and selection, and conditions in which persons attain and revise concepts.

Problems created by rationality per se might yield to changes in procedure such as separating portions of the communique so that it is more difficult for the parts to be compared, or one might distract subjects so that their attention is divided between the communique and another task. Other possible procedures to minimize the rational set of the laboratory might be to sanction inconsistency by convincing subjects that open-mindedness is as much of a virtue as orderliness and consistency, to confront the subject with several issues so that it is more difficult for him to monitor the consistency of his responses, to make experiments less public so that subjects feel fewer pressures to appear consistent or to divorce attitude change experiments from educational settings.

In many ways, the fact that the laboratory is rational may not be too crucial for attitude change research. The principal effect of the rational flavor will be to magnify considerations of consistency. The laboratory may present an accurate portrait of the attitude change process when people are thoughtful, deliberate, and objective. It may provide less information about how persons process a communique when their capacities for critical thinking are subordinated to other interests such as affiliating with a reference group, seeing what a prominent communicator looks like, or "killing time" (see Festinger and Maccoby, 1964, for an example of nonrationality in the laboratory).

The Lonely Laboratory

Hovland (1959) and Sherif, Sherif, and Nebergall (1965) have made the important point that when subjects enter the laboratory they do not leave their reference groups at the door. It is one of the ironies of current social psychology that it has become a psychology of individuals and not of individuals in groups. This emphasis has serious consequences for attitude change research, for many important attitudes are formed and maintained in order to retain ties with persons whose evaluations count.

If a subject is isolated from reference persons in the laboratory, he may exhibit marked attitude change because he is unable to compare his attitudes with those of relevant peers or because he knows that peers are unlikely to find out what stand he took. On the other hand, he may try to act as if the reference group were present and respond to the message in terms of his best guess of how others would respond. Still another possibility is that the subject may convince himself that the reference group really is indifferent about the issue, in which case his concern with the issue would diminish also.

It is understandable that researchers have been reluctant to look at attitude change in anything but an individual setting. It is difficult to compose in the laboratory a set of persons that the subject will take seriously. If intact groups are brought into the laboratory, it is difficult to account for observed attitude change because the effects may be due to some moderating variable that the group members share in common.

There are numerous ways in which one might respond to the fact that the laboratory is a lonely setting. Reexamination of the concept of reference groups would seem to be part of the solution. It is true that social support is important in attitude change. It is also true that social support can originate in many places, whether it be with reference individuals or reference groups. It is commonly assumed that when a person is urged to adopt a discrepant position, he reinstates a prominent group in order to evaluate the consequences of shifting his belief. It would seem equally plausible that a person with several important groups might also search among these groups until he found one that would support the new position.

Most persons have assumed that the reference group is fixed and the attitude is free to vary. We are suggesting that when a subject receives a persuasive communique in a lonely setting, the reverse may occur, namely the attitude is fixed and the reference population is varied. Notice that in most discussions of reference groups there is the presumption that persons are highly dependent on a small number of groups. To phrase this in Thibaut and Kelley's (1959) language, it is presumed they have a low comparison level for alternatives. The effect of the comparison level for alternatives on persuasibility is relatively unknown, but it would seem important to learn the relationship in order to explain what happens when subjects are isolated from groups.

There is still some ambiguity about what role reference groups play when subjects arrive at the laboratory. However, there is no ambiguity concerning the fact that attitude change typically occurs in the company of other persons and that the evaluations of other persons are an important input. Recent concepts such as diffusion of responsibility (Wallach, Kogan and Bem, 1964) and social facilitation (Zajonc, 1965) have striking implications for attitude change. Researchers studying intra-individual processes have been slow to pick up these leads. It is as though researchers, ever since they started to simulate a group by means of a tape recording (Blake and Brehm, 1954), have believed that they were studying social interaction. More accurately, they are studying social *reaction*, not social *inter*action. For this reason they have bypassed one of the crucial ways in which a group can influence attitude change.

Social support implies an *exchange* of views, not merely a recitation of views. Discussions of attitudinal issues are admittedly difficult to control; but rather than ignore exchange because it presents stubborn methodological problems, researchers might more profitably spend time developing procedures to allow the lonely subject to have some company. These procedural refinements could range from improved observational categories to encode influence in ongoing groups (*e.g.*, Hoffman and Maier, 1964) to such devises as the use of multiple-track recorders to convey controlled, quasi-conversational inputs to the subjects (J. Darley private communication, 1966).

As a final point, it should be mentioned that the vice of the lonely laboratory can also be translated into a virtue for at least one important set of questions in attitude research. If a subject is removed from group ties and has few standards to use in evaluating a communication, then perhaps the standards which he adopts are especially sensitive to situational conditions. Our knowledge about the effects of situational variables on the establishment of anchors is quite incomplete. Research by Whittaker (1964) and Schachter and Singer (1962) suggests that significant relationships exist in this area. Uncertainty has high ecological validity in the laboratory, and uncertainty is not as rare in field settings as we might imagine. Ego-involvements may be potent in determining the placement of communications. Still, a person who ignores his surroundings is in for a great deal of trouble in trying to adapt to contingencies.

The Impatient Laboratory

A seemingly innocuous property of many laboratory experiments is that they last for one or two hours. This strict scheduling is often mandatory so that experiments can be coordinated with the class schedules of the subjects. Furthermore, experimenters are always wary that subjects will talk about experimental procedures, regardless of what they promise. One of the best ways to minimize this possibility is simply to run the experiment quickly "before the word gets around." The collapsing of significant persuasion events into one hour has the obvious consequence that we often have theories about immediate reactions to persuasion but know less about long-term effects. However, long-term change is being assessed with greater frequency (*e.g.*, Freedman, 1965; Walster, 1964) so this is not quite the problem that it used to be.

There are other more subtle ways in which impatience has colored some of the conclusions about attitude change that have come from the laboratory. For one thing, most experimenters assume that experimental treatments are engaged immediately and that their effects are not delayed. They also presume that treatments operate simultaneously and throughout the exercise. If there is any lag in the impact of a treatment, it is assumed to be randomly distributed across subjects. Perhaps a more realistic picture of what occurs is that subjects initially are confused by laboratory procedures. Their attention is not focused wholly on the instructions because they are trying to figure out what the experimenter is up to. They are unfamiliar with the experimenter and are getting used to him.

The harassed experimenter who must get everything completed within the hour often does not have time to permit the subject to get acclimated. As a result the subject is often engaged in reading or listening to persuasive materials *before* all of the instructions sink in. Thus, *early* in the experiment his exposure to information is not affected by the manipulations; but in the latter stages his behavior may well be under the control of the manipulation. If a single score is used to measure the impact of the message, it is possible that the partial impact of the manipulation will be obscured, and no differences will emerge. The point is that the treatment may actually be potent, but what has happened is that the manipulation was not in effect the entire time. Closer attention to this phenomenon, and steps to study its effect, might go a long way toward separating stable from unstable laboratory phenomena.

Impatience may take quite a different form. Perhaps our experiments are too long; perhaps we are not impatient enough. A ten-second exposure to a sign in which the persuasive content is varied systematically might produce just as much change as a one-hour exposure. Webb *et al.* (1966) suggest, for example, that traffic signs on highways might be constructed with varying degrees of fearful messages, the behavior of drivers being observed from a helicopter once they pass the sign. Although it may seem ludicrous to compare the impact of a ten-second message with that of a ten-minute or a ten-hour message, there is no reason a priori to expect that one has any more impact than the other. Many of the problems of laboratory settings that we have discussed so far are absent in the ten-second exposure, and there is some evidence that brief events can produce irreversible change (*e.g.,* Davis, 1930).

Attitude change, after all, often boils down to a process where some message initiates activity in the subject, activity which may continue long after he leaves the persuasion setting. There seems to be nothing magical about a one-hour exposure that promises more subsequent activity than a ten-second exposure. In fact, if one takes the Zeigarnik demonstration seriously (*e.g.,* Cartwright, 1942), it is conceivable that a short cryptic communique might produce more deliberation than a self-contained, symmetrical, packaged communique.

Experimenters who believe that significant events occur in one-hour units also may be prone to make incomplete analyses of events that are short-lived. The richness of data obtained over a very short period of time has been dramatically demonstrated in an important book by Pittenger, Hockett, and Danehy (1960) entitled *The First Five Minutes*. These authors have made an exhaustive analysis of only the first five minutes of the first interview between one therapist and one patient. Trivial as this segment might seem when compared with information produced over several therapy sessions, the startling fact is that almost all of the significant themes that later emerged in more detail during the therapy were present in the first five minutes. Furthermore, these themes were *repeated* several times during the first five minutes.

The point seems clear that extending the duration of an attitude change experiment offers no assurance that significant content or attitudinal structure will emerge. A more intensive look at shorter segments of persuasion may produce just as much information as a more cursory look at longer segments. A close look at a short segment has the added advantage that a more restricted range of verbal prods from the communicator are present. Hence, it is easier for the investigator to see relationships between inputs from the communicator and responses by the audience.

Although it may seem that we are belaboring the issue of time, it does seem reasonable that the typical one-hour unit of time for exposing subjects to a communique need not be regarded as prescriptive. If experimenters reexamine their ideas about duration of exposure, they might be better able to devise more potent manipulations, gain a better understanding of the process of attitude change at a molecular level, and even propose some valuable concepts to help explain what occurs during attitude change.

The Sedentary Laboratory

Most subjects who participate in attitude change experiments lead an uncommonly passive life. They are seated, exposed to a communique, evaluate the message, and then are excused, very possibly to leave the laboratory and take some action that will either stabilize or undo the effects of the message which they just heard. Alas, the experimenter will never know, because he remains in the laboratory, comfortable that he has observed a significant portion of the attitude change process.

One of the most common discussions among researchers is that there seems to be a poor fit between attitudes and behavior. Perhaps their puzzlement is not so surprising when we consider that very seldom do they watch attitude change *and* behavior at one sitting in the laboratory. Seldom are subjects given the opportunity to *do* anything about their beliefs. Thus, it should not be surprising that attitudes change in the laboratory but that these changes are fleeting.

The changes might be more stable *IF* the subject could do something to validate or find support for them (*e.g.,* Festinger, 1964). Hovland made a similar point in 1959 (p. 182), yet it has often been overlooked in favor of his more straightforward comparisons of the laboratory and the field. He noted that the field has numerous feedback loops that are absent in the laboratory. One consequence of these loops is that they affect influences that occurred earlier in the persuasion sequence.

Recent research on task enhancement (Weick, 1964, 1966b) shows that if persons agree to work on a task for insufficient reasons, they reevaluate the situation and find additional attractions. More important, when they are actually given the chance to take some action that would validate these revised beliefs, they engage in such behavior to a striking degree. It appears that persons are eager to find support for cognitive realignments, and intense behavioral involvement tends to generate such support. Furthermore, once the belief is validated, it becomes quite stable. It is *not* abandoned as soon as the subject leaves the laboratory.

Failure to provide opportunities for attitude-relevant actions has also meant that researchers have overlooked an especially engaging portrayal of the attitude change process, namely the self-fulfilling prophecy (Merton, 1957). Although there are certain ambiguities about this formulation, it does suggest some interesting questions. The notion here is, of course, that a person makes a false definition of a situation (for example, Negroes are inferior), and this definition evokes a behavior that makes the false conception come true (for example, funds for education are withheld, and Negroes turn out to be inferior and uneducated). Here is an excellent example where actions coupled with feedback loops affect prior beliefs.

Incidentally, one part of Merton's formulation that is generally overlooked is the interesting proposition that there is also a "suicidal prophecy." This is a prophecy that "so alters human behavior from what would have been its course had it not been made, that it *fails* to be borne out. The prophecy destroys itself" (p. 423). If greater attention were paid to actions subsequent to attitude change, it seems probable that researchers might also "discover" this effect. One can think of several instances where prophecies are self-destructive. A person, for example, believes that the skills of Negroes are vastly underrated. He assigns to a Negro employee a task that he is incapable of doing, and because of the erroneous initial definition of the situation, the prophecy fails.

Until researchers take more seriously the old bromide that "the belief fathers the reality" and until they provide subjects with more opportunities to do something about beliefs, they will have to be content both with temporary changes in attitudes and with theories of attitude change that fail to specify mechanisms for stabilization.

The Petty Laboratory

Undoubtedly the most persistent objection to laboratory studies of attitude change is that subjects confront trivial issues, issues in which the latitude of noncommitment is extensive, issues that are not ego-involving. Some warrant is seen for this practice because if a researcher wants to study change, he must choose an issue on which change can occur. But warrant for this practice seems to vanish when theoretical positions differ on the relationship between discrepancy and attitude change. Because the issue of ego-involvement in attitude change has constructively been hounding the laboratory experimenter for some time, it should be examined closely.

At the outset it might be well to mention that ego-involvement can be a seductive label. It is a concept with many meanings, and until its recent operationalizing in the form of the own-categories procedure (Sherif, Sherif, and Nebergall, 1965) it was an elusive target. It was easy, for example, to argue that if social judgmental phenomena did not occur, the subjects were not involved, and if they did occur, that subjects were involved. However, convincing independent checks on involvement were difficult to obtain. Hopefully the recent advances in measurement of ego-involvement will arrest some of the data-free controversy about this variable and direct it toward more specific issues.

If ego-involvement is low in the laboratory, one obvious solution is to heighten it. Experimenters have often been lazy when it comes to choosing an issue and often adopt whatever is uppermost in *their own* minds at the moment. Carolyn Sherif (see Sherif, Sherif, and Nebergall, 1965, p. 184), however, more systematically canvassed students to find out what they were concerned about and found that public affairs were much less important than were issues involving interpersonal problems. Experimenters may be much more out of touch with student life than they realize. Acknowledgment of this fact coupled with greater attention to student concerns might improve the attitudinal content of laboratory studies using student subjects.

Aside from issue content, ego-involvement may be enhanced by pointing out to the subject that his beliefs are vulnerable (McGuire, 1964) or by pointing to inconsistent notions that he has about a topic (McGuire, 1960). One drawback of these procedures is that they could easily shake the confidence that a subject has in his beliefs and make him uncertain. Uncertainty heightens influenceability. The point is that the experimenter might have a difficult time knowing whether attitude change occurred because the subject was uncertain or because he was ego-involved or both.

Ego-involvement can also be enhanced if the subject makes a choice. And it is this issue around which some misunderstanding of dissonance theory has emerged. The misunderstanding has occurred because dissonance researchers have never been very explicit about this point. Temerlin (1963), a psychotherapist, has presented an incisive description of the relationship between choice and involvement. His main point is that a man is his choices or the techniques he uses to avoid making choices. Whenever a person makes a choice, he shows someone else what he is like, and there is always the danger that the impression conveyed will be negative. Temerlin also demonstrates that defense mechanisms can be viewed as ways to avoid choice and responsibility.

The relevant point of all of this seems to be that the mere act of making a choice can heighten ego-involvement. A choice, after all, is a performance, and it is a performance that is open to inspection and evaluation. Thus, even though much dissonance research involves issues that seem trivial, the point is that these issues may become more involving for the subject because he has taken some stand relative to them. A portion of himself is on display that was not earlier. Since it is not immediately clear whether the choice conveys a favorable or unfavorable impression, the person should feel considerable pressure to convince himself, at least, that the choice was credible or to disengage himself from any responsibility for the choice. Thus, it seems that when dissonance research is criticized for using trivial issues the criticism may be misplaced. It is not the issue, it is the choice that produces involvement. Now, if the choice is such that the person is unlikely to see it as an extension of himself, then indeed low ego-involvement is present.

Let us suppose for the moment that it is difficult to get subjects ego-involved in the laboratory. Even if this is true, the situation is certainly not hopeless. Although latitudes of noncommitment may be extensive on issues studied in the laboratory, it would be absurd to presume that all issues have identical latitudes. At least it should be possible to order laboratory issues in terms of those which have greater and lesser latitudes of noncommitment. If this is done, then we have some gradations of ego-involvement, fine as they may be. If the predictions of judgmental theory are valid, differences in placement and attitude change should be evident even in this restricted range.

As a final point concerning the pettiness of the laboratory, it seems possible that "big" issues, significant topics, beliefs in which noncommitment is minimal, may be the exception rather than the rule. The fact that we often have to look so hard to find an ego-involving issue may be less of a commentary about our resourcefulness and more of a commentary on the way things are where we are looking. It is easy to be deceived that because we as experimenters dwell on a single issue and become absorbed in it while writing communiques and quizzing endless subjects that the issue really is prominent and that subjects single it out in real life for a great deal of attention. There is a certain routine about life, a *lack* of confrontation that we may overlook. The academic mind seeks controversy, delights in debate, and devours information. It may, after all, be a rather specific and narrow model on which to base our ideas about attitude change. When issues arise in everyday life, they do not always arise with forewarning and fanfare, nor do persons always see the relevance of an issue to their self-concept or to their group ties. They may have only the vaguest ideas about the implications of an issue. Thus, we might find large amounts of concern and interest without these necessarily being reflected in narrow latitudes of noncommitment.

Maybe all it boils down to is this: Although we may know something about how persons handle dramatic and prominent issues, we probably know very little about mundane attitude change, change on issues that involve the small, relatively insignificant topics which constitute the bulk of a person's daily interaction. There does seem to be a certain amount of drama associated with attitude research. Issues with high ego-involvement may be less prominent in daily interaction than we suppose. For some purposes, reactions to issues on which the person is noncommitted may be just as crucial as those on which he is highly committed.

PROMISES OF THE LABORATORY

Until now we have been discussing limitations of the laboratory with several suggestions about what could be done about the problems. This section describes a few more general solutions to some of the problems that have already been discussed.

Infiltrate Sensitivity Training Groups

A seemingly lucrative and insufficiently tapped source of data about attitude change would seem to exist in T-groups (*e.g.* Schein and Bennis, 1965). These are groups in which persons are together for an extended period of time and in which there is a "joint commitment among interdependent persons to 'process analysis'" (Shepard, 1964, p. 379). T-groups seem to contain most of the properties that we would deem important in the study of attitude change: The groups do become a reference group within a relatively short period of time; there is extended face-to-face contact; almost nothing *but* ego-involving topics emerge; throughout there is an emphasis on the *accurate* placement of communiques, but this emphasis is emergent and permits before and after comparisons; persons are pressed toward expanding their latitudes of acceptance and rejection and narrowing their latitudes of noncommitment; selective exposure is identified and attacked; and there are attempts to help participants tolerate inconsistency and to accept paradox as a part of life.

It might be mentioned in addition that many of the problems associated with asymmetric interaction (Jones and Thibaut, 1958) between the experimenter and the subject in laboratories are absent in T-groups. There is a more equitable exchange, namely the participants provide observations and personal data in return for which they receive help with their concerns. Logically at least, the pressures for ego-involvement are high because the more honest the person is, the more relevant and valuable will be the feedback.

Technically, an investigation of T-groups may not qualify as a laboratory experiment in the usual sense. In this connection it seems important that we avoid being provincial about what a laboratory experiment is. One solution to many of the problems we have detailed is to maintain flexibility concerning *sites* for data collection, while retaining those properties of the laboratory that we have learned to value. Surely, there is no rule that a laboratory has to be in an academic setting.

Diversify Persuasion Tasks

There is considerable sterility among experimenters concerning the format of most persuasion tasks. Not only are these tasks quite transparent to an alert subject, but, as noted earlier, they are only crude analogues of persuasion settings in everyday life. They seldom permit the subject to engage in relevant actions.

A particularly interesting approach to attitude change is the research of Breer and Locke (1965). Basically their notion is that if some attitude (such as cooperation, individualism, or future orientation) is instrumental to task performance and if the task is successfully performed, then the attitude will be adopted more readily by the subject in later situations. Failure at the task will hinder adoption of the attitude. The importance of this work seems to lie not so much in the formulation itself as in the suggestion that crucial beliefs can be embedded in tasks and that, depending on their instrumentality for task accomplishment, beliefs will be adopted or rejected.

Dependent Variable Obsession

It seems ironic that even though persons who study attitude change repeatedly make pronouncements that attitudes are inferred from behavior, they have been negligent in detailing the behaviors from which attitudes are inferred. Instead, most researchers seem preoccupied with independent variables. For the dependent variable, they have settled for crude ratings as the basis to accept or reject hypotheses. It would seem crucial to look more closely for behavioral correlates of attitudes, behaviors such as posture (Scheflen, 1964), facial expression (e.g., Ekman, 1965), gestures (e.g., Krout, 1954), vocal inflections (e.g., Hargreaves and Starkweather, 1963), hesitations in speech (e.g., Goldman-Eisler, 1958), verbal slips (Mahl, 1956), and distances people stand from one another (e.g., Sommer and Ross, 1958).

For example, Hall (1966) presents considerable evidence suggesting that persons who are attracted to one another stand or sit closer together. Proximatic behavior has several implications for procedures in attitude change experiments. Suppose that a communicator tries to change the beliefs of several students. At the conclusion of his presentation, the experimenter tells the subjects and the communicator to fill out some forms in another room before they leave. When the subjects go to the adjacent room they find several folding chairs stacked against the wall. In order to answer the questionnaires they have to set up their own chairs. The dependent variable is simply how far each subject sits from the communicator. Presumably, those subjects who were more persuaded will like the communicator more and will sit closer to him than will those subjects who resisted the persuasion. Admittedly there are some problems with this measure. For example, a person who resists a communicator may feel uncomfortable and want to show the communicator that there was "nothing personal" about the fact that the message was unpersuasive. A subject who felt this way might sit close to the communicator.

Problematic as some of the proposed behavioral measures may be, it seems clear that they are not any more ambiguous than are several of the paper-and-pencil measures that investigators have labored over for years. Refinement of behavioral indices of attitude (*e.g.,* Cook and Selltiz, 1964) coupled with more vigorous attempts to conceptualize linkages between attitudes and behavior (Weick, 1966b) should increase the relevance of attitude change experiments.

Many social psychologists erroneously assume that most of the significant interactions among persons are verbal. There is an ample, sophisticated, and relevant literature concerning nonverbal behavior, showing both that attitudinal content is encoded in body language and that these indices are much more difficult to falsify than are self-reports.

Aside from using nonverbal behaviors to assess attitude change, studies of attitude change would profit from greater use of unobtrusive measures, measures that do not alert the subject that his beliefs are being assessed. An elegant example of an unobtrusive attitude measure is the "lost letters" technique developed by Milgram, Mann, and Harter (1965). The investigator essentially "loses" stamped letters in places such as telephone booths, store counters, and along sidewalks. The letters are addressed to persons with clearly differing beliefs (for example, N.A.A.C.P., White Citizens Council, Friends of the American Communist Party, Medical Research Associates, Mr. Walter Carnap). When a person finds one of these letters, he is free to mail it, destroy it, or ignore it. Presumably his beliefs will be an important determinant of his actions. Thus, with appropriate controls in the form of letters addressed to neutral persons, it is possible to assess for various areas within a city or state, the prevailing sentiment on important issues without the participant realizing that his response is part of an attitude survey.

Incidentally, the use of unobtrusive measures seems to be especially pertinent in testing a judgmental theory of attitude change, because placement of communiques is a crucial process and placement can be affected by measurement procedures. Sherif, Sherif, and Nebergall (1965, p. 228) note, however, that camouflaging an "exhortation to change" can reduce displacement. This would suggest that embedded manipulations and unobtrusive measures would be especially important in testing judgmental theory.

Temper Nature

Much of the folklore concerning experiments and field research suggests that investigators tighten controls in the laboratory, whereas in the field they abandon controls. Both sides of this folklore are clearly unrealistic. Laboratory experiments are frequently less controlled than persons thought, as is shown elegantly in Friedman's (1964) discussion of the "standardization myth." It is also clear now that field observers are *more* obtrusive than had been imagined. They often unwittingly divert and control supposedly natural events. In short, the two research strategies are becoming more alike.

The prospect of subtle manipulative controls in natural settings has some obvious attractions, as indeed the Sherifs (*e.g.*, Sherif, Harvey, White, Hood, and Sherif, 1961) have demonstrated. Recently this strategy of research has been described in detail and has been termed "tempered naturalness." Essentially the idea is as follows:

> The trappings of the natural event are preserved, it unfolds in a conventional manner, but some of its peripheral qualities are qualified. . . . The most common means to accomplish such qualification is to put boundaries around some portion of the ongoing event. This means essentially that participants are exposed to an input that has a beginning and an end, an input that fits into the setting in the sense that it is plausible and expected, an input that is nonreactive and does not arouse suspicion, and an input that permits greater precision in measurement. The input that is referred to is essentially modeled after a laboratory task that has been altered sufficiently in appearance so that it fits into the setting for observation. It is the task which elicits the behavior which the observer records. A directed setting consistent with this model can be created either when an intact task is plausibly "dropped into" the behavior stream (*e.g.*, visitors to a health exposition see films about lung cancer that vary in vividness and their subsequent actions are watched, Leventhal and Niles, 1964) or when the stream of activities is altered so that it contains the essential properties of a task (*e.g.*, the beliefs of a person in a shopping center are mildly or strongly attacked by a communique which she reads during a feigned "man on the street" radio interview, Miller, 1965) (Weick, 1966a).

The use of tempered naturalness seems to have the advantage that it lends coherence to the process of inquiry. When persons advocate that both the field and laboratory should be used as sites for data collection, they sometimes overlook the important point that alternating between the two strategies makes it more difficult to maintain similar or comparable definitions of a concept. When an investigator shifts from the field to the laboratory or vice versa, he typically makes sizeable changes in procedures and measures. When these changes are made, it becomes difficult to tell whether the same process is being studied or whether the potential explanations have multiplied.

One advantage of "tempered naturalness" is that the investigator does not start at one end of the continuum of internal-external validity (Campbell, 1957); instead he starts at a middle point. The advantage of starting at a middle point is that it is easier for the investigator to remove or add properties systematically and to keep track of the ways in which his procedures have been modified. In addition, he can move from the central position to either a field or laboratory setting with fewer changes in procedure. This means that definitions of variables remain essentially intact and there is greater likelihood that the investigator is studying the same process.

It would be incorrect to conclude that we are arguing against those persons who advocate that the field and laboratory be used as complementary sites for data collection. Quite to the contrary. The position maintained here is that both sites are necessary. If both are employed, concepts will become more robust. The point here is if a study originates in a relatively pure laboratory or field setting, the investigator typically must change several features of the basic procedure as he moves to the other setting. As these changes proliferate, there is more danger that a different process is being observed. It would seem that investigators who use both sites have not always been mindful of this possibility.

As a final point concerning tempered naturalness, it should be noted that, since this strategy shares many features found also in the laboratory, there may be the attendant temptation to use this strategy for one-shot investigations. One important advantage of field studies is that they can be extended over time, and, therefore, they often provide a more detailed picture of the process and stability of attitude change. There is a certain compactness about tempered naturalness that may lead the investigator to repeat the error of "impatience" discussed earlier and to look at only a short portion of the attitude change process. It would seem worthwhile in designing a procedure which is based on tempered naturalness to incorporate manipulations and measures that permit greater exploitation of the temporal dimensions of events.

Abolish Quasi-ecological Aims

Much attitude change research suffers from a plurality of self-defeating aims. Many studies begin as an attempt to describe the distribution of opinions among sections of the population. This purpose, however, often becomes blurred when the investigator adds to the study one or more manipulations to address some theoretical issue in attitude change theory. The net result is often a study in which there is a cryptic and inaccurate view of the distribution of opinions, and the manipulations are sufficiently gross and complex that they are difficult to interpret. Neither theory nor description are advanced when aims get mixed in this fashion.

In a sense, the argument here is the complement of the argument associated with tempered naturalness. The rationale for tempered naturalness is that laboratory and field methodologies share significant properties and that portions of both methodologies might be combined in the final design. However, combining methodological properties is *not* the same as combining questions or aims. Tempered naturalness pertains to the *refinement* of procedures, but *as* a procedure it may tempt investigators to ask questions that are less well defined. The seduction occurs because tempered naturalness typically involves a natural setting where a person might well learn about real-world properties of an issue while he also reduces competing explanations by means of appropriate controls. The point is that tempered naturalness does not insure that both aims will be accomplished. The investigator still has to assign priorities in a study. He still has to be clear just what questions he is asking. If the intent of the study is to test theory, then information concerning the distribution of positions in the population will probably be less valid. Similarly, if the intent is to determine the prevailing sentiment on an issue, intrusion into the behavioral stream will have to be held to a subtle minimum. With lesser intrusion, theoretical propositions may be tested less precisely.

Obvious as these points may be, it seems that the running debate within attitude change research concerning the merits of field and laboratory studies has tempted investigators to ask, within the same study, questions that are incompatible. Asking incompatible questions is quite different from employing a set of procedures that involve the best portions of various methodologies. We are simply arguing that research will improve in this area if investigators take care to preserve important differences in their questions while they also search for similarities in strategy.

As questions become clarified, it should be possible for investigators to engage more vigorously in "pure" ecological research, a type of research that is essentially absent from current attitude literature. Even though attitude change research has both field and laboratory data relevant to its questions, there is a significant gap concerning the ecology of natural attitude change. Attitude change theory still lacks a thorough description such as that provided by Barker and Wright (1955), Barker (1963), or Barker and Gump (1964), which describes how persons in everyday life become exposed to communiques, the settings in which exposure occurs, the associates that are around at the time of exposure, the extent to which the issue is discussed when it arises, and so forth. As mentioned earlier, it seems clear that attitude change can occur through several means other than exposure to mass media. Yet our knowledge of these additional sources of exposure is scant, because descriptions of natural attitude change are focused on exposures to mass media.

Persons interested in psychological ecology have recently begun to outfit subjects with radio transmitters so that they can monitor what occurs as these persons go about their everyday activities (*e.g.*, Soskin and John, 1963). It seems likely that recordings obtained under these conditions could be scored for instances of potential and actual attitude change. With these data, investigators might discover neglected variables in the process of attitude change and learn more about factors that impede attitude change (Hovland, 1959, p. 183).

Several additional solutions could be mentioned, but perhaps these are sufficient to suggest that it may be premature to draw conclusions about limitations of the laboratory. As experimenters direct their attention to procedural details that may affect the outcomes of attempts at attitude change, they may be able to discover workable solutions. The first requirement seems to be an accurate identification of the problems. Probably one of the first beliefs that must be abandoned before we advance is the belief that "nothing beyond that which we are now doing is science" (Severin, 1965, p. 282). It would certainly be ironic, as well as a sad commentary on science, if those who devoted their lives to studying attitude change turned out themselves to be the persons who were most reluctant to change their tools for studying change.

But perhaps the best way to summarize this chapter is to return to the letter "D" that I found so useful in relieving my discomfiture at the outset. It is true that experimenters have been derelict, their energies have been diffused in needless controversy, and they have denied or disregarded many relevant criticisms out of defensiveness or despair. However, the issues explored in this chapter suggest that dismay seems unfounded and debunking seems premature. Perhaps these are merely delusions. But, if delusions can generate deliberation, discipline, and daring, perhaps we can look forward to the discovery and not the demise of the laboratory.

REFERENCES

Barker, R. G. (Ed.), 1963. *Stream of behavior.* New York: Appleton-Century-Crofts.

Barker, R. G., and Gump, P. V., 1964. *Big school, small school.* Stanford, Calif.: Stanford Press.

Barker, R. G., and Wright, H. F., 1955. *Midwest and its children.* Evanston, Ill.: Row, Peterson.

Blake, R. R., and Brehm, J. W., 1954. The use of tape recording to simulate a group atmosphere. *J. abnorm. soc. Psychol.,* 49, 311–313.

Braden, Marcia, and Walster, Elaine, 1964. The effect of anticipated dissonance on pre-decision behavior. In L. Festinger (Ed.), *Conflict, decision, and dissonance.* Stanford, Calif.: Stanford Press, pp. 145–151.

Breer, P. E., and Locke, E. A., 1965. *Task experience as a source of attitudes.* Homewood, Ill.: Dorsey.

Campbell, D. T., 1957. Factors relevant to the validity of experiments in social settings. *Psychol. Bull.,* 54, 297–312.

Cartwright, D., 1942. The effect of interruption, completion and failure upon the attractiveness of activities. *J. exp. Psychol.,* 31, 1–16.

Cook, S. W., and Selltiz, Claire, 1964. A multiple-indicator approach to attitude measurement. *Psychol. Bull.,* 62, 36–55.

Davis, J., 1930. Study of 163 outstanding communist leaders. *Proc. Amer. soc. Soc.,* 24, 42–55.

Ekman, P., 1965. Differential communication of affect by head and body cues. *J. Pers. soc. Psychol.,* 2, 726–735.

Festinger, L., 1964. Behavioral support for opinion change. *Publ. Opin. Quart.,* 28, 404–417.

Festinger, L., and Maccoby, N., 1964. On resistance to persuasive communications. *J. abnorm. soc. Psychol.,* 68, 359–366.

Freedman, J. L., 1965. Long-term behavioral effects of cognitive dissonance. *J. exp. soc. Psychol.,* 1, 145–155.

Freedman, J. L., and Sears, D. O., 1965. Selective exposure. In L. Berkowitz (Ed.), *Advances in experimental social psychology.* Vol. 2. New York: Academic, pp. 57–97.

Friedman, N., 1964. The psychological experiment as a social interaction. Unpublished doctoral dissertation, Harvard Univ.

Goldman-Eisler, Frieda, 1958. Speech analysis and mental processes. *Lang. and Speech,* 1, 59–75.

Hall, E. T., 1966. *The hidden dimension.* Garden City, New York: Doubleday.

Hargreaves, W. A., and Starkweather, J. A., 1963. Recognition of speaker identity. *Lang. and Speech,* 6 (2), 63–67.

Hoffman, L. R., and Maier, N. R. F., 1964. Valence in the adoption of solutions by problem-solving groups: concept, method, and results. *J. abnorm. soc. Psychol.,* 69, 264–271.

Hovland, C. I., 1959. Reconciling conflicting results derived from experimental and survey studies of attitude change. *Amer. Psychol.*, **14**, 8–17.

Jones, E. E., and Thibaut, J. W., 1958. Interaction goals as bases of inference in interpersonal perception. In R. Tagiuri and L. Petrullo (Eds.), *Person perception and interpersonal behavior.* Stanford, Calif.: Stanford Press, pp. 151–178.

Kelman, H. C., 1958. Compliance, identification, and internalization: three processes of attitude change. *J. Confl. Resolut.*, **2**, 51–60.

Krout, M. H., 1954. An experimental attempt to determine the significance of unconscious manual symbolic movements. *J. gen. Psychol.*, **51**, 121–152.

Leventhal, H., and Niles, Patricia, 1964. A field experiment on fear arousal with data on the validity of questionnaire measures. *J. Pers.*, **32**, 459–479.

McGuire, W. J., 1960. A syllogistic analysis of cognitive relationships. In M. J. Rosenberg and C. I. Hovland (Eds.), *Attitude organization and attitude change.* New Haven: Yale Univ. Press, pp. 65–111.

McGuire, W. J., 1964. Inducing resistance to persuasion: some contemporary approaches. In L. Berkowitz (Ed.), *Advances in experimental social psychology.* Vol. 1. New York: Academic, pp. 191–229.

Mahl, G. F., 1956. Disturbances and silences in the patient's speech in psychotherapy. *J. abnorm. soc. Psychol.*, **53**, 1–15.

Mausner, B., 1954. The effect of prior reinforcement on the interaction of observer pairs. *J. abnorm. soc. Psychol.*, **49**, 65–68.

Merton, R. K., 1957. *Social theory and social structure.* (Rev. ed.) Glencoe, Ill.: Free Press.

Milgram, S., Mann, L., and Harter, Susan, 1965. The lost-letter technique: a tool of social research. *Publ. Opin. Quart.*, **29**, 437–438.

Miller, N., 1965. Defaming and agreeing with the communicator as a function of communication extremity, emotional arousal, and evaluative set. Paper presented at Eastern Psychol. Assn.

Orne, M. T., 1962. On the social psychology of the psychological experiment: with particular reference to demand characteristics and their implications. *Amer. Psychologist*, **17**, 776–783.

Pittenger, R. E., Hockett, C. F., and Danehy, J. J., 1960. *The first five minutes: a sample of microscopic interview analysis.* Ithaca, New York: Paul Martineau.

Schachter, S., and Singer, J. E., 1962. Cognitive, social and physiological determinants of emotional state. *Psychol. Rev.*, **69**, 379–399.

Scheflen, A. E., 1964. The significance of posture in communication systems. *Psychiatry*, **27**, 316–331.

Schein, E. H., and Bennis, W. G., 1965. *Personal and organizational change through group methods: the laboratory approach.* New York: Wiley.

Severin, F. T. (Ed.), 1965. *Humanistic viewpoints in psychology.* New York: McGraw-Hill.

Shepard, H. A., 1964. Explorations in observant participations. In L. P. Bradford, J. R. Gibb, and K. D. Benne (Eds.), *T-group theory and laboratory method.* New York: Wiley, pp. 379–394.

Sherif, Carolyn W., Sherif, M., and Nebergall, R. E., 1965. *Attitude and attitude change: the social judgment-involvement approach.* Philadelphia: Saunders.

Sherif, M., Harvey, O. J., White, B. J., Hood, W. R., and Sherif, Carolyn W., 1961. *Intergroup conflict and cooperation: the Robbers Cave experiment.* Norman, Okla.: Inst. of Group Relations.

Sommer, R., and Ross, H., 1958. Social interaction in a geriatric ward. *Int. J. soc. Psychol.,* 4, 128–133.

Soskin, W. F., and John, Vera P., 1963. The study of spontaneous talk. In R. G. Barker (Ed.), *The stream of behavior.* New York: Appleton-Century-Crofts, pp. 228–281.

Temerlin, M. K., 1963. On choice and responsibility in a humanistic psychotherapy. *J. humanistic Psychol.,* 3, 35–48.

Thibaut, J. W., and Kelley, H. H., 1959. *The social psychology of groups.* New York: Wiley.

Wallach, M. A., Kogan, N., and Bem, D. J., 1964. Diffusion of responsibility and level of risk taking in groups. *J. abnorm. soc. Psychol.,* 68, 263–274.

Walster, Elaine, 1964. The temporal sequence of post-decision processes. In L. Festinger (Ed.), *Conflict, decision, and dissonance.* Stanford, Calif.: Stanford Press, pp. 112–128.

Watson, G., 1966. *Social psychology: issues and insights.* Philadelphia: Lippincott.

Webb, E. J., Campbell, D. T., Schwartz, R. D. and Sechrest, L., 1966. *Unobtrusive measures: nonreactive research in the social sciences.* Chicago: Rand McNally.

Weick, K. E., 1964. Reduction of cognitive dissonance through task enhancement and effort expenditure. *J. abnorm. soc. Psychol.,* 68, 533–539.

Weick, K. E., 1966a. Systematic observational methods. In G. Lindzey and E. Aronson (Eds.), *Handbook of social psychology.* (Rev. ed.) Reading, Mass.: Addison-Wesley.

Weick, K. E., 1966b. Task acceptance dilemmas: a site for research on cognition. In S. Feldman (Ed.), *Studies of cognitive interaction.* New York: Academic.

Whittaker, J. O., 1964. Parameters of social influence in the autokinetic situation. *Sociometry,* 27, 88–95.

Zajonc, R. B., 1965. Social facilitation. *Science,* 149, 269–274.

5. Laboratory Experiments and Attitude Theory

Bertram L. Koslin

There is a traditional literature reviewing the interrelationships of laboratory and field research in the attitude area. There are few critical analyses available of the *theoretical* significance of our experimental research activities. Here I will attempt an analysis of means-end relationships between experimental research and the purposes of theory construction. It is a skeptical analysis, a kind that is sorely lacking at present.

Our research, like all other scientific endeavors, is directed toward formulating generalizations about the regularities of attitude phenomena. At least this is its aim at an abstract level. We would perhaps agree also that a *theory* of attitudes should organize invariant relationships (laws) into a logical (internally consistent) structure that explains how attitudes are formed and transformed in a wide array of situations. By convention we are taught to value theories that are verifiable, logically consistent, and parsimonious (in the sense that a plethora of empirical particulars are handled with few abstract constructs). Thus, the goal of attitude theory construction is to formulate a logically connected structure of lawful relations that govern how attitudes are formed and changed in the widest possible set of circumstances, during human development and in response to social interaction and persuasion in all social settings the world over.

In the laboratory, controls can be introduced and variables manipulated. Therefore, we ordinarily accept the laboratory experiment as the best means available to confirm or to disconfirm theory. But designating laboratory research as the sole means of testing attitude theory involves a set of knotty problems that require examination.

DISSONANCE BETWEEN FIELD AND
EXPERIMENTAL FINDINGS

Carl Hovland (1959), in a now famous paper, reexamined the question of why attitude change is recorded so frequently in experiments, whereas attitude change is a relatively rare phenomenon in field research. At times the divergence between the findings of laboratory and field research has been ascribed to a difference between methods (*e.g.*, Cohen, 1964; Hovland, 1959; Lipset, Lazarsfeld, Barton, and Linz, 1954). However, in a recent review Cohen (1964) suggested a difference between field and laboratory research more fundamental than a mere matter of method.

> Experiments generally study a set of factors or conditions which are expected on the basis of theory to influence attitude. Towards this end, experimenters try to find issues involving attitudes susceptible of modification through persuasive communications. Otherwise there are likely to be no measurable effects, especially since the experiments are on a small scale. Surveys typically deal with socially significant attitudes which are more deeply rooted and to which people are more highly committed.
> These differences in approach have important consequences for an understanding of the factors underlying attitude change, as two examples will show. Since experimental studies deal with issues which are relatively less involving and where expert opinion is highly involving, opinions may be considerably affected by persuasive communications, and the advocacy of a position considerably discrepant from an individual's own position may lead to a substantial change of attitude. Experimental evidence on the effects of the credibility of the communicator . . . supports this generalization. On the other hand, since surveys usually utilize issues which are basic and involve deep commitment, little change of attitude would be expected, and the more discrepant the individual's position from the communication, the less he might change; he might in fact, even strengthen his original position . . . (p. 131).

Indirectly, at least, Cohen implied that the divergence between the findings of laboratory and field research may be due in part to the experimenter's habitual use of attitudes readily susceptible to modification. If this is the case, a serious question arises: What is the relevance to general attitude theory of experiments making *exclusive* use of issues on which individuals are easily persuaded?

In studies on the effect of communication discrepancies, social judgment research (Sherif and Hovland, 1961; Sherif, Sherif, and Nebergall, 1965) has demonstrated that personal involvement with issues makes a critical difference both in the direction and magnitude of change. Typically, highly involved individuals change less toward a communicator who presents small discrepancies from their stand than do mildly involved individuals. At moderate to large discrepancies from the person's own stand, communications may produce attitude change or a boomerang effect that makes the recipient even more adamant in his own position, depending upon the degree of his involvement. Therefore, with respect to studies manipulating the amount of change advocated by communicators of varying prestige, it would appear that the divergence between laboratory and field studies is, at least in part, a matter of the degree to which involving issues are employed. However, we have little knowledge as to whether attitude change manipulations in experiments on problems other than the attitude-communication discrepancy problem can be generalized from issues of little personal involvement to those of some consequence for the individual.

Some investigators limit the significance of their studies to the formation of attitudes. This limitation has been common in the order effect literature (Lana, 1964). Others limit their studies to the examination of cultural truisms, as McGuire (1964) did in his innoculation studies. Such explicit limitation avoids overgeneralization of results and yields findings that can be fit readily into a general theory of attitudes. On the other hand, to ascribe general significance to findings from experimental manipulations that bear only on issues involving attitudes which the experimenter knows are readily susceptible of modification requires a major assumption.

In the natural sciences, results are also garnered, by necessity, under artificial conditions. However, the extent to which results can be generalized has been tested in engineering or technical studies. It has yet to be demonstrated that many attitude change manipulations have *any* generality. As a result, theories that are supported only by experimental evidence are open to common sense questions about the effects of conditions that did not happen to be included in the experimental set-ups. Brown (1962), for example, apparently limits the generality of balance, incongruity, dissonance models of attitude change by differentiating between attitude change situations involving *intra*personal versus *inter*personal conflict.

A simple disagreement between two persons is not uncommon . . . ; there are numerous . . . discussions that confront one party-line Democrat with one party-line Republican over one partisan issue. The result is a conflict between persons but not a conflict within persons. And somehow we know that in this situation neither participant will change his opinion nor even feel any strong pressure in the direction of change (Brown, 1962, pp. 4–5).

Are we to believe, as Brown suggests, that balance models of attitude change do not apply to the general attitude domain where people know one another's positions in detail and where *inter*personal conflict does not produce *intra*personal conflict? If so, this is a severe restriction, for the products of such confrontations include major decisions affecting mankind. Of course, interpersonal conflict does produce intrapsychic conflict in some conditions. But what are these conditions? Do they apply to the entire attitude domain?

On some issues commonly employed in laboratory studies, individuals may not have any stable attitudes. Is there discontinuity between the psychology of *set* (ephemeral evaluative predispositions or expectations) and the study of attitudes? Ordinarily the universe of discourse in attitude theory refers to relatively *enduring* evaluative predispositions. After all, some psychologists argue that there *are* discontinuities between modes of conflict resolution. For example, it is said that if differentiation is employed as the mechanism of conflict reduction, attitude change does not occur. Why then should we assume that there are continuities between attitudes that are and are not readily susceptible of modification? We should at least entertain the hypothesis that there may be discontinuities between an individual's willingness to reduce conflict in various ways on inconsequential matters and the kinds of things he is willing to do on important issues. It is even likely that the relative probabilities of various modes of conflict reduction may change systematically as issues become more central to the individual.

We have no empirical basis to assume that the conditions creating intrapsychic conflict for individuals with stable attitudes and high familiarity with opposing positions and conditions that induce conflict among a set of relatively inconsequential cognitions are the same. The opposite assumption is equally plausible. Therefore, a central problem for attitude theory is to specify these conditions. It is particularly important that these conditions be specified in circumstances where individuals are free to disagree, diverge, or join with others into conflicting groups. Similarly, the conditions affecting attitude change among conflicting members of the same group need specification. By and large, attitude experiments employ situations in which it is dubious that individuals feel free to diverge. In many others it is difficult to support the argument that interpersonal conflict is really worth the discomfiture it might arouse. Needless to say, matters of attitude are involved in either case.

As a consequence of Freud's work, we know a fair amount concerning the varieties of conflict reduction. What we need to know are the conditions that *produce* intrapsychic conflict for individuals functioning within different patterns of interpersonal relations and that lead to attitude change. Until such conditions are specified, we cannot have verifiable theory. If it can be argued that experimental manipulations produce intrapsychic conflict only when the experimental results fit a theory, then that theory is not verifiable. If various modes of conflict resolution are observed without specifying when attitude change will be the mode adopted, then theory of intrapsychic conflict has little consequence for a general theory of attitudes.

The burden of proof lies with the attitude theorist. Of course, he may utilize neutral and oversimplified experimental situations to demonstrate general principles he intends to employ. But when a theory of attitudes is to be seriously tested, the issues and situations selected need to be varied over the entire range from those which are inconsequential to those which genuinely matter to the subjects. The situations used to test attitude theories need to be varied over conditions in which the pressures to resolve conflict, rather than avoid it or to stabilize it into open conflict, are specifiable.

Recently, Cohen (1964) and Festinger (1964) appear to have become skeptical concerning the significance of attitude manipulations in the laboratory. Each posed a test for the relevance of laboratory studies to attitude change phenomena. The argument takes the following form: Since attitudes (evaluative predispositions) are assumed to have consequences for the way people *behave*—for their *interaction* with others, for their *programs of action* and persuasion—then experimental manipulations shown to produce attitude change should also produce a change in behavior, that is, changes in learning, performance, and interaction. Thus, Cohen (1964) stated that "until experimental research demonstrates that attitude change has consequences for subsequent behavior, we cannot be certain that our procedures for inducing change do anything more than cause cognitive realignments . . ." (p. 138). Parenthetically, this is essentially the same significance test that Asch (1952) proposed many years ago with respect to conformity experiments.

A note of caution is needed before accepting this test as definitive.

Impressive displays of predicted behavior change in the research situation following demonstrated attitude change are not necessarily critical tests of the significance of attitude change manipulations. Nor are they necessarily indications that lasting as opposed to superficial cognitive changes have occurred. The test presumes that behavior is affected by a single variable, namely the subject's attitude. It assumes that the same attitude is aroused by the change manipulation and the behavior test situation. In and of itself, the test does not take into account the variety of attitudes that may be aroused in either situation. Conversely, adequate tests must guard against the possibility that a *common set of extraneous cues* exists across the situations in which attitude and behavior change are measured. Only when such safeguards are introduced would it be legitimate to conclude that a change of attitude produced the behavior in question. Particularly, in highly elaborate situations employed in some attitude experiments, the variables that might have produced attitude or behavior change are complex and confounded (Chapanis and Chapanis, 1964). It would be difficult in such circumstances to insure that the behavior changes that might follow attitude change manipulations were a result of attitude change.

NUGATORY NULL HYPOTHESES

Many experimental situations are fairly unstructured. For the subject, this is particularly true when issues of little consequence to him are employed, when complex manipulations are used, or when the situation simply seems bizarre to him. The experimenter, on the other hand, is entangled in matters of design and executing the procedures; he may be suffering additional anxieties related to his subordinate relationship with the major investigator. In such circumstances, as demonstrated in years of psychological research, subjects organize the situation as best they can, giving meaning to the experience, although perhaps not the same meaning per treatment combination. In arriving at a "definition of the situation" in ambiguous circumstances, subjects are also extremely sensitive to suggestions or cues that are unknowingly generated by the experimenter.

The pattern of implicit and explicit cues that may be operative in experiments has been called the "demand characteristics" of the situation (Orne, 1959, 1962), and they may "overdetermine" the results. Thus the opportunity to affirm the null hypothesis may be precluded. Recent research on the "social psychology of the psychological experiment" has demonstrated how null hypotheses can be made inapplicable. The findings have been obtained in hypnotic (Sarbin, 1950; Orne, 1959; Orne and Evans, 1965; Shor, Orne, and O'Connell, 1966), behavior rating (Rosenthal and Fode, 1963), verbal conditioning (Rosenthal, Kohn, Greenfield, and Carota, 1966), and interview situations (Hyman, 1954). They need to be abstracted and applied to attitude research (*e.g.*, Rosenberg, 1965).

Subject Deception of Experimenters

Orne (1962) has proposed that in psychological experiments

> we might well expect . . . that as far as the subject is able, he will behave in an experimental context in a manner designed to play the role of a "good subject" or, in other words, to *validate the experimental hypothesis.* Viewed in this way, the student volunteer is *not* merely a passive responder in an experimental situation but rather he has a very real stake in the successful outcome of the experiment (p. 778).

If we assume that the subject shares with the experimenter a common concern in advancing science, and that the "good subject" is concerned with the utility of his work in this regard, then probabilities of accepting the null hypothesis simply are not those assumed in making statistical tests of the results. There is a greater possibility of "overdetermined" results.

The situation is serious enough in any psychological experiment using human subjects. However, there is even *less* likelihood that the null hypothesis can be tested in some attitude research. In the complex, unstructured, or brain-tickling type of experiment, the subjects are more apt to generate hypotheses, associations, and a variety of other cognitions and motive states in order to give meaning to the situation. The usual motive to be a "good subject" may then combine with the cognitions that have been differentially aroused in different treatment conditions because the context of the various manipulations is itself confusing. Not only is a nugatory null hypothesis produced, but, in addition, the effects of the treatments are apt to be hopelessly confounded with these unforeseen events. The complex gimmick-ridden experiment designed to deceive the subject as to its purpose thus has an additional weakness. It leaves the critical reader and at times the experimenter (but not always, *cf.* Chapanis and Chapanis, 1964) without basis for inquiry into what variables may have been confounded to produce the results. Without such basis "experimental control" loses its meaning.

Experimenter Bias

In unstructured circumstances there is the risk of mutual deception by the experimenter and subject. As Orne and Scheibe (1964) noted, the "subjects' behavior can be differentially manipulated by altering the implicit and explicit cues in the experimental situation, and . . . subjects may react to social cues, or demand characteristics, in such a way as to confound experimental results" (p. 11). Therefore, not only does the subject himself confound some attitude experiments in his own attempts to give meaning to the situation, but the experimenter contributes his share by providing "demand characteristics" that the subject in turn seizes as guides for understanding what is expected of him.

Especially when the investigator personally applies the experimental manipulations or uses his own behavior as a variable, the desired results may be obtained without his awareness that he is also providing cues that guarantee the results. By the time the experiment has been sent through a series of pretests (which may unintentionally insure that the extraneous cues applied with each experimental manipulation cluster properly), the risk of experimenter self-deception is very large. The unhappy result is a report of conclusions that do not state accurately what produced the findings.

The "demand characteristics" of the situation, the cooperative subject with a stake in the research (perhaps even as the investigator's student), and the unstructured nature of many experimental situations may be responsible for the considerable difficulty in replicating findings in the attitude field. It is apparent that if phenomena reported in attitude experiments are to be obtained by those who do not share the in-group "understandings" of the theorist, steps must be taken to minimize confounding variables while maximizing the likelihood that accepting the null hypothesis is truly a possible experimental outcome.

Controls for Bias

Good experimentation, especially with human subjects, requires more than exercise of superficial experimental and/or statistical controls. If an attitude experiment is to demonstrate something of consequence, there must be many more possibilities for the hypothesis to be negated than affirmed. It would represent a considerable improvement in methodology if attitude experiments were designed to show (or at least to specify logically) that the alternatives against the hypothesis were equally as likely as the desired experimental result.

Even a skeptical stance on the part of researchers would help. We need to guard against shaping results by choosing only the "type" of material traditional to the theoretical viewpoint under investigation, by altering instructions with no explicit reason, or by tinkering with the procedures in a series of pretests without including the explicit steps as part of the research itself. Once the experimental design is formulated, we should take active steps toward insuring that the demand characteristics of the experimental situation have been minimized. The addition of control groups will help at times, but very often the "demand factors" change when the experimental manipulations are omitted for control groups. Nevertheless, it is feasible to employ methods used in the discovery of the "overdetermined" multiple choice test item. It is possible to inquire whether subjects generate the results without having *experienced* the experimental manipulations.

The test of significance for experimental manipulations should be that their effects be demonstrated in situations where the risk of "overdetermining" the results is minimal. Such situations have to ensure that the subject has cognitive clarity concerning the instructions, the response alternatives available, and the like. Such situations need not be highly structured in order that the subject have a clear *understanding of his task*. For example, the purpose of the research may be to determine the effect of manipulations in unstructured or uncertain situations. It is possible to make the subject's task clear to him while making it highly improbable that he can infer what the desired result might be. In the investigation of some problems it is also possible to use abstract tasks which minimize the likelihood that subjects will be able to bring to bear past experiences that might bias the results. The autokinetic situation (Sherif, 1936) is a good example. The task was clear to the subject. The impact of the particulars from subjects' past histories was minimized while the range of possible responses was allowed to vary freely. At the same time, knowledge of the purpose of the research was not sufficient to direct the subject to specific patterns of behavior that would substantiate the hypotheses.

The "Shaped" Hypothesis

In all experimentation there are many more alternatives that would disconfirm the predicted result other than the few outcomes that are included in the experimental design. By the time decisions are made concerning how the research hypothesis is to be tested through a given set of manipulations and subjects in a particular design, the experimenter's *selectivity* has already filtered various alternatives in order to test his predictions against a particular alternative(s). In attitude studies the research design frequently sets up alternatives that operate like straw men against the experimenter's hypothesis. The experimenter's selection of experimental procedures and issues, types of response scales, and means of data analysis reduce the probabilities that any of the straw men can remain standing while enhancing the probability of obtaining the predicted result. The experimenter would be justified in attributing significance to his laboratory findings if he could demonstrate the effect of experimental manipulations in a variety of contexts with various methods. An attitude change manipulation that is worth its salt should produce effects across situations in which numerous transformations in experimental design are made.

It is ironic that the laboratory experiment loses its sacrosanct stature for some psychologists when the data are negative. Apparently for some, the logical beauty or the simplicity of a theory leads to the deep conviction that it must be true despite negative evidence. Positive results, on the other hand, are taken as impressive demonstrations of what was known more surely by intuition. There is little justification (except transcendentally) for such a Kantian outlook. On the other hand, there is equally as little to support the extreme view that laboratory findings have ontological priority over findings generated by other methods. It is a strange commentary on the current scene that the two often appear hand in hand.

THEORY AND NATURAL PHENOMENA

Ordinarily it is a requirement of scientific investigations that the constructs of theory have established correspondences with empirical events, that is, there is a demand for operational definitions of terms. However, the desired relevance between theory and phenomena is not limited to those phenomena which can be displayed only in the laboratory under special conditions. If the purpose of formulating attitude theory is to organize into a logical structure a set of invariant relationships explaining the greatest possible number of particulars, then naturally occurring phenomena should not be ruled out as beyond the pale of science and precluded from disconfirming theory. As John Stuart Mill (1904) stated some time ago, "principles of evidence and theories of method are not to be constructed *a priori*" (p. 545).

If laboratory findings are at variance with field research or with data garnered by any of a variety of methods, then, as Sherif (1954) has pointed out, either the laboratory or field findings or both are wrong. The obvious approach is to inquire into the discrepancy between the findings and not to select arbitrarily one set of phenomena as more "real" than the other, as less "tainted" by the selectivity of observers or of methods. However, in order to compare what divergences exist among laboratory and field or naturalistic findings for constructive purposes, it is necessary to have a theory that is stated in a form appropriate to data gleaned by a variety of methods. It is difficult to bring social phenomena, as reported by observers in a variety of cultures, to bear on some current theories of attitude change. Some of these theories and their concepts preclude the possibility that empirical phenomena can provide any relevant evidence for their disconfirmation (Chapanis and Chapanis, 1964).

What is required is not theory that leads merely to a flurry of laboratory or field activity, for such a flurry is often mistakenly considered by definition an indication of the theory's fertility. What is required is theory that can be confirmed or disconfirmed *outside as well as inside* the laboratory. What is needed is theory that orders situations along dimensions, that differentiates between ephemeral and more enduring evaluative predispositions, and that aspires to explain the following phenomena: mass changes as well as private attitude change; attitude change during development; attitude change as a consequence of changes in group and intergroup relations, of a shift in reference groups and of personal agitation and sensory deprivation.

A general theory must encompass the phenomena of attitude change as they are known by a variety of methods. Laboratory findings lose value for general theory when they fail to correspond to empirical phenomena and when this failure is ignored or slighted. A comparison of findings between laboratory and more "real life" situations may enable us to develop the psychological experiment as a more useful tool in the verification of general attitude theory, if indeed we want general theory.

REFERENCES

Asch, S. E., 1952. *Social psychology*. Englewood Cliffs, N.J.: Prentice-Hall.
Brown, R., 1962. Models of attitude change. In R. Brown, E. Galanter, E. H. Hess, and G. Mandler. *New directions in psychology*. New York: Holt, Rinehart and Winston, pp. 3–85.
Chapanis, N. P., and Chapanis, A., 1964. Cognitive dissonance: five years later. *Psychol. Bull.*, **61**, 1–22.
Cohen, A. R., 1964. *Attitude change and social influence*. New York: Basic Books.

Festinger, L., 1964. Behavioral support for opinion change. *Publ. Opin. Quart.* **28**, 404–417.

Hovland, C. I., 1959. Reconciling conflicting results derived from experimental and survey studies of attitude change. *Amer. Psychologist,* **14**, 8–17.

Hyman, H. H., 1954. *Interviewing in social research.* Chicago: The Univ. of Chicago Press.

Lana, R. E., 1964. Three theoretical interpretations of order effects in persuasive communications. *Psychol. Bull.,* **61**, 314–320.

Lipset, S. M., Lazarsfeld, P. F., Barton, A. H., and Linz, J., 1954. The psychology of voting: an analysis of political behavior. In G. Lindzey (Ed.), *Handbook of social psychology.* Reading, Mass.: Addison-Wesley, pp. 1124–1175.

McGuire, W. J., 1964. Inducing resistance to persuasion. In L. Berkowitz (Ed.), *Advances in experimental social psychology.* New York: Academic, pp. 192–229.

Mill, J. S., 1904. *A system of logic, book VI.* (8th ed.) New York: Harper.

Orne, M. T., 1959. The nature of hypnosis: artifact and essence. *J. abnorm. soc. Psychol.,* **58**, 277–299.

Orne, M. T., 1962. On the social psychology of the psychological experiment: with particular reference to demand characteristics and their implications. *Amer. Psychologist,* **17**, 776–783.

Orne, M. T., and Evans, F. J., 1965. Social control in the psychological experiment: antisocial behavior and hypnosis. *J. Pers. soc. Psychol.,* **1**, 189–200.

Orne, M. T., and Scheibe, K. E., 1964. The contribution of nondeprivation factors in the production of sensory deprivation effects: the psychology of the "panic button." *J. abnorm. soc. Psychol.,* **68**, 3–12.

Rosenberg, M. J., 1965. On eliminating evaluation apprehension from attitude measurement. *J. Pers. soc. Psychol.,* **1**, 28–42.

Rosenthal, R., and Fode, K. L., 1963. Psychology of the scientist: V. three experiments in experimenter bias. *Psychol. Rep.,* **12**, 491–511.

Rosenthal, R., Kohn, P., Greenfield, P. M., and Carota, N., 1966. Data desirability, experimenter expectancy, and the results of psychological research. *J. Pers. soc. Psychol.,* **3**, 20–27.

Sarbin, T. R., 1950. Contributions to role-taking theory: I. hypnotic behavior. *Psychol. Rev.,* **57**, 255–270.

Sherif, Carolyn W., Sherif, M., and Nebergall, R. E., 1965. *Attitude and attitude change.* Philadelphia: Saunders.

Sherif, M., 1936. *The psychology of social norms.* New York: Harper.

Sherif, M., 1954. Integrating field work and laboratory in small group research. *Amer. sociol. Rev.,* **19**, 759–771.

Sherif, M., and Hovland, C. I., 1961. *Social judgment.* New Haven: Yale Univ. Press.

Shor, R. E., Orne, M. T., and O'Connell, D. N., 1966. Psychological correlates of plateau hypnotizability in a special volunteer sample. *J. Pers. soc. Psychol.,* **3**, 80–95.

6.   Attitude Research and the Jangle Fallacy

Eugene L. Hartley

It is my understanding that the purpose of this volume is to serve as "primarily a stock-taking of some of the significant problems and trends in theory and research." Within that context, I shall address myself to three items of concern, only the first of which is represented in the title of this chapter. Essentially I should like to provoke further consideration and clarification of some special topics under the following general rubrics: first, the nature of attitudes; second, identification; and third, the measurement of ego-involvement.

THE NATURE OF ATTITUDES

Not so very long ago, as some people reckon time, psychologists included in their introductory courses and basic texts consideration of what might be called philosophical problems. One such problem commonly discussed, for example, was the "mind-body problem." Along with such discussions would often be a review of the fallacy of reification, the tendency to believe that an abstraction has concrete actuality. I can remember that early in my teaching career I used to discuss with my students the speed of a race horse: how speed could be defined, measured, and transmitted by heredity (else why such high stud fees?). Yet if we were to dissect a race horse we would not be able to locate its speed. From there we would move on to the concept of reification and the frequency with which the study of psychology was confused by this error. For example, in thinking about intelligence and personality characteristics, were we dealing with abstract descriptions of human functioning or a concrete entity or "thing" in the person?

Small wonder that somewhere (I regret I can no longer assign the source) someone discussed reification as the tendency to believe that because we had a word for it, a name, there must be such a thing. And further, that there was the jingle fallacy and the jangle fallacy. People seem to believe that if two things are called by the same name they are the same thing; and this might be designated the jingle fallacy. On the other hand, we have the jangle fallacy, the tendency to assume that if two things are labeled differently, called by different names, then they *are* different.

Now obviously I could have gotten to this point via Korzybski or Piaget or via any number of other routes. The particular route chosen is not important. What is of importance is confronting the question of the nature of social attitudes as they relate to our conception of the general psychological nature of man. I strongly suspect that most of us tend to reify the concept and in our discussions tend to manifest both the jingle and jangle fallacies as well. Just what do we really mean by an attitude, psychologically speaking?

We need not here review the host of definitions that the literature provides. The Oxford English Dictionary (Murray *et al.*, 1933) suggests that in our language the term derives from a late seventeenth-century usage in the fine arts to describe the posture of a figure in statuary or painting and used in a fashion closely related to the original (and literal) use of "disposition." From here it is not a far cry to the nineteenth-century usage that denotes customary behavior as representative of a state of mind and the mode of regarding an object of thought. Consider, for example, the late nineteenth-century publication, not ordinarily thought of as a psychological treatise yet one that certainly mirrored prevailing concepts and orientations, by W. S. Gilbert and Arthur Sullivan entitled "H.M.S. Pinafore." Here we find in Act I:

> A British tar is a soaring soul,
>   As free as a mountain bird,
> His energetic fist should be ready to resist
>   A dictatorial word.
> His nose should pant and his lip should curl,
> His cheeks should flame and his brow should furl,
> His bosom should heave and his heart should glow,
> And his fist be ever ready for a knock-down blow.
> His eyes should flash with an inborn fire,
>   His brow with scorn be wrung;
> He never should bow down to a domineering frown,
>   Or the tang of a tyrant tongue.

His foot should stamp and his throat should growl,
His hair should twirl and his face should scowl;
His eyes should flash and his breast protrude,
And this should be his customary attitude.

Along with this general background of usage in the English language, there is the related orientation of the early and more explicitly psychological researches in the laboratories of Germany. Remember the early reaction-time studies, the discovery of the importance of the subject's *set*, whether he had a stimulus set or a response set, and the experimental control of *Einstellung* for the further research?

In contemporary social research we tend to regard "set" as representing a relatively *transitory* state and "attitude" as representing a relatively *enduring* disposition. But we have never given operational definition to the distinction. We have never really worked through the interrelations of set, situational determination of social behavior, development and stabilization of attitudes, habituation, and overlearning. How can we profit from the developments in learning theory and such specific efforts to contribute to our thinking as the paper by Professor Schoenfeld (1965) and the researches by many others, if we permit our evaluative categorizations to structure our perceptions in such fashion that we restrict our concerns to what we conventionally consider attitude study rather than to the valid psychological matrix, whatever it might be?

Let me claim the privilege of sharpening my comments by reference to some of the work of colleagues. In their recent book *Attitude and Attitude Change,* the Sherifs try to establish the nature of an attitude (Sherif, Sherif, and Nebergall, 1965). Precisely because of my essential agreement with their position, I shall use their discussion to raise issues that still need to be clarified. They provide the statement that attitudes cannot be observed directly but are inferred from characteristic or consistent patterns of behavior toward objects or classes of objects. So far so good. But then they go on to say:

> However, not all characteristic behavior indicates an attitude. For example, the fact that we customarily walk downstairs instead of tumbling down does not require explanation in terms of an attitude, nor does the characteristic response of eating when a hungry person is offered food (p. 19).

The text goes on to emphasize the *evaluative* component of behavior that identifies the attitude. The hungry man eats: that is *not* attitude-behavior. When he selects one food rather than another, he is reflecting evaluation, and that is attitudinal in nature. This seems fair enough, but I have difficulty in accepting it. I first read this statement shortly after recovering from abdominal surgery, and I thought I had very definite attitudes about walking downstairs. The pain or fear of pain contributed to what would otherwise have been an habitual act. When we learned to walk downstairs, as children, we did have attitudes. Later, as the behavior was overlearned, did we lose our attitudes and retain the behavior? Still later, is it that special circumstances might place the behavior in an attitudinal context again? What fundamentally is involved? When the rat learns to turn to the right in a maze to avoid an electric shock and to gain access to food, does he have an attitude at the choice point? When the pigeon learns to discriminate between a red and a green light and to peck for food only under appropriate illumination, is he developing an attitude toward the colored lights? Does the rat, the pigeon, do I, lose the attitude as we pass some threshold point of habituation? I am sure my dogs like me; their behavior tells me so (and what if I am anthropomorphic for a bit?), but what is the "evaluative" component that I perceive? Is it simply the differential behavior toward me and toward strangers? But this is habitual. At some point such questions should be answered.

If attitudes are inferred from behavior, but not from *all* behavior, then the characteristics of the relevant behavior must be clearly, objectively, and operationally differentiated from the nonrelevant behavior. Today, I am not sure that the terms "consistent" and "evaluative" are adequate. What does "evaluative" mean behaviorally? How do we define "consistency"? We know that a person can be consistent as long as he is observed operating within the framework of a particular role, but he may be inconsistent if we view him in a variety of roles.

But let us turn to another problem on which I need help. Speculating about the meaning of "evaluative" induces a certain amount of introspection and leads to another area where I have difficulties. In many phenomenological approaches to attitude study we find discussions of stereotypes, the "pictures in our heads" so convincingly described by Walter Lippmann (1922). Extension of this concept into attitude research was, of course, spearheaded by the classical studies of Dan Katz and Kenneth Braly (1933; 1935). But what are stereotypes? I am not asking what stereotypes are in attitude research but in psychology.

In my current undergraduate courses in general psychology I find myself trying to link the following: direct sensory-perceptual experience, after-images, memory images, symbols in thinking and problem solving, *common social symbols or stereotypes,* and idiosyncratic personal symbols in dreams and fantasies. Am I wrong, or do stereotypes represent the same psychological phenomenon that we find in other imagery important in studies of thinking? I am not talking of social origins versus personal, not questioning the degree of social consensus. What I am suggesting is that concern with stereotypes as a form of attitude study necessarily places attitudes in the context of thinking and problem solving.

Let us turn again, but now we can be somewhat briefer, for we are approaching more familiar territory. The traditional approaches to attitude measurement along a linear continuum derive from an affective-conative emphasis in human behavior. We measure the degree for or against a social stimulus, the degree of favorableness-unfavorableness, the like-dislike continuum, to represent a person's attitude. The development of the so-called "functional" approach to attitude theory has put this emphasis into a more coherent and systematic formulation. But as we pursue the descriptions of the functions served by social attitudes, it is difficult to disentangle attitudes from other processes that serve similar or identical functions. Clearly, the study of attitudes must involve our understanding of emotions and motivation.

But perhaps we ought to shift our stance to help coordinate the perspective. Gordon Allport recently undertook to reassess his conception of personality traits after an interval of some 36 years (Allport, 1966). During that time (from 1931 to 1966) there had been many developments in attitude research as well as personality study. As we now review the discussion of traits, it is clear that most of the propositions could be directed to social attitudes with equal validity. In fact, in his concluding paragraph, Allport states:

> Finally, there are several problems connected with traits that I have not attempted to revisit. There are, for example, refinements of difference between trait, attitude, habit, sentiment, need, etc. Since these are all inside tendencies of some sort, they are for the present occasion all "traits" to me. Nor am I here exploring the question to what extent traits are motivational, cognitive, affective, or expressive (p. 9).

Can this provide additional support for integrating in attitude study an index of ego-involvement? But does it not also call attention to the need to clarify the relation between traits of personality and social attitudes? Should my attitudes toward women with brown hair come under the heading of personality study, whereas my attitudes toward women with dark skin be considered social psychology? Is there really a different psychology for my attitudes toward brunettes and my attitudes toward Arabs? Do they really represent different pyschological processes, or is the difference in the social matrix?

Now let us go back to our original problem: what is the nature of an attitude, *psychologically*. Attitudes are learned, are inferred from behavior, are relatively stable, are represented in personal imagery, have motivational and cognitive and affective and expressive facets, and integrate with the personality of the individual. But is not everything? Is there a psychological function that does not have these properties? Memories? Thoughts? Personal goals? Self concepts? Is there any *unit* that can be established, even theoretically, as an attitude? Are we not reifying? Are we not displaying the jingle fallacy in unifying the learned behavior, the image, the evaluative-categorization, the motivational, the personality function into what we choose to call social attitudes? Perhaps we can derive a meaningful unit to be called attitude from a social analysis, but do we really expect it to be a psychological unit? If you share my pessimism about identifying a psychological unit that we can establish as *attitude*, then ought we not study the attitude facets in their proper contexts? The social judgment-involvement approach is related to other studies of judgment, in the laboratory and in the field, not necessarily to studies of stereotypes. Studies of stereotypes should be placed in the context of imagery and symbols in thinking. Let us not fall into the error of the jangle fallacy and fail to see the similarities between our attitude studies and the basic psychological processes simply because they have a different name.

Here I am addressing myself primarily to the psychologically oriented social psychologists and urging that we recognize the variety of component processes we have chosen to fuse into our unit, the social attitude. But the reverse of the coin also bears a message. The social psychologist has been concerned with study of the various psychological processes in a social context. Just as he should pay more attention to his basic roots, so he has findings that contribute to general psychology—not as a final chapter in an introductory textbook, unrelated to what has gone before—but as an integral part of our basic understanding. Discussions of motivation now include status striving, but do not put it in the reference group context; learning discussions integrate studies of social reinforcement but do not include canalization; we find discussions of person perception as well as thing perception but no real integration, no real analysis of stimulus factors in social perception. There is discussion of generalization, both stimulus and response generalization, but no studies of role behavior in that context. Let us not forget that we are treading on a mall, with even more interplay than a two-way street provides. Our understanding of the basic processes might well be improved if the findings from the studies of social attitudes were not discriminated against, if they were desegregated and integrated properly into the larger community of knowledge.

With respect to social attitudes, it seems to me that we have to transcend the old question, What are the personal and social influences in the determination of X attitudes? The unit that is a social attitude derives its unity from a societal definition, not a psychological approach as psychologists have been traditionally conceiving the problem. We cannot resolve the difficulties by definitions. The analysis of attitudes in terms of the psychological representation of the sociological units is available in the studies of the interiorization of reference group norms, the identification with reference groups, and their symbolic representations in the form of reference individuals. As social psychologists, it might be well for us to address ourselves to more analytic study of the psychology of reference groups, the units and processes of reference-group functions within the individual, the dynamics among the ego-involvements of the individual, rather than excessive preoccupation with the traditional and more specialized psychological processes such as motivation or perception or even judgment. And we must develop much more sociological sophistication to place the individual and his reference groups in a proper context to see how norms for a group are differentiated and defined for psychological processing.

I like the own-categories technique for attitude study, not because it serves a better definition of attitudes but because it builds toward a more adequate cognitive mapping of the individual's social field. It locates the boundaries for positive and negative valences and gives a synthesis of cognitive and conative components in a manageable manner. These values inhere in our requirements for study of nonsocial as well as social stimuli as a function of the nature of man and his psychological organization. We do science a disservice if we seem to be restricting our studies to the "attitude" realm when we are in actuality studying *psychology*. We are also somewhat delinquent if we study psychology in the guise of attitude research and pursue the psychological leads without regard to the *social* psychological requirements of a sociological anchorage.

IDENTIFICATION

Here I would like to get help in understanding the significance of the difference between personal and impersonal anchors of social attitudes. For about a year I have been nagged by some possible implications of the studies of the "sleeper effect" and the lack of attention to the problems they pose. Perhaps I can get temporary relief by ventilating my questions here. Ultimately, of course, it will take a good deal of research to satisfy my needs.

In the World War II Studies in Social Psychology, Hovland, Lumsdaine, and Sheffield (1949) described the sleeper effect, presented data, and suggested some explanations. Subsequently, Hovland and Weiss (1952) and Kelman and Hovland (1953) reported studies that tested and confirmed the hypotheses offered in the earlier publication. The later studies analyzed source or communicator credibility in delayed measurement of opinion change rather than the simple sleeper effect. The part of these studies that I find particularly challenging is the separability of the source and the content of the communication in the functioning of the subjects. Communications from a source of low credibility had little immediate effect on opinion but significant effects when tested after a lapse of time. Apparently the rate of decay, the forgetting curve, is different for source and content.

What is the role of a personalized anchor in psychological functioning? Before we had television available, problems raised by its predecessor, the radio, were the subject of a variety of interesting studies. The findings were not always consistent, and we have not pursued the matter to discover why the results sometimes demonstrated that "live" presentations, communications with the speaker present, were more effective than the same communication electronically mediated, as in the study by Walter Wilke (1934), and sometimes not. But clearly the presence or absence of the speaker made a significant difference under many conditions.

Consider a little study reported by Gordon Allport in 1936. A group of subjects was exposed to presentations from two sources simultaneously. One source broadcast a short story while the second, standing before the group, simultaneously read a different story of equal length. The subjects could listen as they chose. After the conflict of voices was over, the subjects were asked to write whichever story they felt better able to write. Of 40 stories written, 35 were the story read by the speaker physically present, only one came from the loud speaker, and the remainder (4) were too fragmentary to be identified.

That the presence of a person makes a difference in our psychological adjustments is abundantly clear from even the most casual of phenomenological observation. That personalization of material alters our "handling" of it also seems to be supported in such studies as have been referred to above. But there is further confirmation from many sources. Remember the 1948 version of Flesch's readability yardstick (Flesch, 1948)? He needed two formulae: one for reading ease based on word length and sentence length and one for human interest based on the number of "personal words" and personal sentences. Both indices proved important in the assessment of readability, the mechanics of language and the involvement of persons.

This sampling of empirical studies provides ample support for a belief in the importance of a personal-impersonal (or attenuated) anchorage differential in psychological function. The literature of the clinicians is full of emphasis on transference phenomena and the importance of the identification process. With another emphasis, Milton Rokeach suggested that the cognitive organization of belief-disbelief systems included a central-peripheral dimension (1960). I am not sure that I want to accept his emphasis on linearity here, but it is interesting. He suggested that it would be helpful to conceive the organization thus:

> (1) A *central* region represents what will be called the person's "primitive" beliefs. These refer to all the beliefs a person has acquired about the nature of the physical world he lives in, the nature of the "self" and of the "generalized other" (G. H. Mead, 1952).
> (2) An *intermediate* region represents the beliefs a person has in and about the nature of authority and the people who line up with authority, on whom he depends to help him form a picture of the world he lives in.
> (3) A *peripheral* region represents the beliefs derived from authority, such beliefs filling in the details of his world-map (pp. 39–40).

And with his conceptualization of the open and closed mind, Rokeach extends this formulation of the central-peripheral dimension into some very interesting experiments on party-line thinking with its obvious implications for the analysis of social behavior in the open community.

But perhaps this is enough to illustrate the nature of my concern. About 20 years ago, Muzafer Sherif and S. S. Sargent (1947) addressed themselves to an analysis of ego-involvement and the mass media. These authors recognized the importance of "human interest" in the variety of stimulus material offered in the media but seemed to deal with it simply as a device for arousing more intense ego-involvement. Human interest features in the newspapers, radio, and magazines, and the basic nature of most movies afford maximum opportunity for identification, they note. We find statements like the following:

Ego-involvements may be quite general, or they may become personalized and specific (p. 12).

. . . an individual may become ego-involved with a particular newspaper or magazine columnist or radio commentator and depend unconsciously upon the views expressed for his own ideas and attitudes (p. 12).

However, in the movies the personalized sort of ego-involvement is even more striking (p. 12).

This personal identification is especially intense in the case of youth (p. 13).

The content of the press is far more varied than that of movies or even the radio. Conditions are less conducive to identification, which takes place mostly with respect to that part of the newspaper devoted to human interest stories, pictures, cartoons, comics and some of the features. It may, however, play a part when one reads signed columns, editorials and even straight news reports (p. 14).

The major ego-attitudes and hence the ego are derived primarily from the values of the group or groups with which we identify ourselves. The very character of identification is built up on the basis of attitudes formed in relation to the person, group or institution. The continuing process of our personal identity consists mainly of the constellation of established attitudes in relation to groups and individuals (p. 10).

What is the relation between personal identification and ego-involvement? Is ego-involvement with a group the same as with an individual? Is identification with a group the same as with an individual? Of course we can phrase our questions in terms of stimulus materials: is an unsigned editorial in a newspaper as effective as the same content in a column with a known by-line and possibly a photograph? Are attitudes anchored in self, in other individuals, in groups or apparently unanchored, of equal stability? What is the relationship needed between the kind of attitude anchorage and the kind of propaganda for greatest effectiveness? Obviously these are rhetorical questions not properly phrased for research purposes. Research needs hypotheses to be tested. As yet, I do not believe that the problem has been sufficiently explored for the hypotheses to be abstracted and organized. There is much evidence of the kind suggested in my samples above and in varied theoretical writings that indicates the problem is of importance.

On the methodological side, experimentation need not be too difficult, nor is descriptive measurement. We have the recently developed own-categories technique for securing an index of ego-involvement.

The study of attitude anchorage is also quite feasible. Suggestive of possible approaches, I would like to mention an exploration I undertook recently with an adaptation of George Kelly's Role Construct Repertory Test, commonly known as the Rep Test (Kelly, 1955). The Rep Test was devised to assist in personality study, but we adapted it to examine some social attitudes. In our study we were concerned with orientations toward various civil defense programs. We identified six different programs and six possible reference individuals or groups. In the original Rep Test, the stimulus materials are presented to the respondents in triads. In our form, one unit was always one's own beliefs and values, one unit was the belief and value system of a potential reference individual, and one was a defense position. The reference individuals and the defense positions were rotated so that each was presented with each other and with the self. The instructions, in part, required the respondents to study the three items identified and to decide "In what important way are two of these three belief systems alike, and at the same time, essentially different from the third?"

In this form it was thus possible for the respondents to bracket themselves with a leader, the leader with a position, or themselves with a position. Data were secured from 39 of our students at The City College of New York. Several different analyses were made, providing a variety of findings that were interesting. For the present context I will report that when we studied the data for the structural analysis, there were about 15 bracketings of self and leader, a mean of 14.4 pairings of leader and position, but only an average of 8.8 pairings of self and position. At the time of this study our data suggest the students were, in general, relatively little involved. Though if asked to do so, they would articulate a position, basically these positions seemed to be "peripheral" in the Rokeach sense, structured psychologically as derived from reference individuals or groups with whom or which they identified or were involved (Hartley, 1966).

Objective techniques are available and can be adapted and improved. How about some good hypotheses so that we can get on with the research in meaningful fashion?

THE MEASUREMENT OF EGO-INVOLVEMENT

For this third, and final, section of the chapter I shall sound a cautionary note. The introduction of the own-categories technique for attitude study makes simple linear measurement obsolete. It will undoubtedly have a decided impact on personality study. It is, however, still in its early stages of use, and it would be unfortunate if there were a premature rigidification of the interpretation of the data. At present a variety of studies seem to be supportive of the use of the size of the latitude of rejection, either absolute size or in relation to the size of the latitude of acceptance, as an index of the degree of ego-involvement. With stronger ego-involvement we can expect firmer anchorage in one's own position, possibly (because of less assimilation) a smaller latitude of acceptance, but more certainly a significant broadening of the latitude of rejection at the expense of the latitude of noncommitment. In theory this seems sound and is confirmed in a number of empirical analyses to date.

But perhaps the measure can be influenced by situational factors. Perhaps there will be kinds of ego-involvement that operate a bit differently or at least issues that provoke responses that contaminate the measure. Maybe there are even cultural factors that lead to different findings. I know that confirmation has come from a variety of groups, but they all have been, as far as I know, subcultures within the general Western European sphere. I have not forgotten the lesson of that elegant little monograph, *The Psychology of Social Norms* (M. Sherif, 1936).

I raise the question here because I would like to share some tentative findings from a little study executed by Miss Loveleen Bhatia at The City College of New York, whose analysis is not yet complete. In her study, Miss Bhatia used 50 subjects: 20 Indians, 10 Pakistanis, and 20 Americans, all residents in New York. Part of the procedure called for the subjects to sort statements into piles in accordance with the own-categories technique. This procedure was gone through twice, once with the 46 statements taken from each form of the scale developed by Grice as the Remmers generalized scale of attitude toward any group (Remmers, 1934). The sorts were made applying the statements to "Indians and Pakistanis" in general. After sorting each form, of course, they indicated own position, latitudes of acceptance, and latitudes of rejection. For purposes of first analyses, the two sorts by each subject were combined to provide a single measure. Because of the small number in the samples, the Indian and Pakistani subjects were combined into one group to compare with the American subjects. The results were interesting and quite the reverse of what had been predicted.

First, with respect to the number of categories used, no differences appeared between the presumed uninvolved Americans and the presumably involved Indians and Pakistanis. The means were: Indians and Pakistanis 8.20, Americans 8.35; $F = .0464$.

When the analysis shifted from number of categories to number of items in the three latitudes, the results were as follows:

	Indian and Pakistani	Americans	F	p
Latitude of acceptance	34.30	20.25	29.67	.01
Latitude of noncommitment	14.16	22.30	5.80	.03
Latitude of rejection	38.60	45.15	5.17	.03

In this adaptation of the own-categories procedure with materials designed to measure attitudes toward Indians and Pakistanis, when we compared Indian and Pakistani subjects with American subjects, we found the *latter* had significantly larger latitudes of rejection and noncommitment and significantly smaller latitudes of acceptance. I do not think we can readily accept the hypothesis that our Americans were more ego-involved than the Indians and Pakistanis.

In another part of the study subjects were binaurally exposed to conflicting Indian and Pakistani propaganda concerning the Kashmir issue. They were then asked to report as much as they could remember. The recalled protocols were scored for number of Indian elements and number of Pakistani elements included and a selectivity index computed. The Americans showed significantly less selectivity than did the Indians and Pakistanis. We would expect selectivity to be associated with ego-involvement, of course, and this part of the study confirmed our expectations.

However, perhaps the Americans were more ego-involved when the general issue of attitudes toward Southern Asians was raised, yet were uninvolved in the Kashmir dispute as far as favoring one side or the other was concerned. Perhaps the Indians and Pakistanis were comparatively uninvolved in a generalized attitude that lumps the two nations together but very much involved when the dispute between the two nations was at issue. If we do not accept these reversals of our original expectancies about involvement, then we must question complete reliance on the relative size of the latitude of rejection as a direct index of comparative degrees of ego-involvement.

Perhaps we need more study of some of the factors in the experimental situation that might influence performance. Was there something about Miss Bhatia's manner or appearance that led to more acceptance and less rejection among her fellow countrymen and their near neighbors and the reverse for the American respondents? Are there cultural differences? After all, there is still a great difference in social institutions between the countries of the two groups. The joint family, with possibly greater variety of views, still prevails in India and Pakistan, as contrasted with the nuclear family which is common here. Are there cultural differences in readiness to display hostility and rejection? Does the status of visitor in this country put people in a special state which creates artifacts?

We could go on asking many more questions, but it is answers we need. For the present, the answers are not available in empirical form. It might be well to explore the more significant leads so that we establish some of the limits on the use of the measurement method before hasty overextension leads to artifacts in data that contribute to dismaying "conclusions."

It is difficult to conclude a discussion such as this. Clearly a recapitulative summary is not in order. I will confess that these days I feel much like the veteran nursery school teacher who was asked why she had been so brusque with the children that day. "Joe," she responded, "I've been teaching four-year-olds to put on their overshoes for seventeen years. Don't you think it's about time they'd learned something?"

The final paragraph of the 1937 edition of that foundation tome of our present day discipline, *Experimental Social Psychology* by Gardner and Lois Murphy and Ted Newcomb, reads as follows:

> All in all, we are led to reiterate our conclusions regarding the determinants of "single" attitudes. Interrelated attitudes are rarely individual affairs, but are largely borrowed from groups to which we owe strongest allegiance. Individual variations such as age, sex, and various personality characteristics have much to do with the nature of the groups with which one becomes affiliated, and with the degree and permanence of such affiliations. Individual experiences, whether of accidental or occasional nature, on the one hand, or those occasioned by family membership or residential community, on the other, are also instrumental in determining group membership. This is by no means to deny the importance of purely psychological factors. But such experimental evidence as is available has led us to the conclusion that the latter are effective largely through their power to select this rather than that group affiliation, to react to it with greater or less intensity and, to some extent, perhaps, to modify it. The social psychology of attitudes is the sociology of attitudes illuminated by an understanding of the psychological factors which determine individual susceptibility to group influences (pp. 1045–6).

Despite these guidelines, researchers continue to study attitudes and attitude change without regard to reference groups. Almost all aspects of an experimental situation are described except for the nature of the social group which *is* the experiment: the local norms and expectancies for the subject role and the relationship between the experimenter and the subject.

The theoretical importance of such considerations has long been recognized; research approaches have long been available. Information has come from many sources, and a number of outstanding studies have been reported. In a much smaller way, for example, some of my own studies have helped demonstrate that race attitudes of individuals derive from social norms, that in the course of development there is increasing integration of the psychological processes reflecting attitudinal effects in individual function, that the conformity component is important in the differentiation of the relatively tolerant and intolerant personalities, that multiple group involvements of the individual are a significant factor in accounting for variability in attitudinal expressions. Ruth Hartley has demonstrated the integration of racial identification in ego development. In her work on sex roles she has clarified the interrelation of self identification, role definition, and evaluative judgment of the behavior of others, as well as the importance of reference group identification in defining judgments. The generalizations about social attitudes from a social-psychological point of view seem very well grounded in empirical studies. Now that we have available more sophisticated statistical techniques for multivariate analysis and computer technologies for the analyses of complex sets of data, there seems little excuse for continued failure to employ what we know in designing our studies.

Years ago, Muzafer Sherif and I were graduate students together. He was then working in the laboratory with the autokinetic phenomenon, and I was in the field studying the development of children's race attitudes. We had many long talks, and in general our points of view were very similar. There was one item of research strategy, however, about which we did not agree. Muzafer insisted on the importance of "demonstrating the obvious," and I felt that we ought to explore new frontiers, that we ought not "waste" time on the obvious. Well, let me confess there has been a sleeper effect; my judgmental frames have shifted considerably, and I am ready to demonstrate the convergence of our norms.

There is a great need to consolidate our thinking about the nature of attitudes and attitude change processes, for only by so doing can we contribute to the conduct of future research on an *improved* basis.

To that end, I suggest we do the obvious thing and covenant, minimally (1) to be sensitive to the social atmosphere within the framework of which we develop our research undertakings; (2) to endeavor to identify and report the nature of the reference groups dominant for the respondents at the time and under the conditions of the data collection; and (3) to explore, even if only speculatively, how under different circumstances, with different reference groups evoked, the same subjects might respond differently to the same materials. Perhaps in this fashion we can clarify the contexts for our work and make our findings more readily cumulative. Perhaps in this fashion, new principles will become obvious.

REFERENCES

Allport, G. W., 1936. The radio as a stimulus situation, *Acta Psychologica*, 1, 1–6.

Allport, G. W., 1966. Traits revisited, *Amer. Psychologist*, 21, 1–10.

Bhatia, Loveleen, 1966. Unpublished masters thesis, The City College, New York, in process.

Flesch, R., 1948. A new readability yardstick. *J. appl. Psychol.*, 32, 221–223.

Gilbert, W. S., and Sullivan, A., H.M.S. Pinafore. In *The complete plays of Gilbert and Sullivan*. New York: The Modern Library, pp. 114–115.

Hartley, E. L., 1966. Prediction of American public response to a damage limiting program. Unpublished memorandum, ORNL.

Hovland, C. I., Lumsdaine, A. A., and Sheffield, F. D., 1949. *Experiments on mass communication.* Princeton: Princeton Univ. Press.

Hovland, C. I., and Weiss, W., 1952. The influence of source credibility on communication. *Publ. Opin. Quart.*, 15, 635–650.

Katz, D., and Braly, K. W., 1933. Racial stereotypes of 100 college students. *J. abnorm. soc. Psychol.*, 28, 280–290.

Katz, D., and Braly, K. W., 1935. Racial prejudice and racial stereotypes. *J. abnorm. soc. Psychol.*, 30, 175–193.

Kelly, G. A., 1955. *The psychology of personal constructs.* New York: Norton.

Kelman, H. C., and Hovland, C. I., 1953. "Reinstatement" of the communicator in delayed measurement of opinion change. *J. abnorm. soc. Psychol.*, 48, 327–335.

Lippmann, W., 1922. *Public opinion.* New York: The Macmillan Co.

Murray, J. A. H., Bradley, H., Craigie, W. A., Onions, C. T. (Eds.), 1933. *The Oxford English Dictionary.* London: Oxford Univ. Press, The Clarendon Press.

Remmers, H. H., 1934. Studies in attitudes: a contribution to social psychological research methods. *Bull. Purdue Univ., Stud. Higher Educ.*, 35, No. 4.

Rokeach, M., 1960. *The open and closed mind.* New York: Basic Books.

Schoenfeld, W. N., 1965. Learning theory and social psychology. In O. Klineberg and R. Christie (Eds.), *Perspectives in social psychology.* New York: Holt, Rinehart and Winston, pp. 117–135.

Sherif, Carolyn W., Sherif, M., and Nebergall, R. E., 1965. *Attitude and attitude change: The social judgment-involvement approach.* Philadelphia: Saunders.

Sherif, M., 1936. *The psychology of social norms.* New York: Harper.

Sherif, M., and Sargent, S. S., 1947. Ego-involvement and the mass media. *J. soc. Issues,* **3,** 8–16.

Wilke, W. H., 1934. An experimental comparison of the speech, the radio, and the printed page as propaganda devices. *Arch. Psychol., N.Y.,* No. 169.

Part III

7. Attitude as the Individual's Own Categories: The Social Judgment-Involvement Approach to Attitude and Attitude Change

Muzafer Sherif and Carolyn W. Sherif

Problems of attitude and attitude change are urgent and crucial today, perhaps more than in previous periods of human history. Man's mastery of his physical environment—especially his foreshortening of the time required to exchange words, goods, people, and missiles—has created a new world. People differing drastically in attitude find themselves in contact, whether they like it or not and whether for good or ill. At the same time, man's changing environment, both physical and social, demands new modes of adaptation that presume attitude change on a broad scale.

Attitude problems of man's social development and his relations with his fellows have long been recognized as central in social psychology. Research into these problems has flourished for well over three decades. To those familiar with the literature, it is astonishing how little theoretical progress in specifying attitude problems has been made since the formulations of W. I. Thomas, the sociologist, or William McDougall, the psychologist who dealt with attitude problems both in his treatment of social "instincts" and "sentiments." The now traditional approaches to measurement of attitudes, on the other hand, developed with amazing independence from such theoretical treatments. Therefore, it is not surprising that much of the research literature has little or no bearing on the significant theoretical problems that made attitude a central concept in social psychology.

In this chapter we shall summarize an approach to problems of attitude and attitude change that has developed from concern with the nature of attitudes, with their significance for social-psychological theory, and with measurement techniques veridical to their nature and significance. The label for this approach, the social judgment-involvement approach, reflects the empirical bases for the concept of attitude and for the measurement techniques developed. On the one hand, the approach is based on findings from the experimental study of judgment, both psychophysical and social. Here, we rely heavily on experimental psychology. On the other hand, the approach rests on empirical findings about the involvement of the person's self or ego in an ongoing event or situation. In the latter aspect, we rely on sociologists and the long thin line of psychologists since William James who have stressed that attitudes are not discrete elements in human psychology, but are, on the contrary, constituents of the person's self system.

After discussing briefly the background of the approach, we shall inquire specifically into the nature of attitudes, then present operational measures of attitude, representative findings, and predictions about reactions to communication and attitude change.

BACKGROUND OF THE APPROACH

The social judgment-involvement approach is not presented as a formal model derived logically from a limited set of untested assumptions, although its development follows a logical sequence. This assertion does not reflect disdain for comprehensive theory nor for formal models. On the contrary, the desired goal in the behavioral sciences, as in any science, is theory that is truly comprehensive and models that are *valid*. Our concern is with the means to attain this goal.

Those sciences dealing with human behavior are in their infancy, despite their popularity and despite the pretensions we may maintain with our students, colleagues, or potential buyers of our skills. Man's astonishing mastery of his physical environment in the last two centuries still contains breaks and gaps. His efforts to develop the scientific process for studying his own fate with his fellows cover little more than a century.

There is a fundamental step for the scientific process during the early development of inquiry. The first step in such inquiry is to learn about the phenomena in question. As applied to problems of attitude and attitude change, this step means learning from the actualities of events as persons uphold a position or disdain another, as they react to communication from others with satisfaction or tension, as they categorize that communication as resembling or differing from their position in some degree, and as they change their attitudes and behavior or become more confirmed in their customary grooves, as the case may be.

Of course, the mere description of phenomena is not science in itself. It is, however, a first step, as noted by such diverse authors as the psychologist MacLeod (1951) and the mathematicians Allendoerfer and Oakley (1959), the latter in a college textbook of mathematics.

The next steps involve the laborious specification of the conditions in which the phenomena and their variations are manifested. The aim is to condense these conditions into conceptual terms as variables that can be specified sufficiently to predict the occurrence and the alteration of the phenomena. Without specification of the factors or variables that affect observed phenomena, there may be theory, but it is not scientific. There may be formal logic, but it proceeds from untested premises. In the domain of social behavior, theory then becomes a game. At this stage of development, the behavioral sciences need fewer games and more examination of the assumptions from which their games are played, fewer formal expressions of models limited to an arbitrary set of variables and more empirical specification of the *significant* variables that need to be included in an adequate model.

These are among the reasons that, at this stage of development, the social judgment-involvement approach welcomes the charge of being primitive or even crude. It welcomes the charge because its aim is to examine the nature of the phenomena in question—attitudes and their change—and to specify major variables that are bound to affect these phenomena in all of their variations.

Thus the approach is not merely concerned with how people behave when they experience tension, dissonance, incongruity, or imbalance but in specifying the conditions (variables) that will *produce* such experiences. Its aim is to predict the degree of discrepancy between a communication and the person's attitude that will arouse psychological discomfiture, to predict his reaction to the communication, and to predict how it will or will not affect his attitude. It aims to specify the conditions in which an individual will be susceptible to attempts to change his attitude or be resistant to change even *before* anyone has attempted to alter his view.

These pretensions required a concept of attitude based on assumptions that are empirically valid. They require research into attitude problems that are personally significant and critical. They require a perspective on these problems broader than that provided by an inspection of one or a few samples of persons comfortably situated in an environment that has never challenged their cherished values or has so sheltered them from critical decisions that they see no alternatives but their own limited field. The time has long since passed when the social scientist can generalize about attitude problems on the basis of phenomena observed in a small fraction of a tiny portion of the educated population in one or two of the world's advantaged countries.

Finally, the social judgment-involvement approach has the pretension of developing concepts and operational measures for the *structure* of the person's attitude and his degree of personal involvement in the matter at hand. In these early stages of development, the pretension is to demonstrate the kind of measurement techniques required by an adequate theory. Many technical improvements and elaborations are feasible, some of them suggested by other contributors to this volume (*cf.* Diab, Chapter 8, and Triandis, Chapter 12). Certainly, the use of multidimensional analysis is the obvious next step.

In short, the social judgment-involvement approach has been long in the making, even for a field of inquiry as new as attitude research. Its most recent and complete statement was *Attitude and Attitude Change* (Sherif, Sherif, and Nebergall, 1965). The survey of findings on judgment was presented in *Social Judgment* (Sherif and Hovland, 1961), along with a program of research initiated in 1948. The literature on attitudes and self (ego) involvement was surveyed and summarized in *The Psychology of Ego-involvements* (Sherif and Cantril, 1947).

Because a *valid* model of attitude and attitude change is the ultimate goal, it is all the more important that we proceed from assumptions that are established empirically. Assumptions based on analogy with the more established sciences have not helped but hindered the progress toward this aim.

For example, traditional attitude measurement has been based largely on such models. In research practice the individual's attitude has been represented as a point on a scale derived by analogy from a physical model. Thus, an attitude has been represented as an arithmetic mean of acceptances (positive) and rejections (negative), as a point on an interval scale or a ratio scale with a zero point (as in the measurement of temperature), as a point in two, three, or n dimensional space, or as a point on a cumulative scale (as in the measurement of physical distance in Euclidean space). Too often the measurement model and the particular measurement itself have not been referred back to the phenomena they purported to measure.

Although it is true that a two-inch segment of matter is included in a total measurement of ten inches, it is by no means true that a social attitude representing a lesser position will be included in the range of positions acceptable to a person strongly committed to an extreme position. Opposing sides in a conflict, each desiring peace but committed to emerge victorious, need not see a negotiated peace as a position included in their scale. "Desegregation at a reasonable pace" will be jeered by a person committed to "desegregation now" and placed in the detestable category of tokenism.

Therefore, at the outset, the present approach inquires into the nature of the scales to which attitudes are referable. Every attitudinal reaction implies that the person has compared, evaluated, or chosen among alternatives. These are examples of a judgment process. What are the judgment scales that the person uses as his basis for comparison, evaluation or choice? Here it is useful to distinguish between judgment scales that can be assessed relative to physical units—that is, *psychophysical* scales—and those that on the whole cannot be so assessed—that is, *psychosocial* scales.

Psychophysical and Psychosocial Scales

In laboratory research on judgment, the word "psychophysics" is associated with studies assessing judgments relative to the units of a physical continuum or at least to physical gradations. The psychophysical scale is certainly not entirely foreign to the study of social judgment. For example, conceptions of speed and distance can be gauged both against standard measures of these continua and against the distances and speeds that the person has experienced using various social tools. We know that these conceptions differ considerably for a peasant with a donkey and a jet pilot. Thus, while rooted in social experiences, the differences in their conceptions are referable to a scale of physical units.

In social life, however, there are matters of strong concern for which no physical measures are available, such as those for speed and distance. Even the value of a given monetary unit is subject to lengthy and complex decisions, resting ultimately on agreement among those who exchange the money. We are not suggesting that the principles of judgment for psychophysical scales are necessarily invalid for judgments relative to psychosocial scales. On the contrary, we suggest that the way to discover whether these principles are operative is to understand first the nature of psychosocial scales. The same principles may be operative if we take into account both the nature of psychosocial scales and the new factors that enter into the judgment process, factors that may be less important or even absent in psychophysical judgments.

We are not alone in suggesting that psychosocial scales may have properties differing from those of psychophysical scales. Decades ago the sociologist Emile Durkheim (1915) stated forcefully that events of social life are not merely carry-overs of physical events and cannot, therefore, be extrapolated from them on the same continuum.

What are some major properties of psychosocial scales that distinguish them from physical continua? It is not sufficient to point out that psychosocial scales require the consensus of given sets of people, for so do time, weight, distance, and many other physical scales. Two differences between psychophysical and psychosocial scales will suffice to clarify our point in this context.

First, the psychophysical scale based on consensus is, at some point, referable to physical events and can be checked against them. The Indian groups whose calendars were calculated inaccurately soon found the planting season falling in the wrong months. However, psychosocial scales are typically referable only to other social facts: the ways of life, the relationships within and between groups, and their value systems.

Second, psychosocial scales are based on consensus that also establishes limits of acceptability and the limits of what is objectionable. The direct referent for such evaluative boundaries is the consensus itself. The limits not only vary from culture to culture and group to group but in the same groups during different periods of history. For example, a hundred years ago the possibility of a federal graduated income tax in this country was highly objectionable to the great majority; it was supported only by a few radical groups who were thought to be "crackpots." Currently, there is a variety of positions about raising or lowering the tax and about which groups should benefit, but very few persons seriously advocate abolishing it altogether.

What we are saying here is that a psychosocial scale reflects the stands taken by groups, by strata or by an entire society at a given period in their history. They have regularities, and they are patterned, as are the groups that uphold the various stands. In fact the existence of regularities and changes in the patterns is essential if there is to be a social science, for a science cannot be built about a collection of wholly unique events. However, it cannot be assumed that these regularities have the same properties as physical scales.

At any given time, individual differences in attitude can be gauged relative to the regularities and patterns of social organization, the current patterns of acceptability and rejection, and their changes. In fact the individual's attitudes must be gauged relative to the stands taken by others in his own group and in other groups. Thus, the study of attitudes cannot be strictly psychological. The yardsticks that can be developed for valid assessment of individual attitudes are derived from the stuff that should be the domain of study for sociologists, anthropologists, political scientists, and economists.

In order to proceed with an analysis of the judgment process when a person with an attitude on some topic is faced with a communication or other event relevant to it, let us ask some simple questions whose answers will give our direction in research.

WHAT IS AN ATTITUDE?

The present approach starts by asking the following crucial questions: *What is it* that is to be changed when a person is exposed to some attempt to change his attitude? What is it that is resistant to change?

Clearly, the way we answer these questions will affect what and how we study. The need for answers was indicated recently by Allen of the University of Wisconsin (1966) when he wrote: "One of the shortcomings of traditional research in the attitude area is the excessive preoccupation with changing a response on an isolated (and apparently randomly selected) issue in the laboratory at the expense of research on the nature of attitudes" (p. 284).

From studies labeled research on attitude and attitude change, we might conclude that attitude is a blanket term covering any old judgment or opinion that the individual renders. Are we dealing with factors governing the individual's guesses about the number of beans in a jar, or leaves on a tree, or sand pebbles on a square yard of beach? Or are we concerned with his views on his family, on how he sees himself as a person relative to his contemporaries, on the worth of his religion, his politics, his profession, his country, or his way of life? It is one thing to attempt to change a person who uses a toothbrush to switch from one brand to another. It is quite another thing to persuade someone who has never brushed his teeth that a toothbrush should be used.

In short, when we talk about attitude change are we talking about any change in behavior whatsoever? Or are we talking about changes in the person's stands towards other persons, objects, groups, beliefs, and institutions that he accepts or rejects as related to himself, with all of the commitments, identifications and emotional reverberations associated with such stands?

In order to answer these questions, we need to examine the properties that have made attitude a central problem in social psychology, to characterize the data from which an attitude is inferred, and to formulate a definition of attitude that fits these properties and the data.

Criteria of Attitude

When an attitude is discussed we are not talking about something that can be observed directly. We are speaking of a psychological concept designating something *inside* the individual. Just as we can never directly observe pain, psychological tension, or an unspoken idea, we cannot see an attitude. Nevertheless, the concept of attitude has several characteristics that differentiate it from other concepts referring to internal states of the individual.

Attitudes are not innate. They belong to that domain of human motivation variously studied under the labels of "social drives," "social needs," "social orientations," and the like. It is assumed that the appearance of an attitude is dependent on learning.

Attitudes are not temporary states but are more or less enduring once they are formed. Of course, attitudes do change; but once formed they acquire a regulatory function such that, within limits, they are not subject to change with the ups and downs of homeostatic functioning of the organism or with every just-noticeable variation in the stimulus conditions.

Attitudes always imply a relationship between the person and objects. In other words, attitudes are not self-generated, psychologically. They are formed or learned in relation to identifiable referents, whether these be persons, groups, institutions, objects, values, social issues, or ideologies.

The relationship between person and object is not neutral but has motivational-affective properties. These properties derive from the context of highly significant social interaction in which many attitudes are formed, from the fact that the objects are not neutral for other participants, and from the fact that the self, as it develops, acquires positive value for the person. Therefore, the linkage between self and the social environment is seldom neutral.

The subject-object relationship is accomplished through the formation of categories both differentiating between the objects and between the person's positive or negative relation to objects in the various categories. The referent of an attitude constitutes a set that may range, theoretically, from one to a large number of objects. However, in actuality the formation of a positive or negative stand toward one object usually implies differential attachment to others in the same domain. For example, a singular attraction to one person typically involves a comparison with other persons who are similar and different. The attitude toward the person, therefore, necessarily includes the views toward others with whom he is compared. Needless to say, this process need not be a conscious and deliberate one.

The referents of an attitude, as differentiated from other internal states by the above criteria, may be objects in the person's environment that are nonsocial, in addition to social objects.

As the above criteria imply, the formation of attitudes is integral to the process of forming a self concept. In fact, through the establishment of a constellation of subject-object relationships, the self concept is delineated. Through this process, the groups in which the child is born become not merely external realities to which he must adapt but *reference groups* with which he identifies or strives to identify himself.

Because the criteria for attitude include the person's relatedness to relevant objects on a conceptual level, the present approach is a cognitive approach. However, it is also a motivational-affective approach, for attitudes are not neutral affairs. Finally, it is a behavioral approach because the only possible data from which attitude can be inferred are behaviors, verbal or nonverbal. Attitudes are necessarily cognitive-motivational-behavioral. Any sharp separation of these is bound to be arbitrary and to distort the nature of the phenomena. In actual research practice, treatment of these aspects as "components" typically amounts to using samples of *behavior* in different tasks or situations assigned at different points in time. Although this is legitimate research practice, we should not let our research techniques blind us to the undeniable blending of cognitive-motivational-behavioral in *any* specific situation or task that arouses an attitude.

Defining the Concept

As noted above, attitudes are necessarily inferred from behavior. In defining an attitude, we need to take special note of what *kind* of behavior is evidence for an attitude.

Definitions of attitude have had certain essential features in common. Almost invariably, one of these is that attitudes are acquired or learned. Another is that attitudes are inferred from modes of behavior by the same individual over a time span that are *characteristic, consistent,* and *selective.* Such specification of the data for attitude study was made by the sociologists Thomas and Znaniecki (1918) and included by the psychologists Murphy, Murphy, and Newcomb (1937); G. W. Allport (1935); Donald Campbell (1950; 1963); Smith, Bruner, and White (1956); and by the authors of the series of volumes from the Yale Communication Research program directed by Carl I. Hovland (*e.g.,* Hovland, Janis, and Kelley, 1953; Rosenberg, Hovland, McGuire, Abelson, and Brehm, 1960).

A definition of attitude should also point to operational tools for assessing attitude and attitude change. It should be formulated in a way that takes into account the nature of psychosocial scales so that the person's attitude can be located relative to a communication intended to change it, beyond the vague statement that it is "similar" or "discrepant."

The definition developed in our approach is based on a body of evidence (*cf.* Sherif and Hovland, 1961; Sherif, Sherif, and Nebergall, 1965). It leads to methods for specifying the structure of an individual's attitude. Briefly it stems from evidence that the characteristic, consistent, and selective modes of behavior from which attitude is inferred are based on characteristic standards and scales for comparison. A judgment process underlies the behavior in which the individual uses a set of categories for *comparing* and *evaluating* items within the stimulus domain in question.

The judgment process in this case is not neutral. In selecting one alternative over others, in seeking some and avoiding other alternatives, in consistently preferring some to others, the individual both discriminates among the alternatives and *evaluates* them. It is as though he were saying "I like and want this one" or "This is the one for me," while avoiding others as objectionable, disgusting, or "definitely not my kind."

Accordingly, the present approach developed the following definition of attitude:

Operationally, an attitude may be defined as the individual's set of categories for evaluating a stimulus domain, which he has established as he learns about that domain in interaction with other persons and which relate him to various subsets within the domain with varying degrees of positive or negative affect.

The data from which attitudes are inferred, therefore, are the person's *consistent* and *characteristic categorizations*, over a time span, of relevant objects, persons, groups, or communications into acceptable and objectionable categories. Change is inferred from the alteration of the individual's acceptance-rejection pattern. A closer understanding of this acceptance-rejection pattern and the analysis of measurable changes has been one of the main tasks in the present approach. From this analysis it has proven possible to make predictions about reaction to communication based on well-known principles governing anchor effects on judgment.

LATITUDES OF ACCEPTANCE, REJECTION, AND NONCOMMITMENT

Proceeding from the definition of attitude, let us specify three concepts for purposes of assessing the structure of an attitude:

1. *Latitude of acceptance:* If a person voluntarily states his view on a topic, he usually gives the position most acceptable to him. The latitude of acceptance is simply this most acceptable position *plus* other positions the individual also finds acceptable.

2. *Latitude of rejection:* The position most objectionable to the individual, the thing he most detests in a particular domain, *plus* other positions also objectionable to him define the latitude of rejection.

3. *Latitude of noncommitment:* While accepting some and rejecting others, the individual may prefer to remain noncommittal in regard to certain positions. Ordinarily, these are the "don't know," "neutral," "undecided," "no opinion," or "no comment" responses in public opinion surveys. In all of our research, the individual has been required *only* to indicate the most acceptable and objectionable positions, being free to accept or reject others but not forced to do so. The positions that he does *not* evaluate as either acceptable or objectionable under these circumstances constitute his *latitude of noncommitment.* As we shall see, some of the most useful predictive indicators discovered in our research are closely related to the size of this latitude of noncom-

mitment, that is, the positions on which the person prefers to remain noncommittal.

What are the advantages of specifying the structure of the person's attitude in terms of latitudes of acceptance, rejection, and noncommitment? *First,* individuals finding the same position as most acceptable *do* differ in their tolerance for other positions and in the range of their rejections. *Second,* the latitudes of acceptance, rejection, and noncommitment differ systematically for persons upholding different positions according to their degree of involvement in the issue at hand.

In translating the concept of attitude into research procedures, we have developed two techniques for assessing latitudes of acceptance, rejection, and noncommitment that differ sufficiently to be spelled out in some detail (*cf.* Sherif, Sherif, and Nebergall, 1965). Although both techniques are closely related to the conception of attitudes, the research procedures, the advantages and disadvantages of each are different, as we shall see. Here, we shall call one procedure the Method of Ordered Alternatives. The second is known as the "Own Categories" Procedure.

Method of Ordered Alternatives for Assessing the Structure of Attitude

Briefly, the Method of Ordered Alternatives (positions) starts with a survey of existing stands upheld by different groups or significant persons on an issue. From the statements obtained through content analysis of the social field, a number are selected to secure latitudes of acceptance, rejection, and noncommitment. Those positions selected represent the entire range of positions sampled, from one extreme to another. The only assumption about their scalar properties is that they do represent the range of the various positions on the issue and that they can be *ordered* reliably from one extreme to the other by anyone acquainted with the issue in question. No assumptions about the intervals between the available alternatives are made.

The Method of Ordered Alternatives has been used to secure latitudes of acceptance, rejection, and noncommitment on a variety of social issues both in this country and abroad (*cf.* Sherif, Sherif, and Nebergall, 1965; Diab, 1965a, 1965b; Whittaker, 1965; Bieri *et al.*, 1966). In order to obtain measures of the three latitudes, the subject is simply asked to indicate the position most acceptable to him (his own position), any others that are acceptable or not objectionable, the position most objectionable to him, and any others that may be objectionable. Note that he is not asked to respond successively to every statement. In fact many subjects prefer not to do so, and the positions which they *neither* accept nor reject constitute the latitude of noncommitment.

In order to summarize a considerable mass of data briefly here, we utilize findings from a study of the 1960 presidential elections (Sherif, Sherif, and Nebergall, 1965). After presenting illustrative data, we shall draw certain conclusions based on these findings, on a similar study conducted in 1956 (Sherif and Hovland, 1961), on studies of the prohibition issue (Hovland, Harvey, and Sherif, 1957), studies of farm policy by Whittaker (1965), the labor-management issue by Alvar Elbing, the desegregation issue by L. LaFave, and the issue of reapportionment of state legislatures according to population by John Reich (*cf.* Sherif, Sherif, and Nebergall, 1965).

All of the issues mentioned are controversial, and in each case active participants on each side of the controversy have been subjects along with less concerned parties (for example, college students from general classes, school teachers, unselected adult citizens, etc.). Still, for reasons that will become apparent as we continue, certain limitations are imposed upon our generalizations by the subject populations available. For this reason, we take particular note of the work of Diab in circumstances where partisanship is more intense and significant in the lives of individuals (*cf.* this volume, Chapter 8).

Figure 7.1 is a summary of the relative sizes of latitudes of acceptance, rejection, and noncommitment on the 1960 election issue. Although these particular data were obtained in the Pacific Northwest, it should be noted that data obtained in the southwestern region, which has a different population and history, do not differ significantly from these.

The figure presents the mean number of positions in the latitude of acceptance, rejection, and noncommitment for persons adopting each of nine positions as *most acceptable* to them (their own positions). The person's own position is given on the baseline from A, the most extreme Republican, to I, the most extreme Democratic position. The ordinate represents the mean number of positions responded to in different ways. Solid dots indicate the mean number of acceptances, X's the mean number of rejections, and the white circles represent the mean number for noncommitment.

Note that the means for the latitude of acceptance form almost a straight line near three acceptances, regardless of a person's own position. The dip at E (the noncommittal position) reflects the heterogeneity of these persons: About 17 percent of the subjects at E (which

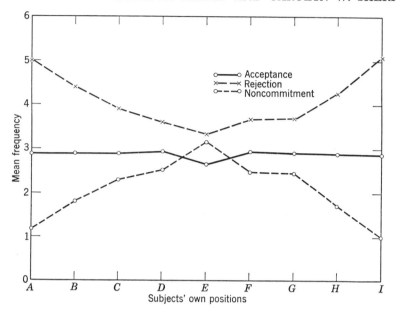

Figure 7.1 Size of lattitudes of acceptance, rejection and noncommitment for persons adopting each of nine positions as most acceptable. The locations represent means for subjects in a study of the 1960 presidential election (from Sherif, Sherif, and Nebergall, 1965, p. 52).

is nonpartisan) found only the E position acceptable, whereas another 40 percent were "leaners," accepting only one other position on either the Republican or Democratic side. Relationships between the size of the latitude of rejection and the person's own stand and between noncommitment and the person's own stand are both significant.

Certain generalizations are possible from the data in Figure 1 and the other studies mentioned above.

1. The latitude of rejection increases in size as a function of the extremity of the person's position, and the function is curvilinear for bipolar issues such as these.

2. The latitude of noncommitment is inversely related to extremity of commitment, approaching zero for persons with the most extreme commitment.

3. The relative sizes of the latitude of rejection, the latitude of acceptance, and latitude of noncommitment are clearly different for person's upholding the various positions. Relative to the latitude of acceptance, the latitude of rejection is disproportionately greater and

the latitude of noncommitment smaller as the person's own position becomes more extreme.

There is considerable evidence from earlier research showing that persons who adopt extreme stands are more likely to be highly involved than those with moderate stands (*e.g.*, Cantril, 1946). Conversely, there is evidence from data on ratings of personality dimensions that the person who is highly involved in a particular personal characteristic is likely to give extreme ratings on that dimension (Tajfel and Wilkes, 1963). In fact a recent review of research on the latter problem concludes that extremity of ratings on personal characteristics varies with the personal importance attached to the characteristic when research procedures do not "impose" the dimension to be rated upon subjects (O'Donovan, 1965, p. 365).

Significant as the association between extremity of position and personal involvement may be, our interest has been in the effects of varying ego-involvement, not in extreme attitudes per se. There are several reasons for this interest. In the first place, extremity of position is frequently identified by psychologists in this country as a sign of pathology. For this reason it is particularly significant that in the review of the literature on extreme ratings of personal attributes, O'Donovan (1965) found evidence that the "pathology-polarization hypotheses are supported by studies in which rating dimensions are imposed upon the subject," and "the meaningfulness-polarization hypotheses are supported by studies in which the subject has the opportunity to provide his own personally meaningful dimensions" or to select dimensions that are more significant to him personally (p. 365). Perhaps our view of persons who take extreme stands has been colored excessively by a norm of "liberal moderation." In other settings extreme stands may be viewed as strong convictions (*cf.* Diab, 1965a) rather than as symptoms of personal disturbance.

Second, in our research on the 1960 presidential election, *variances* around the mean latitudes for persons upholding different own positions (Figure 7.1) differed significantly only for those who adopted the E (non-partisan) position. This finding means that (with the exception of the heterogeneous lot who chose to remain nonpartisan) the distributions around the means in Figure 7.1 were similar for subjects upholding each position as most acceptable. Thus, there were a number of subjects who chose moderate positions as most acceptable but gave considerable other evidence of being highly involved in the election. These persons also rejected as many as five or six positions out of nine.

Third, although our earlier research had led us to expect that the size of the latitude of acceptance would decrease with extremity of positions, it is clear from Figure 7.1 that the mean latitude of acceptance did not vary significantly with own position. There is sufficient evidence from other studies to show that *relative* sizes of the latitudes of acceptance and rejection do differ according to extremity of position and that highly involved subjects do indeed have narrower latitudes of acceptance than uninvolved subjects (*cf.* Whittaker, 1965; LaFave and Sherif, 1962; Reich and Sherif, 1963). However, the size of the latitude of acceptance was not sufficient as an indicator of involvement across varying own positions on the election issue.

The purpose of our concern in securing an indicator of ego-involvement was to make predictions about the placement of five communications on the election issue by subjects upholding different positions. Noting that the size of the latitude of rejection varied systematically with own position and that the variances of subjects upholding different positions did not differ significantly, we adopted size of the latitude of rejection as an operational index of involvement in the issue. As we shall see presently, individuals thus differentiated as to involvement do show systematic differences in their perception of the position presented in communication.

Since noncommitment increases markedly with moderateness of position (Figure 7.1) and is much more frequent for issues less involving than a national election immediately prior to the event, we have suggested that the relative frequency of noncommitment on several issues may serve as a predictive indicator of the individual's susceptibility to change on these issues. Although research is underway to assess this suggestion, very little has been done to specify all of the conditions associated with high noncommitment. It is an important area of research, since subjects with a large latitude of noncommitment are particularly likely to change their attitudes in response to a communication (Sherif, Sherif, and Nebergall, 1965). Larimer (1966) has recently shown, with French-speaking and English-speaking Canadians as subjects, that a communication falling within the latitude of noncommitment is evaluated much more favorably than a communication falling within the person's latitude of rejection.

The data obtained by the Method of Ordered Alternatives reveal systematic variations in the structure of an attitude according to extremity of position and according to relative involvement in the issue. The structures revealed are, however, almost starkly geometric. In order to understand the processes underlying the results, we turn now to a consideration of the judgment process when a person appraises stimulus material relevant to his attitude.

In fact, in the present approach, the partitioning of Ordered Alternatives into latitudes of acceptance, rejection, and noncommitment was based on study of the judgment (categorization) process, not on sheerly logical grounds. The judgment process is best revealed through the use of the Own Categories Procedure, to which we now turn.

THE INDIVIDUAL'S OWN CATEGORIES

What psychological processes underlie the differences obtained between latitudes of acceptance, rejection, and noncommitment according to the person's relative involvement? Several psychological theories have proposed that category width (latitude) reflects a personality trait or "style." However, available studies that have correlated the same person's category widths for issues of varying personal involvement have found that personal consistency across issues accounts for no more than 10 to 15 percent of the total variance (e.g., Sherif, 1961; Glixman, 1965). Therefore we sought a theoretical basis for the phenomena sufficiently broad to incorporate idiosyncratic variables and to account for the fact that an individual may tolerate differences on issues of little concern to him (even to the point of self-contradiction) while seeing a matter of high personal concern in terms of "black and white." The theory also had to be sufficiently broad to include the fact that the ranges for tolerance and condemnation vary from one human group to another.

We found such a basis in the psychology of judgment, studied for nearly a century in psychological laboratories in various countries. Our account of the principles essential to the approach is necessarily sketchy here (cf. Sherif, Sherif, and Nebergall, 1965).

Systematic Variations in Judgment

Whether the object of judgment is a weight, the length of a line, the color of a person's skin, or the beauty of a girl, judgment is rendered relative to the immediate stimulus context in which it appears and to preceding contexts. For example, a statement on the issue of segregation in the public schools ("We must keep the future interests of school children in mind") is appraised differently when preceded by other statements opposed to segregation, on the one hand, or by statements favoring segregation, on the other.

However, all stimuli present or just preceding the object of judgment do not have equal weight in affecting the outcome, not even in the psychophysical laboratory where the stimuli are usually neutral. In one of the orthodox psychophysical methods, the standard stimulus that is presented with each new comparison stimulus is more influential than those less frequently presented or not designated as a standard (Helson, 1959, p. 591). Such frequently presented stimuli, or those designated as standards, become anchors for the individual's judgments. Lacking an explicit standard, the individual typically uses the most extreme stimuli presented to him as anchors in sizing up the intermediate values. The end stimuli thus contribute more than others to his judgment of a particular member of a series (Parducci, 1963).

An anchor enhances accuracy of judgment for items coinciding with it in value; but it produces systematic shifts or "displacements" in judgments of objects differing from it in varying degrees. An anchor differing slightly from the object of judgment results in displacement *toward* the anchor: this is an *assimilation effect,* well known in studies of perception and now in judgment (*cf.* Sherif, Taub, and Hovland, 1958; Parducci and Marshall, 1962; Helson, 1964). With increasing discrepancies between the anchor and the object of judgment, assimilation ceases, and, after a transition, displacement begins to occur in a direction *away* from the anchor: the difference between the anchor and the object is exaggerated. This is the well-known *contrast effect.* Assimilation and contrast in judgment are complementary phenomena governed by the relationship between anchor and objects of judgment; they are not separate mechanisms, as Helson (1964) has also stressed.

Years ago, Hunt and Volkmann (1937) showed that contrast effects could be produced in the laboratory by instructing the subject to *imagine* the most extreme representative of the dimension being judged. Thus, it is evident that the person's *internal standards* have to be taken into account, as well as the stimulation that he faces within a limited time period.

The foregoing findings provided the basis for the logic in explaining shifts in judgment of attitude statements that occurred according to the person's own attitude in studies of the Thurstone method of equal-appearing intervals (Hovland and Sherif, 1952; Sherif and Hovland, 1953). In these experiments, the subject's task was objective. He was to categorize a series of 114 statements developed by Hinckley according to how favorable or unfavorable they were to the status of Negroes. In one condition, he was to use eleven categories *imposed* upon him by the experimenters' instructions. In the other, he was left free to use any number of categories in any way he chose, in

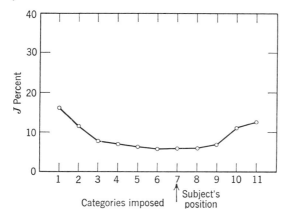

Figure 7.2 Percentages of items (J percent = Judgment percent) placed in eleven categories imposed by instructions by moderately pro-Negro subjects (data from Sherif and Hovland, 1953).

order to differentiate among the statements. In short, the Own Categories Procedure was used. Some of the subjects were highly involved in the issue, either as the first Negro students at a previously segregated institution or as active white participants in the desegregation movement.

Before presenting illustrative findings from this research, it is important to note that the pool of statements ranged from extremely pro- to extremely anti-Negro statements and also contained a large number of intermediate items having high Q values (high variability). In this and subsequent studies using the Own Categories Procedure, the stimulus materials have contained a large number of items that are categorized by unselected subjects with great variability.

The subject's task is to sort the pool of items into any number of piles or categories that seems necessary so that items within each category seem to him to "belong together." Typically, a category at one extreme is defined by instructions. The person subsequently numbers and labels his own categories relative to that extreme. Upon completion of the task, he may be asked to indicate which categories are acceptable or objectionable to him, if a direct report of latitudes of acceptance, rejection and noncommitment is desired.

Figure 7.2 presents results with *imposed* categories for moderately favorable subjects (indicated by the arrow at seven on the baseline, with eleven being most favorable). It represents the relative frequen-

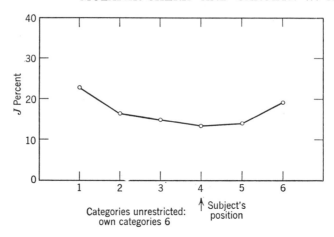

Figure 7.3   Percentage of items (J percent = Judgment percent) placed in own categories by moderately pro-Negro subjects (data from Sherif and Hovland, 1953).

cies of judgment in each of the eleven categories imposed by the instructions. It can be seen that these moderate subjects did a fair job in using the eleven categories about equally, with a slight concentration at each end. They distributed their judgments even more equitably among categories when they sorted the same statement with the Own Categories Procedure, as shown in Figure 7.3.

Figures 7.4 and 7.5 present comparable data for persons who were highly involved in the Negro issue with own positions at eleven, the most favorable extreme. Under the *imposed* categories condition (Figure 7.4), these subjects neglected the intermediate categories imposed on them by instructions, producing bimodal distributions of the items with a small mode at the favorable end and a disproportionately high mode at the extreme farthest away from their own stand on the issue.

The bimodal distribution was greatly accentuated under the Own Categories Procedure (Figure 7.5), owing especially to the tendency for highly involved persons to use fewer categories than less involved subjects. On the average, the most militant Negro subjects used fewer than four categories, placing 65 of the 114 statements in a single objectionable category and 27 in a category acceptable to them. In comparison, unselected white students used more categories, on the average, placing 43 statements in objectionable categories and 38 in categories they later indicated were acceptable.

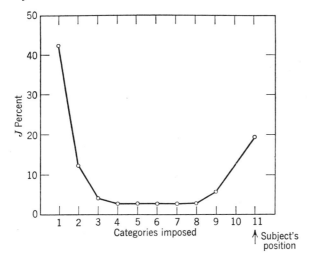

Figure 7.4 Percentage of items (J percent = Judgment percent) placed in eleven categories imposed by instructions by extremely pro-Negro subjects (data from Sherif and Hovland, 1953).

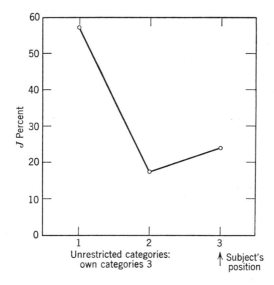

Figure 7.5 Percentage of items (J percent = Judgment percent) placed in own categories by extremely pro-Negro subjects (data from Sherif and Hovland, 1953).

In that early research, the results for anti-Negro subjects were not a clear reversal of the distributions for pro-Negro subjects. It was suggested that the anti-Negro subjects were less involved in the issue, but it was possible to specify this only by pointing to the striking differences between their activity pertinent to the issue and that of the pro-Negro subjects. Therefore, it is particularly interesting that Vaughan (1961) did obtain the reverse of the distributions in Figures 7.4 and 7.5 for *anti* subjects, in a situation where the normative trend to appear "liberal" about minority groups was not strong, namely in south Texas. In this case, the *anti* subjects were negative toward Texans of Latin-American origin.

Accounting for the Bipolar Variations in Judgment

Proceeding directly from the findings on assimilation-contrast effects in psychophysical judgments, we can account for both the bimodal distributions in judgments (Figures 7.4 and 7.5) and the related finding that the latitude of rejection is disproportionately greater than latitude of acceptance for highly involved subjects. The additional assumptions needed to do so are supported by experimental evidence (Sherif, Sherif, and Nebergall, 1965).

1. If a person has an attitude toward a stimulus domain, his judgments of specific objects in that domain are, to some extent, made relative to his own reference scale, in addition to the context of immediate and preceding stimulation. This reference scale is composed of the individual's own categories. (See the definition of attitude presented earlier.)

2. To the extent that the stimulus domain has high priority in his self system (degree of ego-involvement), the task of categorizing stimuli becomes an *evaluative* task for him, even though he is told to judge according to objective, nonevaluative criteria. Although instructed to heed only the stimulus attributes of the items and to categorize them on an impersonal dimension, the highly involved individual performs the task in terms of his agreements-disagreements with the items. (Vaughan reported that her anti-Latin subjects often objected to the instruction that they sort items only according to how pro- or anti-Latin they were because, in their words, so many of the statements *simply were not true.*) One may *force* the involved person to follow instructions by insisting that he compare one item with another, as in the method of paired-comparisons. He *can* discriminate among the items (*cf.* Kelley *et al.*, 1955); but barring special arrangements forcing him to do so, he does not divorce the task

of categorizing items from his evaluations of them. This is the basic reason why the Own Categories Procedure suggests itself as an indirect or disguised method for attitude and personality assessment (Sherif and Sherif, 1964).

3. To the degree that he is ego-involved, the person uses his own position as the main standard for placing items related to it. Since, in our own research, predictions from this postulate have invariably been more accurate when we considered the bounds (limits) of the latitude of acceptance, we are forced to conclude that the involved person also has a clear concept of "how far he will go" and that the latitude of acceptance itself acquires an anchoring function.

The psychological process when the individual is presented with a specific set of stimuli to classify is then analogous to that in the judgment laboratory: Using his own position as an anchor, he is more discriminating about admitting items to acceptable categories than about placing items in objectionable categories. His threshold for acceptance is raised. His latitude of acceptance is comparatively small because he is "choosy" about admitting positions to it. At the same time, however, the use of own position as an anchor results in an assimilation effect. The raised threshold for acceptance is a *relative* matter, for the own position anchor also results in assimilation of positions close to it. This assimilative trend is revealed in the small mode at the acceptable end of Figure 7.5 and in the tendency for subjects to rate statements more favorably when they are near their own positions (*cf.* Zavalloni and Cook, 1965; Sellitz, Edrich, and Cook, 1965).

Concomitantly, use of own position as an anchor reduces discrimination for positions widely discrepant from it: the threshold for rejection is *lowered* because discrepant items are *contrasted* to the acceptable position and seen as *more* discrepant than they would be by a person who is not involved in the issue. As a result, items that might seem "moderate" to a less involved person are lumped together into one or a few broad categories as *objectionable*. Hence, the highly involved person has a latitude of rejection disproportionately greater than his latitude of acceptance.

4. On a controversial issue (bipolar), the highly involved person uses *fewer* categories than a less committed person, a fact that is probably related to the assimilation-contrast effects relative to his own stand. Logically, at least, these systematic displacements would result in a need for fewer categories.

The twin phenomena, namely a restricted number of categories and unequal use of categories, are intensified by the degree of personal involvement. The evidence stems from two kinds of experiments using the Own Categories Procedure: (a) experiments comparing categorizations of the same materials by subjects whose public activities indicate varying involvement (e.g., LaFave and Sherif, 1962; Vaughan, 1961; Reich and Sherif, 1963) and (b) experiments varying the stimulus material according to their relative involvement for the same subjects (e.g., Sherif, 1961; Glixman, 1965; Koslin, Waring, and Pargament, 1965).

Using the latter method, Koslin and others had Peace Corps volunteers categorize series of statements on five issues that subjects ranked according to how much time they spent talking on the topic. Using the latter criterion of involvement, the investigators found that latitudes of acceptance decreased and latitudes of rejection increased in width from the least involving issue (housing in India) to the most involving issue (segregation in the United States). The latitude of rejection was greater than the latitude of acceptance for the latter issue. Furthermore, repetition of the task with items added to each extreme produced significantly *less* shifting of items in the more involving than the less involving issue. In other words, *consistency* in categorizing the items common to the two tasks was greatest for the more involving issue.

More recently, Koslin (1966) had Peace Corps volunteers assess two sets of different statements on motives for joining the Corps, using a modified Own Categories Procedure. The sets of statements were matched by an independent determination of their standard scores derived from paired-comparison judgments. By correlating the mean value of statements the subjects placed into their different categories on the two tasks, Koslin has shown that *consistency* of categorization (reliability) is very high indeed on such an involving topic, even when the specific statements in the two sets differed. The lowest correlation obtained was .95.

Since the systematic displacements and variations in number of categories according to degree of involvement occur even when the person is not instructed to reveal his attitude, we have suggested the Own Categories Procedure as an indirect or disguised test of attitude. For similar reasons, the technique is admirably suited for cross-cultural comparisons and for a nonconfrontive method in locating areas of personal concern in the study of personality. Although the specific content can be adapted to cross-cultural and interpersonal differences, the logic of the method should be invariant since it is based on general principles of human judgment.

PLACEMENT OF COMMUNICATION IS BASIC TO
PROBLEMS OF ATTITUDE CHANGE

Attempts at attitude change—whether in interpersonal, group, or mass communication situations—involve some form of communication. The basic information for predicting a person's reaction to a communication is *where* he places its position and the communicator relative to himself. The way that a person appraises a communication and perceives its position relative to his own stand affects his reaction to it and what he will do as a result.

If the foregoing propositions be granted, it becomes apparent that a theory of attitude change has to be capable of predicting the person's judgment of communication. From at least the time of William James, various authors have noted the phenomena of tension, irritation, and discomfiture in response to a situation violating values of some personal importance. The observation is not new. In recent years, a number of theories have developed to predict how the individual will respond to this internal tension, imbalance, incongruence, or dissonance. However, study of the variables affecting whether a communication will or will not arouse such internal tension has not been systematically undertaken within these theoretical frameworks.

By systematic study of the placement and evaluation of communication, the present approach to attitude change has developed a set of generalizations concerning the process of appraising communication. They are basic in predicting whether attitudes change or do not change. As these generalizations indicate, the person's reaction to a communication is predicated upon a patterned psychological process that precludes certain behavioral alternatives and promotes others. Theories that do not take such patterning into account, proceeding instead to predict reaction to communication on the basis of logical alternatives, will necessarily be found to err at some point. The logical alternatives turn out to be related psychologically, such that a person may adopt more than one and in varying degrees. The behavioral outcome is governed by the patterning of a set of variables that are specified in the sections to follow.

Discrepancy between Communication and the Person's Stand

The determination of a discrepancy between a communication and the person's position at the time must be made relative to that person's own categories (his attitude). When groups of individuals are involved, such determination amounts to specifying the position of a communication relative to the psychosocial scale established in the particular group to which the individual belongs (his reference group). On the basis of such specification, the following generalizations were reached about placement and evaluation of communication:

A. To the extent that a communication lies within the latitude of acceptance or nearby in the latitude of noncommitment, it is judged as *closer* to the own position (*assimilated*) and is simultaneously perceived as factual, unbiased, fair, and pleasing (Sherif and Hovland, 1961; Sherif, Sherif, and Nebergall, 1965; Larimer, 1966).

B. As the position of communication becomes more discrepant from the latitude of acceptance and increasingly within the latitude of rejection, it is increasingly judged as *more* discrepant and simultaneously perceived as biased, propagandistic, and false (Sherif and Hovland, 1961; Sherif, Sherif, and Nebergall, 1965; Larimer, 1966; Sherif and Jackman, 1966).

In other words, placement of communication and evaluation of it occur as patterned aspects of the same judgment process governed by the relationship between the communication and the latitudes of acceptance, rejection, and noncommitment.

In studying placements of five communications presenting different positions on the 1960 election campaign, we were able to specify some of the major variables affecting the occurrence of assimilation-contrast effects and the accompanying evaluations of communication. These are presented briefly in terms of the range of positions within which assimilation and positive evaluation will occur.

Degree of Involvement. If the person is not involved at all in an issue, discrepancy relative to his own stand becomes a minor issue. The experience of tension, imbalance, or incongruity presumes a discrepancy from a position to which the individual attaches some importance.

In a study of placement of five communications presenting different positions on the 1960 election, ego-involvement was defined operationally in terms of the size of the *latitude of rejection*, with the greater latitude indicating greater involvement in the issue. Discrepancy of the communication was calculated in terms of position steps that it was removed from the limit of the person's latitude of acceptance. The consistent finding was that *less* involved subjects (with smaller latitudes of rejection) assimilated the communication toward their own view over a much wider range of discrepancies than did highly involved persons. Highly involved persons with the same latitude of acceptance as the less involved persons revealed a *narrower* range of asssimilation. Conversely, the highly involved person revealed a contrast effect when appraising a communication that a less involved person assimilated. In a recent study, Eagley and Manis (1966) reported a related finding: ego-involved subjects responded more negatively to a discrepant communication than less involved subjects.

We conclude that the range of assimilation is inversely related to the degree of personal involvement.

Structure of the Communication. The structure of the communication may be defined operationally in terms of the number of alternative interpretations (placements) it permits. Certain properties of issues (for example, complexity), of statement (for example, ambiguity) and of position (for example, moderate versus extreme) decrease the degree of structure as so defined. Although a great deal remains to be studied about communication structure, available evidence indicates that the effects of varying involvement cannot be specified without considering this variable.

A. Clear-cut statements of extreme positions are not subject to assimilation-contrast effects to an appreciable degree. It is the somewhat less extreme (Zavalloni and Cook, 1965; Selltiz, Edrich, and Cook, 1965) and especially the intermediate statements (LaFave and Sherif, 1962; Koslin *et al.*, 1965; Sherif, Sherif, and Nebergall, 1965) that are subject to systematic displacement. These findings are probably related, on the one hand, to the fact that extreme positions are frequently stated in unambiguous form and, on the other, to the tendency of advocates of extreme stands to simplify the issue. Definition of the communication variables conducive to lack of structure in the intermediate range will probably require further specification of the nature of verbal ambiguity (*cf.* Zimbardo, 1960; LaFave *et al.*, 1963). Moderate positions are not necessarily ambiguous (*cf.* Sherif and Hovland, 1961; Zavalloni and Cook, 1965), yet the greatest variability in categorizing usually occurs in the intermediate range (*cf.* Edwards, 1946). Further study of the structure variable might well be related to studies of fluid social situations where rumors are rife (*e.g.*, Cantril, 1941). In such situations the individual's use of his own standards in assessing the rumors produces variations that resemble assimilation-contrast effects.

B. The relationship between ego-involvement and communication structure is clear when the communication presents just *two* alternatives, as in the debate format or a systematically counterbalanced statement presenting both sides of an issue with no conclusion (Sherif,

Sherif, and Nebergall, 1965). In the 1960 study of election communications, we found that such communications, especially the actual
television debates between the two candidates, were highly conducive
to assimilation. Proportional to the extremity of their positions, partisan
of each side saw their candidate's performance as superior. However,
the assimilation trend was much stronger for subjects who were *less*
ego-involved. The general trend of assimilation was confirmed more
recently in a laboratory study presenting material from the same debates well after the elections, with the interesting difference that some
Republican subjects defected toward the then-elected Democratic
candidate, Kennedy (Rosnow, 1965).

On the basis of present evidence, we may conclude that the range
of assimilation increases as the structure of communication decreases
but that high ego-involvement restricts the assimilation range.

Source of the communication. Although little research has been
conducted on placement of the position presented in a communication
as a function of its source, it is clear that the source is an important
variable. When the source is unidentified, the listener typically sizes
up his views and, depending upon his placement of the position,
attributes the source to an organization friendly or inimical to his
reference group, as the case may be (*cf.* Sherif, Sherif, and Nebergall,
1965; Sherif and Jackman, 1966).

Future study of effects of different sources must include more systematic investigation of the person's reference groups and of their
friendly or hostile relationship to other groups. Most research in recent
years has dealt with the communicator chiefly in terms of his "credibility," a descriptive label that implies a judgment on the part of the
subject. The variables affecting judgments of "credibility" are certainly
crucial to an adequate theory for reactions to communication. Many
years ago, Asch (1940) showed that reaction to communications
varied according to whether the communicator was presented as a
member of a "congenial" or "antagonistic" group. Subjects went to
considerable pains in trying to interpret a communication so that
it "fit" the stand of the communicator's group. Such findings would
indicate that "credibility" is a complex judgment reflecting both the
recipient's reference groups and the particular attributes prized in
its scheme of values.

On the basis of available evidence, the present approach postulates
that a source with high status for the individual's reference groups
will increase the range of assimilation. The possible interactions be-

tween source, the person's involvement in the issue at hand, and his involvement as a group member remain to be explored, insofar as they may affect his placement of communication.

PREDICTIONS ABOUT ATTITUDE CHANGE

The social judgment-involvement approach makes some definite predictions about when attitudes will change, when they will not, and when they will be strengthened in response to communication. These predictions require that the position of communication be specified relative to the person's latitudes of acceptance, rejection, and noncommitment.

The first prediction concerns *susceptibility* to change regardless of the particular communication presented with the intent to change a person's attitude. Susceptibility to change will vary according to the sizes of the person's latitude of noncommitment and latitude of rejection. There is considerable evidence that "moderate" subjects (with large latitudes of noncommitment and small latitudes of rejection) change in laboratory experiments approximately twice as frequently as highly committed subjects with small latitudes of noncommitment and large latitudes of rejection (Sherif, Sherif, and Nebergall, 1965). Therefore, regardless of the discrepancy of the position presented, we predict that the more the person is involved in the issue (the more important it is to him), the *less* susceptible he will be to short-term attempts to change his attitude.

Specification of the structure of a person's attitude in terms of latitudes of acceptance, rejection, and noncommitment permits further predictions about the direction and pattern of change among those who are susceptible. In the study of the 1960 election campaign, the attitudes of partisans on both sides and those adopting moderate stands were assessed twice about a week apart. Eliminating the most extreme subjects who could only change by becoming less extreme, blind predictions of the direction of change were made based on the pattern of acceptances and rejections during the first session. Accurate prediction was made for over 70 percent of the subjects who changed. The possibility of predicting both susceptibility and direction of change on such a basis remains to be explored further.

The frequency and the extent of change as the position presented in communication differs increasingly from the person's own stand can be predicted on the basis of the same variables affecting placement of the communication. Central to these is the degree of personal involvement. Although the "balance" and "dissonance" theories have included statements qualifying their predictions according to the "importance" or "relevance" of the matter at hand, none has included a theory of self (ego) that leads to operational measures of this variable. The typical measure has been self-ratings by the subjects. The recent emphasis by a number of researchers within and outside of the "dissonance" movement on the need for specifying the variable of "importance" may hopefully lead to new developments (*cf.* Walster and Festinger, 1962; Brock and Becker, 1965; Zajonc and Burnstein, 1965; O'Donovan, 1965). Meanwhile, the social judgment-involvement approach has suggested a basis for operationalizing the variable, namely the process of social judgment as it occurs when significant constituents (attitudes) of the self are situationally involved.

Because the theory of cognitive dissonance has not included a theory of ego-involvements nor of systematic variations in judgment produced by ego-involved stands, its predictions about attitude change differ from those of the present approach in important respects. Notably, the present approach does not predict a linear increase in frequency or extent of attitude change as the discrepancy increases between communication and the person's stand. The present approach predicts increasing frequency and extent of attitude change with increased discrepancies *only within the range of assimilation,* which is, we repeat, affected by the person's involvement in his stand, the structure of the communication, and the source. Beyond the assimilation range, the prediction is *decreasing* frequency and extent of attitude change proportional to the increasing discrepancy between the person's stand and the position of communication.

Given some involvement in this issue, we predict a curvilinear relationship between attitude change and communication discrepancy. With extreme discrepancies and high personal commitment, the person will *never* react to a transitory communication by changing his attitude. He will feel irritated, he may derogate the communicator, or speak to his friends about it; but he will never see changing his own attitude in the direction of the communication as a viable alternative. On the contrary, he is more apt to retrench in his own stand or to shift *away* from the communication.

Various writers have pointed to an apparent contradiction in findings on attitude change as it relates to communication discrepancy. The contradiction *is* apparent, for it disappears when the conditions of the various experiments are fully specified. As the social judgment-involvement approach predicts, those experiments reporting increased change with increasing discrepancies have been performed under one or more of the following conditions:

1. Low ego-involvement or no attitude at all at the outset.

2. Ambiguous communications or highly unstructured situations to be judged.

3. Limited ranges of discrepancies.

4. Sources valued highly in terms of the individual's reference groups (including the experimenter as a source for college students).

Studies reporting a curvilinear relationship between change and discrepancy of communication (e.g., Whittaker, 1965; Aronson et al., 1963; Freedman, 1964; Johnson, 1966) have included involving topics, moderately valued sources, and/or broad ranges of communication discrepancies.

The evidence to date, therefore, falls into a pattern. Low involvement, unstructured stimulus situations, and highly valued sources increase the range of assimilation, within which communication is increasingly effective in producing attitude change. High ego-involvement, structured communications, and less valued sources restrict the range of assimilation, beyond which decreasing frequency and extent of attitude change occurs as the communication becomes more discrepant. Accurate predictions about attitude change can be made only when these variables, at least, are clearly specified.

On our part, we are interested in utilizing the methodological advantages gained from the present approach in further studies of the formation and change of attitudes within the person's reference groups. Attitudes are seldom acquired or changed in lonely situations involving only the individual and a single communicator. The most significant attitudes are acquired with reference to his fellow men with whom he has ties, claims for recognition, and for amounting to something as a person. In previous experiments, interaction among individuals facing common problems or moved by common motives was found to be a potent context for the formation of highly involving attitudes toward other groups and for their change (Sherif, Harvey, White, Hood, and Sherif, 1961). Intensive studies of natural groups (Sherif and Sherif, 1964) have shown that the person's ego-involvements are related to his group membership and that the latitudes of acceptance and rejection differ both for members of different groups and for members of the same group according to their roles and the importance of an issue to that group.

Eventually, accurate prediction of attitude change hinges upon our ability to specify the individual's relative involvement in a variety of value domains, a matter closely related to his roles in various reference groups and to their values. Such specification presumes adequate measurement of his attitudes. The present approach can be extended in these directions to the mutual benefit of research on attitudes and research on group processes, which are undeniably the context for the formation and change of attitudes most significant and consequential for the individual and for his fellow men.

REFERENCES

Allen, Vernon L., 1966. Review: Attitude and attitude change. *Amer. sociol. Rev.*, **31**, No. 2, 283–284.

Allendoerfer, C. C., and Oakley, C. O., 1959. *Fundamentals of freshmen mathematics.* New York: McGraw-Hill.

Allport, G. W., 1935. Attitudes. In C. Murchison (Ed.), *A Handbook of social psychology.* Worcester, Mass.: Clark Univ. Press.

Aronson, E., Turner, Judith A., and Carlsmith, J. M., 1963. Communicator credibility and communicator discrepancy as determinants of opinion change. *J. abnorm. soc. Psychol.*, **67**, 31–37.

Asch, S. E., 1940. Studies in the principles of judgments and attitudes: II. Determination of judgments by group and by ego standards. *J. soc. Psychol.*, *SPSSI Bull.*, **12**, 433–465.

Bieri, J., Atkins, A. L., Briar, S., Leaman, R. L., Miller, H., and Tripodi, T. 1966. *Clinical and social judgment: the discrimination of behavioral information.* New York: Wiley.

Brock, T. C., and Becker, L. A., 1965. Ineffectiveness of "overheard" counter-propaganda. *J. Pers. soc. Psychol.*, **2**, 654–660.

Campbell, D. T., 1950. The indirect assessment of social attitudes. *Psychol. Bull.*, **47**, 15–38.

Campbell, D. T., 1963. Social attitudes and other acquired behavioral dispositions. In S. Koch (Ed.), *Psychology: a study of a science.* Vol. 6. New York: McGraw-Hill.

Cantril, H., 1941. *The psychology of social movements.* New York: Wiley.

Cantril, H., 1946. The intensity of an attitude, *J. abnorm. soc. Psychol.*, **41**, 129–135.

Diab, L. N., 1965a. Studies in social attitudes: I. Variations in latitudes of acceptance and rejection as a function of varying positions on a controversial social issue. *J. soc. Psychol.*, **67**, 283–295.

Diab, L. N., 1965b. Studies in social attitudes: III. Attitude assessment through the semantic differential. *J. soc. Psychol.* **67**, 303–314.

Durkheim, E., 1915. *The elementary forms of religious life.* London: Allen and Unwin.

Durkheim, E., 1938. *The rules of the sociological method.* Chicago: The Univ. of Chicago Press.

Eagley, Alice H., and Manis, M., 1966. Evaluation of message and communicator as a function of involvement. *J. Pers. soc. Psychol.*, **3**, 483–485.

Edwards, A. L., 1946. A critique of "neutral items" in attitude scales constructed by the method of equal-appearing intervals. *Psychol. Rev.*, 53, 159–169.

Freedman, J. L., 1964. Involvement, discrepancy and change. *J. abnorm. soc. Psychol.*, 69, 290–295.

Glixman, A. R., 1965. Categorizing behavior as a function of meaning domain. *J. person. soc. Psychol.*, 2, 370–377.

Helson, H., 1959. Adaptation level theory. In S. Koch (Ed.), *Psychology A study of a science.* Vol. 1. New York: McGraw-Hill.

Helson, H., 1964. Current trends and issues in adaptation-level theory. *Amer. Psychologist*, 19, 26–38.

Hovland, C. I., Harvey, O. J., and Sherif, M., 1957. Assimilation and contrast effects in communication and attitude change. *J. abnorm. soc. Psychol.*, 55, 242–252.

Hovland, C. I., Janis, J. L., and Kelley, H. H., 1953. *Communication and persuasion.* New Haven: Yale Univ. Press.

Hovland, C. I., and Sherif, M., 1952. Judgmental phenomena and scales of attitude measurement: Item displacement in Thurstone scales. *J. abnorm. soc. Psychol.*, 47, 822–832.

Hunt, W. A., and Volkmann, J., 1937. The anchoring of an affective scale. *Amer. J. Psychol.*, 49, 88–92.

Johnson, H. H., 1966. Some effects of discrepancy level on responses to negative information about one's self. *Sociometry*, 29, 52–66.

Kelley, H. H., Hovland, C. I., Schwartz, M., and Abelson, R. P., 1955. The influence of judges' attitudes in three methods of scaling. *J. soc. Psychol.*, 42, 147–158.

Koslin, B. L., 1966. Personal communication.

Koslin, B. L., Waring, P. D., and Pargament, R., 1965. Measurement of attitude organization with the "own category" technique. Prepublication report, Princeton University.

LaFave, L., and Sherif, M., 1962. Reference scales and placement of items with the own categories technique. Norman, Okla.: Institute of Group Relations (mimeographed).

LaFave, L., Szczesiak, R., Yaquinto, J., and Adler, B., 1963. Connotation as a supplemental variable in assimilation-contrast principles in psycho-social scales. Fuller report of paper to Amer. Psychol. Assoc. Annu. Meetings, Philadelphia (mimeographed).

Larimer, G., 1966. Social judgment approach to the investigation of French and English Canadian attitudes. Paper presented to annual meetings, Eastern Psychol. Assoc., New York City, April.

MacLeod, R. B., 1951. The place of phenomenological analysis in social psychology. In J. Rohrer and M. Sherif (Eds.), *Social Psychology at the crossroads.* New York: Harper.

Murphy, G., Murphy, Lois B., and Newcomb, T. M., 1937. *Experimental social psychology.* New York: Harper.

O'Donovan, D., 1965. Rating extremity: Pathology or meaningfulness? *Psychol. Rev.*, **72**, 358–372.

Parducci, A., 1963. Range-frequency compromise in judgment. *Psychol. Monogr.*, **77**, 2, No. 565.

Parducci, A., and Marshall, L. M., 1962. Assimilation vs. contrast in the anchoring of perceptual judgments of weight. *J. exp. Psychol.*, **63**, 426–437.

Reich, J., and Sherif, M., 1963. Ego-involvement as a factor in attitude assessment by the own categories technique. Norman, Okla.: Institute of Group Relations (mimeographed).

Rosenberg, M. J., Hovland, C. I., McGuire, W. G., Abelson, R. P., and Brehm, J. W., 1960. *Attitude organization and change.* New Haven: Yale Univ. Press.

Rosnow, R. L., 1965. Bias in evaluating the presidential debates: A "splinter" effect. *J. soc. Psychol.*, **67**, 211–219.

Selltiz, Claire, Edrich, H., and Cook, S. W., 1965. Ratings of favorableness of statements about a social group as an indicator of attitude toward the group. *J. Pers. soc. Psychol.*, **2**, 408–415.

Sherif, Carolyn W. 1961. Established reference scales and series effects in social judgment. Doctoral dissertation, The Univ. of Texas.

Sherif, Carolyn W., and Jackman, N., 1966. Judgments of truth in collective controversy. *Publ. Opin. Quart.*, **30**, 173–186.

Sherif, Carolyn W., Sherif, M., and Nebergall, R. E., 1965. *Attitude and attitude change. The social judgment-involvement approach.* Philadelphia: W. B. Saunders.

Sherif, M., and Cantril, H., 1947. *The psychology of ego-involvements,* New York: Wiley; Wiley Science Series (paperback), 1966.

Sherif, M., Harvey, O. J., White, B. J., Hood, W. R., and Sherif, Carolyn W., 1961. *Intergroup conflict and cooperation. The Robbers Cave experiment.* Norman, Okla.: Univ. of Okl. Book Exchange.

Sherif, M., and Hovland, C. I., 1953. Judgmental phenomena and scales of attitude measurement: Placement of items with individual choice of number of categories. *J. abnorm. soc. Psychol.*, **48**, 135–141.

Sherif, M., and Hovland, C. I., 1961. *Social judgment: Assimilation and contrast effects in reaction to communication and attitude change.* New Haven: Yale Univ. Press, paperback edition, 1965.

Sherif, M., and Sherif, Carolyn W., 1964. La méthode des catégories personnelles et les recherche sur les attitudes. *Bull. du C.E.R.P.* (Centre National de la Recherche Scientifique, Paris, France), **13**, No. 4, 185–197.

Sherif, M., and Sherif, Carolyn W., 1964. *Reference groups: Exploration into conformity and deviation of adolescents.* New York: Harper.

Sherif, M., Taub, D., and Hovland, C. I., 1958. Assimilation and contrast effects of anchoring stimuli on judgments. *J. exp. Psychol.*, **55**, 150–155.

Smith, M. B., Bruner, J. S., and White, R. W., 1956. *Opinions and personality*. New York: Wiley.

Tajfel, H., and Wilkes, A. L., 1963. Salience of attitudes and commitment to extreme judgments in the perception of people. *Brit. J. soc. clin. Psychol.*, **2**, 40–49.

Thomas, W. I., and Znaniecki, F., 1918. *The Polish peasant in Europe and America*. Chicago: The Univ. of Chicago Press.

Vaughan, Kathryn B., 1961. A disguised instrument for the assessment of intergroup attitudes. Master's thesis, Texas Coll. of Arts and Industries.

Walster, Elaine, and Festinger, L., 1962. The effectiveness of "overheard" communications. *J. abnorm. soc. Psychol.*, **65**, 395–402.

Whittaker, J. O., 1965. Attitude change and communication-attitude discrepancy. *J. soc. Psychol.*, **65**, 141–147.

Zajonc, R. B., and Burnstein, E., 1965. The learning of balanced and unbalanced social structures. *J. Pers.*, **33**, 153–163.

Zavalloni, Marisa, and Cook, S. W., 1965. Influence of judges' attitudes on ratings of favorableness of statements about a social group. *J. Pers. soc. Psychol.*, **1**, 43–54.

Zimbardo, P. G., 1960. Verbal ambiguity and judgmental distortion. *Psychol. Rep.*, **6**, 57–58.

8. Measurement of Social Attitudes: Problems and Prospects

Lutfy N. Diab

The concept of attitude, more than any other concept in the field of social psychology, has been widely used in attempts to explain and predict behavior. Needless to say, the degree of success in these attempts depends mainly on two major assumptions, namely (1) that the attitude measure being used is valid, and (2) that the attitude being measured relates to a highly ego-involving issue and, therefore, may be a major causative factor for the behavior in question. Failure to predict behavior will be proportional to the degree in which either of these two assumptions is not justified.

In this chapter, the second assumption is met by dealing only with important and highly ego-involving social attitudes and issues. Therefore, the following sections deal mainly with the first assumption through discussion of problems involved in the measurement of social attitudes (1) by means of conventional attitude scales such as those developed by Thurstone, Likert, and Guttman; (2) through the social judgment-involvement approach developed by Sherif and others (Sherif and Hovland, 1961; Sherif, Sherif, and Nebergall, 1965); and (3) through the semantic differential procedure devised by Osgood and others (Osgood, 1962; Osgood, 1964; Osgood, Archer, and Miron, 1963; Osgood, Suci, and Tannenbaum, 1957). Recent cross-cultural evidence (Diab, 1965a; 1965b; 1965c; 1965d; 1966), some of it unpublished, will be included in further support of the viewpoint that is discussed. Finally, a suggested synthesis of the social judgment-involvement approach and the semantic differential procedure will be presented.

140

MEASUREMENT OF ATTITUDES THROUGH CONVENTIONAL ATTITUDE "SCALES"

The so-called attitude "scales" have been the most widely used techniques for the measurement of attitudes. These scales, exemplified by the Thurstone, Likert, and Guttman scales, have at least two characteristics in common:

1. They all represent the individual's attitude towards an object by a single preference score or average "most acceptable" position on a continuum of positions ranging from highly favorable to highly unfavorable.

2. In every case the individual is fully aware that his attitude on the issue in question is being measured (Krech, Crutchfield, and Ballachey, 1962; Sherif and Sherif, 1956).

Although this presentation will be concerned mainly with the first characteristic of attitude scales mentioned above, there is no doubt that the second characteristic is immensely important in attitude measurement. It does make a great deal of difference whether the subject is aware that his attitude is being measured. Consequently, indirect attitude assessment techniques, such as the "own-categories" procedure (Sherif, Sherif, and Nebergall, 1965) constitute a great improvement over the conventional direct attitude scales.

With respect to the first characteristic mentioned above, the conclusion reached by Sherif, Sherif, and Nebergall (1965) is adopted here, namely "that the individual's stand is not represented adequately as a point along a continuum" (p. 222). Scores obtained on the basis of conventional attitude scales have dealt almost invariably with the preferences of the individual for one or more positions on a continuum to the exclusion of any positions which he may possibly reject. In line with Sherif's theorizing and research, it appears that a consideration of *ranges* of acceptance *and* rejection of various positions on an issue would result in a more realistic representation of the individual's attitude. The next section presents some of the main problems involved in the measurement of social attitudes through direct attitude scales.

The Meaning of a Point Along a Continuum

The most critical question that can be asked concerning the adequacy of representing attitude as a point along a continuum of positions is the following: How much alike or how different are the attitudes of two persons with identical scores on an attitude scale? The-

oretically, two individuals with identical attitude scores ought to exhibit identical attitudes towards the object in question. In other words,
individuals endorsing the same position on a controversial social issue
should constitute a homogeneous grouping with respect to their stands
on the issue in question.

However, as pointed out by Sherif and others (Hovland, Harvey,
and Sherif, 1957; Sherif, 1960; Sherif and Hovland, 1961; Sherif, 1961;
Sherif, Sherif, and Nebergall, 1965), two individuals selecting the
same position on a continuum of positions as representing their "most
acceptable" stand could, nevertheless, have *different* attitudes. In fact,
Sherif (1961) has stated emphatically "no two individuals in the same
group uphold the norms to the same degree, nor are cases of noncon-
formity involving different individuals ever identical" (p. 182).

The convenience of dealing with an individual's attitude through
a single score or average has resulted in an inadequate and unrealistic
representation of attitudes. Hence, the introduction of the concepts
of latitude of acceptance, latitude of rejection (Sherif, 1960; Sherif
and Hovland, 1961), and latitude of noncommitment (Sherif, Sherif,
and Nebergall, 1965) in the measurement of social attitudes has been
a much needed corrective.

To have an attitude towards an object does not mean simply the
adoption of one single position out of a number of possible or prevalent positions on the issue in question. Having an attitude implies
a certain relatedness on the part of the individual to the remaining
positions that he did *not* select as representing his "most acceptable"
stand, whether the attitude scale uncovers this information or not.
To say that a person accepts a certain position as most representative
of his own stand on an issue is definitely informative, but it is also
incomplete. Knowledge of his stand toward the remaining positions
on the issue becomes highly important, particularly for the prediction
of his behavior in situations relevant to the issue in question.

MEASUREMENT OF ATTITUDES THROUGH
ASSESSMENT OF LATITUDES OF ACCEPTANCE,
REJECTION, AND NONCOMMITMENT

The superiority of assessing attitudes through latitudes of acceptance, rejection, and noncommitment, rather than through single
preference scores or averages, has been substantiated in recent research utilizing the controversial social issue of Arab unity. Subjects
with a moderate stand towards the Arab unity issue, as represented
by their "most acceptable" positions on the evaluative dimension of
Arab unity, were found, quite unexpectedly, to show selectivity in

mass communication media highly similar to subjects opposed to Arab unity (Diab, 1965c). In an attempt to account for this unexpected finding, two procedures were followed: (1) consideration of the latitudes of acceptance, rejection, and noncommitment rather than the "most acceptable" positions alone (see Table 8.1), and (2) consideration of the degree of the subject's commitment to his "most acceptable" position (Diab, 1965b).

Latitudes of Acceptance, Rejection, and Noncommitment

The data presented in Table 8.1 show the latitudes of acceptance, rejection, and noncommitment for individuals upholding different positions favoring or opposing Arab unity. In constructing this table, the procedure used by Sherif was followed (Sherif, 1960; 1961).

The table consists of three parts, to be read starting at the top with Latitude of Acceptance. At the extreme left, the positions checked by the subjects as "most acceptable" are listed as rows, from A (extremely pro-Arab unity) to I (extremely anti-Arab unity), with E representing an indecisive statement. Reading across the rows, one can see the percentage of subjects endorsing a particular position as "most acceptable" who also accept *other* positions (arrayed in the columns from A . . . E . . . I).

Moving down to the part labeled Latitude of Rejection, the percentages of the *same* subjects who rejected various positions are presented. Finally, at the bottom, the percentages of noncommitment are given for the same subjects.

It is clear from Table 8.1 that the great majority of moderate subjects (those checking positions D, E, or F as "most acceptable" to them) rejected the favorable end of the evaluative continuum of Arab unity and remained noncommittal to the positions representing the unfavorable end of the continuum. Only persons checking position D as "most acceptable" included *both* ends of the continuum in their latitude of rejection. Thus, a consideration of the subjects' latitudes of acceptance *and* rejection reveals the resemblance between these so-called "moderate" subjects (particularly those at positions E and E) and the anti-Arab unity subjects.

The unexpected selectivity in mass communication media exhibited by moderate subjects now becomes understandable in the light of this additional information provided by knowledge of their latitudes of acceptance and rejection.

Degree of Commitment to "Most Acceptable" Position

In a study on variations in latitudes of acceptance and rejection as a function of varying own positions on the Arab unity issue (Diab,

Table 8.1 *Latitude of Acceptance, Rejection, and Noncommitment as Related to the Position "Most Acceptable" on Arab Unity* [Percentages Adopting Positions in Rows from extremely Pro-Arab Unity (A) to Extremely Anti-Arab Unity (I) Who Accept (top), Reject (below) or Remain Noncommittal (bottom) to Nine Positions on the Issue]

Positions Checked Most Acceptable	N	Latitude of Acceptance									Latitude of Rejection									Latitude of Noncommitment								
		A	B	C	D	E	F	G	H	I	A	B	C	D	E	F	G	H	I	A	B	C	D	E	F	G	H	I
A	100	100	98	60	21	1	1	—	—	—	—	—	2	10	33	61	82	98	89*	—	2	38	69	66	38	18	2	11
B	60	77	100	53	28	7	—	—	—	—	3	—	—	3	23	42	78	100	82*	20	—	47	69	70	58	22	—	18
C	19	28	72	100	67	6	—	—	—	—	11	6	—	—	23	24	76	91	75*	61	22	—	33	71	76	24	9	25
D	25	5	19	57	100	57	19	—	—	5	53	9	—	—	—	27	39	78	57*	42	72	43	—	43	54	61	22	38
E	21	6	—	17	39	100	39	28	—	11	68*	64	30	5	—	10	15	40	34	26	36	53	56	—	51	57	60	55
F	7	—	—	—	—	100	86	29	14	—	86*	86	71	29	—	—	—	—	29	14	14	29	71	100	—	14	71	57
G	6	—	—	—	17	83	100	100	—	—	83*	100	100	50	—	—	—	—	17	17	—	50	83	17	—	—	83
H	7	—	—	—	14	86	71	100	43	—	86*	100	71	71	14	—	—	—	—	14	—	29	29	72	14	29	—	57
I	11	—	—	—	—	17	51	100	100	—	91*	100	56	44	33	11	—	—	—	9	—	44	56	67	72	49	—	—

* Indicates positions checked "most objectionable" *and* "also objectionable." For each asterisk, the proportion of subjects checking the same position "also objectionable" rather than "most objectionable" are as follows: A (6%), B (28%), C (12%), D (9%), E (20%), F (14%), G (0%), H (0%), and I (11%).

1965b), it was found that the individual's degree of commitment to his "most acceptable" stand is significantly associated with the relative sizes of his latitudes of acceptance and rejection on this issue. Thus, subjects who "strongly" upheld a moderate position on the Arab unity issue rejected a significantly greater number of items than they accepted. On the other hand, moderates who expressed "mild" commitment to their position accepted *more* items than they rejected. Furthermore, "moderate" subjects who felt "strongly" about their stand on the Arab unity issue *rejected* significantly *more* positions than did the moderates who expressed only "mild" feeling about their position (Diab, 1965b).

These results suggest that *moderate* subjects, as determined by the moderate positions chosen "most acceptable" to them, cannot be considered as representing a homogeneous category. Further, no group of subjects classified on the basis of "most acceptable" position may be considered homogeneous. One way of differentiating among individuals endorsing the same position or stand is to take into consideration the strength of commitment of the individual to his stand. There could be *mildly held* extreme positions as well as *strongly upheld* moderate positions.

Since degree of commitment to one's stand is related to the relative size of the individual's latitudes of acceptance, rejection, and noncommitment, it should be sufficient to determine these latitudes in order to be able to differentiate in this respect among individuals upholding the same position. As Sherif, Sherif, and Nebergall (1965) conclude:

> The latitude of rejection, therefore, appears to be the most useful indicator for singling out moderate individuals highly involved on an issue as well as extremists not highly involved. The level of noncommitment is suggested as an indicator of the general level of involvement in one issue as compared to another (p. 59).

Thus, for example, the attitudes of moderate subjects who *reject* more items or positions on an issue than they accept are obviously not identical to those of moderates who *accept* more positions than they reject. Clearly, it would be important also to know the specific positions that are accepted or rejected.

Extremity of Individual Stand and Latitudes of Acceptance, Rejection, and Noncommitment

In reporting the study by Sherif and Hovland utilizing the issue of the 1956 presidential election in the United States, Sherif (1960) states:

The statements were designed to prevent a "ceiling effect." In fact, our results reveal a reluctance to endorse extreme end items (statements *A* and *I*), even by subjects selecting a position next to the extreme as the one most acceptable and actively committed to one of the major parties as campaign workers (pp. 206–207).

Sherif and Hovland (1961) emphasize these results as follows:

> In fact, only about 46 percent of the subjects checking *B* or *H* position as most acceptable selected *A* or *I* position as also acceptable to them. Nearly 20 percent of the subjects at *B* or *H* position rejected the statements at the nearby extreme. On the other hand, no less than 90 percent of subjects checking *B* or *H* positions as most acceptable included, respectively, the *C* or *G* statements in their latitudes of acceptance (p. 138).

The results obtained on the Arab unity issue (see Table 8.1) differ appreciably from those of Sherif and Hovland reported above, although the various statements (*A* to *I*) were worded in essentially the same way as those used by Sherif and Hovland in their 1956 presidential election study. The nine final statements are listed:

A. The achievement of Arab unity is absolutely essential from all angles in the Arab people's interests.
B. On the whole, the interests of the Arab peoples will be served best by the achievement of Arab unity.
C. It seems that the Arab people's interests would be better served if Arab unity is achieved.
D. Although it is hard to decide, it is probable that the Arab people's interests may be better served if Arab unity is achieved.
E. From the point of view of the Arab people's interests, it is hard to decide whether Arab unity would be advantageous or disadvantageous.
F. Although it is hard to decide, it is probable that the Arab people's interests may be better served without Arab unity.
G. It seems that the Arab people's interests would be better served without Arab unity.
H. On the whole, the interests of the Arab peoples will be served best without Arab unity.
I. The achievement of Arab unity is completely detrimental from all angles in the Arab people's interests.

The end positions (*A* and *I*) were worded very strongly in the Arab unity study, as in the 1956 presidential election study, in order to prevent a "ceiling effect." However, as may be seen in Table 8.1, subjects checking position B as "most acceptable" also selected position A (77 percent) as acceptable. However, only 53 percent of these subjects selected position C as also acceptable, and only 3 percent rejected position A.

Although the number of subjects checking position H as "most acceptable" is small, Table 8.1 shows that 43 percent of these subjects accepted position I, and 71 percent checked position G as also acceptable. None of them rejected the I position (most extreme anti-Arab unity). The difference between these results and those of Sherif and Hovland may be attributed to the greater ego-involvement with the present issue on the part of Arab subjects than was the case with American subjects in their national elections.

In commenting on their subjects, Sherif and Hovland (1961) state that "among the subjects were members of political organizations active in the campaign. Some of these persons were disrupting the routine of their daily lives to contribute to the victory of their candidates" (p. 138). In spite of this relatively high involvement of the American subjects with the election issue, the kind of involvement which Arab subjects have in the Arab unity issue may very well be more basic and much less temporary or transitory in their daily lives.

Among the Arab subjects who responded on the Arab unity issue, a large proportion belonged to political organizations or parties that strive actively for the achievement of Arab unity against odds. Some of these subjects, therefore, are constantly involved in various kinds of activities (cultural as we as political) revolving around the issue of Arab unity. In doing so, these individuals are under the possible threat of university disciplinary action (for example, political demonstrations or rallies as well as distribution of pamphlets containing political material are forbidden on the university campus). Furthermore, they may at times be subject to arrest by government officials. Thus, high involvement with the Arab unity issue means much more than mere disruption of daily routine for a specific period of time. It means, on the one hand, constant activity and concern on the part of the individual and, on the other hand, the possibility of serious or even dangerous consequences for him.

The issue of Arab unity is, in addition, a much more challenging and basic issue than the issues studied by Sherif and Hovland (for example, repeal of prohibition or election of national officials). If a state or county goes "wet," the individual does not have to drink alcohol. If the Democrats win the presidential election, the individual can remain a member of the Young Republicans and hope to win in the local elections or, perhaps, in the next presidential election. However, the situation is different with the Arab unity issue.

The issue of Arab unity involves the creation of a new state and the dissolution of a number of countries, including one's own. Such a change is quite drastic and involves the very self-identity of the individual. In a study (Diab, 1966) on reaction to a moderately anti-Arab unity "communication" (actual position at F) by pro-Arab unity subjects, the contrast effect (judging the communication as anti-Arab unity) was much more pronounced than the contrast effect obtained in the Hovland, Harvey, and Sherif study utilizing the prohibition issue (1957).

Although the importance of both latitudes of acceptance and of rejection on an issue for understanding reaction to communication and attitude change was stressed, Sherif and Hovland (1961) actually used only the distance of the position advocated on the "communication" from the limits of the subjects' latitudes of acceptance in analyzing their data (Hovland, Harvey, and Sherif, 1957; Sherif, 1960; Sherif and Hovland, 1961). Analysis of the results obtained with the Arab unity issue (Diab, 1966) shows that the subjects' reactions to a moderately unfavorable communication could not be explained adequately by considering only the distance of the communication from the limits of the subjects' latitudes of acceptance. In brief, it was found that knowledge of the subjects' latitudes of acceptance *and* rejection, rather than an estimate of the subjects' "own stands" alone or their latitudes of acceptance alone, accounted much more adequately for the subjects' reactions to the "communication" (Diab, 1966).

In line with Sherif's work (Hovland, Harvey, and Sherif, 1957), the same subjects used in studying the Arab unity issue (Diab, 1966) were asked to evaluate a moderately anti-Arab unity paragraph (communication) in the following way: "Indicate your feelings as to how fair, realistic, reasonable, good, and honest this paragraph is in relation to analyzing the issue of Arab unity." Each of these five adjectives was presented on a four-point scale (for example, very fair, fair, unfair, very unfair). The subject was asked to check only one of the four alternatives for each of the five adjectives. The "communication" presented to the subjects (representing the F position in the original series ranging from A to I) was as follows:

> Though certainty in prediction is somewhat difficult, yet it may be stated that because of the many political, social, and economic differences which exist among the Arab countries, unity may possibly do more harm than good to the Arab people in general and to the relatively more advanced countries in particular.

The only information given to the subjects about the communication was that it was a quotation from a text on "Arab unity." No additional information was given as to the identity of the author, the publisher, or the place of publication. Consequently, the subject's attention was focused mainly on the *content* of the communication. In line with Hovland, Harvey, and Sherif (1957), it was expected that "reactions to a communication will decrease in favorableness as the distance between S's own stand and the position advocated in the communication increases" (p. 245).

Results concerning evaluation of the communication by subjects with different stands on the issue are presented in Figure 8.1. The subject's own position (based on the mean of statements checked acceptable) is indicated on the abscissa, and the percentage of favorable evaluations of the mildly unfavorable communication is represented along the ordinate.

The findings in the Arab unity study are indicated by the solid line in Figure 8.1. The dotted line represents similar data from the prohibition study (Hovland, Harvey, and Sherif, 1957). In line with the latter study, favorable reactions to the communication increased as the distance between the subject's own stand and the position advocated in the communication decreased. However, the present results show a higher percentage of favorable reactions for subjects with extremely unfavorable positions on the Arab unity issue than for those holding moderate positions. Similar results by Sherif and

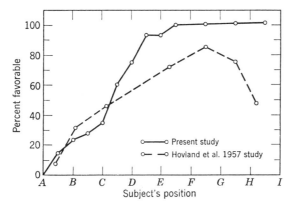

Figure 8.1 Percentage of favorable evaluations of a mildly unfavorable communication (at *F*) by subjects holding various positions on the Arab unity issue (based on mean acceptable position).

Hovland (1961) showed that "the maximum favorable reaction for the moderate communication is found among those holding a moderate position" (pp. 154–155). The reasons why subjects at positions *G, H,* and *I* in this study did not show the expected decrease in favorable evaluations of the communication is not immediately clear. However, these same subjects revealed a strong contrast effect in relation to the same communication (Diab, 1966, *cf.* Figure 8.1 of this volume). In other words, these subjects are so extreme in their negative attitude towards Arab unity and so highly ego-involved in the issue that a "moderate" anti-Arab unity communication was not acceptable to them. Phrases included in the moderately anti-Arab unity paragraph (communication), such as "though certainty in prediction is somewhat difficult" and "unity may possibly do more harm than good" were interpreted as *favorable* to Arab unity because, from the point of view of these subjects (those at Positions *G, H,* and *I*), Arab unity is detrimental to their interests in various degrees. For them, it is *not* hard to decide about the relative advantages of Arab unity, as statement *F* and the communication state. To them, Arab unity is simply *unacceptable* in various degrees. Why, then, did they react to the communication favorably?

Perhaps a look at the reference group ties of these individuals may help to shed some light on the paradox. In one degree or another, 94 percent of these subjects actually belonged or aspired to belong to groups that express extreme dislike for Arab unity. Some actually belonged to anti-Arab unity political groupings or parties; others stated that *if* they were going to join any political parties or groupings, they would prefer or definitely like to join the same anti-Arab unity parties. Still others stated that the groups which they would *not* want to join under any circumstance are the *pro-*Arab unity parties or organizations. The political parties to which these anti-Arab unity subjects belonged or aspired to belong (their reference groups) are characterized both by their extremely negative stand towards Arab nationalism and Arab unity and by the stress which each places on alternative kinds of nationalisms and unities—mainly "Lebanese" nationalism, "Syrian" nationalism, and their unity. It might be stated here that the only element which combines these two nationalisms is their common hatred for Arab nationalism. Otherwise, they are equally hostile to one another. Their extreme hostility towards each other was overcome by their overwhelming hostility to their "common enemy" Arab nationalism. Thus, we can see that anything opposed to this enemy might be rated favorably, even though placement of the arguments was affected by their attitudes. Such a moderately unfavorable statement as Arab "unity may possibly do more harm than good" was reacted to as a highly favorable statement to Arab unity. These results are in line with the findings of Hovland and Sherif (1952) and Sherif and Hovland (1953) with highly ego-involved subjects categorizing "neutral" items on the highly important controversial social issue of Negro segregation.

Measurement of Attitudes by the Semantic Differential

Findings on the Arab unity issue have shown that subjects with extreme stands exhibited greater consistency among their attitude dimensions than did moderate subjects (Diab, 1965b). This finding held for the extreme *pro-Arab* unity subjects but not with equal clarity for extreme anti-Arab unity subjects. Thus, the greatest consistency between the two dimensions studied (that is, the "evaluative" and the "possibility" dimensions of Arab unity) was for the extreme pro-Arab unity subjects. Specifically, it was found that 94 percent of the extremely pro-Arab unity subjects felt that Arab unity would definitely be achieved at some time in the future. However, only 50 percent of the subjects who were extremely anti-Arab unity on the evaluative dimension were also extremely pessimistic about the possibility of Arab unity.

In accounting for this lack of consistency on the part of subjects with extremely *unfavorable* attitudes towards Arab unity, the possible differential effects of positive and negative ego-involvements were considered as well as the operation of *reality checks* that worked against the subjects' endorsement of such extreme positions on the possibility dimension as: "it is almost certain that Arab unity will not be achieved at any time in the future" (position H) or "there is no doubt whatsoever that Arab unity will never be achieved at any time in the future" (position I).

Extreme negative stands on the possibility dimension are simply opposed to reality: Arab unity *did* take place during 1958, and although it lasted only till 1961, the present study was made during the first three months of 1963 when negotiations were going on in Cairo for the formation of a new United Arab Republic to be composed of Egypt, Iraq, and Syria. Thus, although subjects adopting extremely anti-Arab unity positions on the evaluative dimension rejected an average of 3.21 positions and remained noncommittal on 3.25 positions, extreme anti-Arab unity subjects on the *possibility* dimension rejected on the average 2.75 positions and remained noncommittal on 3.70 positions. In other words, subjects who believed

that Arab unity was disadvantageous rejected more items and remained noncommittal on relatively fewer items on the evaluative dimension than did subjects who believed that Arab unity would not
be achieved in the future (the possibility dimension). In fact, contrary
to expectations, subjects who were extremely anti-Arab unity on the
possibility dimension did not reject significantly more items than they
accepted (Diab, 1965b). This is in contrast to extreme anti-Arab
unity subjects on the *evaluative* dimension who rejected significantly
more items than they accepted (Diab, 1965b, *cf.* Table 8.1 of this
volume).

It is apparent, therefore, that the latitudes of acceptance, rejection,
and noncommitment for subjects holding similar stands could be
different on different *dimensions* of the same issue. Thus, the study
of the individual's patterns of acceptance, rejection, and noncommitment on more than one dimension of the issue becomes imperative,
particularly in those instances where the attitudes in question are
multidimensional in nature. Krech, Crutchfield, and Ballachey (1962)
comment on this point by saying "if an investigator insists upon uni-
dimensional scales, he eliminates the possibility of studying persons
whose attitudes are not patterned unidimensionally" (p. 177).

On the basis of data collected with the semantic differential procedure, Osgood, Suci, and Tannenbaum (1957) conclude that judgments
of an attitude object usually vary along three main dimensions,
namely, an evaluative dimension, a potency dimension, and an activity
dimension, along with a number of other less important dimensions.
Osgood (1964) summarized the issue as follows:

> Despite deliberate and independent variations in the sampling of
> scales, of concepts, and of subjects, three dominant and independent
> (orthogonal) factors have kept reappearing: an Evaluative Factor
> (represented by scales such as *good-bad, pleasant-unpleasant,* and
> *positive-negative*), a Potency Factor (represented by scales such as
> *strong-weak, heavy-light,* and *hard-soft*), and an Activity Factor
> (represented by scales such as *fast-slow, active-passive,* and *excitable-
> calm*) (p. 173).

Of the above three dominant factors in the affective meaning system, evaluation is the most important factor followed by potency
and then activity. In the various factor analyses, Osgood and others
(1957) found that the evaluative dimension accounted "for the largest
proportion of the total variance" (p. 190). According to Osgood and
others, attitude is identified as the evaluative factor of the total semantic space.

In order to measure attitude, Osgood and others (1957) proposed that in addition to the evaluative factor ". . . we usually include a considerable number of scales representing other factors—this is done both to obscure somewhat the purpose of the measurement and to provide additional information on the meaning of the concept as a whole, aside from the attitude toward it" (p. 191). For example, two individuals may agree in judging Arab unity as "very good" but, at the same time, may disagree as to how potent or active it is. On the other hand, two persons may agree in judging Arab unity as highly potent and active but, nevertheless, evaluate it unfavorably. Consequently, on the basis of evidence presented by Osgood and others (1957), the semantic differential provides "a richer picture of the meaning of the attitude object than just the evaluative dimension . . ." (p. 195). By combining judgments made on a number of semantic differential scales representing the evaluative as well as other factors of meaning, "additional information can be obtained and prediction presumably improved" (p. 198). In addition, accumulated evidence by Osgood and his colleagues (Osgood, 1964; Osgood, Archer, and Miron, 1963) demonstrated the cross-cultural and cross-linguistic existence of the same three independent factors of meaning, namely, evaluation, potency, and activity.

In order to clarify some of the findings arrived at in studies utilizing the controversial issue of Arab unity (Diab, 1965b; 1965c), a number of semantic differential scales representing the three main independent factors were used to assess the meaning of the concept "Arab unity" to subjects upholding various positions on this issue (Diab, 1965d). These semantic differential scales, representative of the evaluative as well as other factors in the semantic space of Arab subjects, were taken from a mimeographed report by Osgood and others (1963). The use of the semantic differential procedure in assessing attitudes towards the Arab unity issue (Diab, 1965d), in comparison to the use of a continuum of positions representing the evaluative factor alone (Diab, 1965b; 1965c), resulted in a more complete picture about Arab unity and *did* help to explain and predict the behavior of the subjects. In line with the findings of Osgood and others (1957), it was clearly shown that "two people may have identical *attitudes* toward a concept (as determined by allocation to the evaluative dimension alone), and yet have quite different meanings of the concept (as determined by the profiles as wholes)" (p. 198).

The main findings of this study on attitudes toward Arab unity (Diab, 1965d) dealt with differences in the *meaning* of Arab unity for subjects who evaluated the concept differently. Thus, it was found that subjects who evaluated Arab unity as "very good" were not equally extreme on the other dimensions. In fact, they rated Arab unity as being "slightly potent," as "quite active, real, possible, and predictable," but also "slightly near" and "slightly difficult" to achieve. On the other hand, subjects who evaluated Arab unity as "very bad" were found to have equally extreme ratings on scales representing factors other than the evaluative factor. They rated Arab unity as "very weak and slow," "quite passive," and "very far, difficult, imaginary, impossible, as well as unpredictable." Finally, subjects who evaluated Arab unity as "equally good and bad" were found to judge Arab unity, in a manner somewhat similar to anti-Arab unity subjects as "quite slow and emotional" as well as "slightly far, impossible, unpredictable" and "quite difficult" to achieve.

The above findings on the meaning of the concept "Arab unity" to subjects with extreme as well as moderate stands towards the Arab unity issue (Diab, 1965d) have helped to clarify some of the results of other studies (Diab, 1965b; 1965c). For example, the similarity in selectivity in mass communication media found previously between moderate and anti-Arab unity subjects (Diab, 1965c) becomes understandable in the light of this additional information on the *meaning* of the attitude object obtained through the semantic differential procedure. In spite of differences in evaluation of Arab unity between moderate and anti-Arab unity subjects, similarities exist in connection with the other dimensions of meaning that, consequently, contributed to similarities in selectivity in mass communication media. Furthermore, the greater selectivity exhibited by extreme anti-Arab unity subjects, in comparison to extreme pro-Arab unity subjects, could have been predicted from their consistently unfavorable ratings of Arab unity on scales representing dimensions other than the evaluative factor.

THE SOCIAL JUDGMENT-INVOLVEMENT
APPROACH AND THE SEMANTIC
DIFFERENTIAL PROCEDURE: A SYNTHESIS

In concluding this presentation of research utilizing different approaches to the measurement of social attitudes, the following generalizations may be suggested:

1. The representation of an individual's attitude by means of a most acceptable "point" or an average preference "score" along a continuum is not adequate or realistic. Thus, two individuals having

identical "scores" on an attitude scale could differ widely in their "stands" on the other remaining positions on the same attitude scale.

2. The assessment of latitudes of acceptance, rejection, and noncommitment is a definite improvement over the conventional scales in the realistic representation of an individual's attitude along a continuum of positions. Assessing attitudes in terms of these latitudes or ranges becomes highly essential for understanding the individual's reactions to and evaluations of various relevant social stimulus situations.

3. The use of the semantic differential procedure to assess the individual's judgment of the attitude object on all important dimensions of meaning is more informative than the measurement of "attitude" alone, as represented by ratings on one dimension, namely, the evaluative dimension. The measurement of social attitudes on dimensions representative of evaluation as well as of *other* factors of meaning is necessitated by findings which showed that differences in evaluation of an attitude object are not necessarily associated with similar differences along other dimensions. Thus, for instance, one individual may rate a concept as "good, strong, and active" whereas another may rate the same concept as "good, weak, and passive."

On the basis of the above generalizations, it is evident that the semantic differential procedure does give more information about the meaning of the attitude object than can be obtained from the evaluative dimension alone, and consequently, helps to improve prediction of the individual's behavior in situations involving the attitude object.

However, the semantic differential procedure is subject to the same criticism that was made previously of conventional attitude scales. The semantic differential procedure is superior to conventional attitude scales in providing additional information about the meaning of the attitude object; *yet,* it is similar to these attitude scales in representing the individual's ratings on various semantic scales by a single preference "point" or "average" preference score. Thus, two persons giving the same ratings for an attitude object on a number of semantic differential scales need not necessarily have identical meanings of that attitude object, particularly in the case of "neutral" ratings. Different individuals may give identical "neutral" ratings of a concept on a number of semantic differential scales, yet these "neutral" ratings could have any one of a number of possible meanings.

First, these "neutral" *ratings across* all scales may mean that the individual has really no attitude towards the concept in question or, as Osgood maintains, the meaning of the concept would be at the origin of a hypothetical semantic space, which he defines as complete "meaninglessness." In short, this category would include the "indifferent" individual who does not really care one way or the other about the issue in question.

Second, "neutral" ratings may mean, however, that the subject judges the concept as actually falling midway on a number of semantic scales. Thus, he judges it as "equally good or bad," "equally strong and weak," rather than "neither good nor bad," "neither strong nor weak." In other words, the subject here has mixed feelings about the attitude object and not "lack" of feelings. He sees certain "good" aspects of the attitude object, but he is at the same time aware of certain "bad" ones; he is equally cognizant of its strengths and weaknesses. In short, this category would *include the strongly committed "neutral" or "moderate"* person on the issue in question.

Finally, the *third* possible meaning of "neutral" ratings is the case of an individual who, for various reasons, believes in the "desirability" of a middle-of-the-road stand but who, consciously or unconsciously, may be either for or against the issue in question. Consequently, the problem in using the semantic differential procedure becomes one of differentiating among individuals with apparently identical ratings of an attitude object, particularly in the case of the so-called "neutral" ratings.

In order to handle the above problem, a synthesis of the social judgment-involvement approach and the semantic differential procedure was suggested previously (Diab, 1965a; 1965d). It simply consists of asking the subject to rate a concept on a number of semantic differential scales representative of the three main independent factors of meaning and appropriate to the concept in question. However, on each of the scales, the subject is asked to indicate the position "most acceptable" to him as well as other position(s) "also acceptable." The subject's score would be the mean value of his latitude of acceptance. Furthermore, the subject is also asked to indicate on each scale the position "most objectionable" to him as well as other position(s) "also objectionable." The subject's score would be the mean value of his latitude of rejection. Thus, for each of the semantic differential scales, the subject's rating of the concept or attitude object is represented by latitudes of acceptance, rejection, and noncommitment as well as by an average preference score, an average rejection score, and an average noncommitment score. Thus, for instance, the strongly committed "moderate" or "neutral" individual will be recognized not only by his "neutral" ratings of the concept on the various semantic differential scales but, mainly, by his rejection of both ends of the scale continuum. Similarly, a "moderate" person who rejects the favorable and accepts the unfavorable end of the scale continuum would be obviously different from another "moderate" who rejects the unfavorable and accepts the favorable end of the same scale continuum. Differences among individuals with identical extreme positive or negative stands could be revealed in differences in the patterning of their latitudes of acceptance, rejection, and noncommitment. Consequently, it appears that this synthesis of the social judgment-involvement approach and the semantic differential procedure should result in improving prediction of the subject's reactions to and evaluations of social stimulus material relevant to the concept or attitude object in question. However, the usefulness of this suggestion remains largely to be explored in future research.

REFERENCES

Diab, L. N., 1965a. Some limitations of existing scales in measurement of social attitudes. *Psychol. Rep.*, **17**, 427–430.

Diab, L. N., 1965b. Studies in social attitudes: I. Variations in latitudes of acceptance and rejection as a function of varying positions on a controversial social issue. *J. soc. Psychol.*, **67**, 283–295.

Diab, L. N., 1965c. Studies in social attitudes: II. Selectivity in mass communication media as a function of attitude-medium discrepancy. *J. soc. Psychol.*, **67**, 297–302.

Diab, L. N., 1965d. Studies in social attitudes: III. Attitude assessment through the semantic-differential procedure. *J. soc. Psychol.*, **67**, 303–314.

Diab, L. N., 1966. Reaction to a communication as a function of attitude-communication discrepancy. *Psychol. Rep.*, **18**, 767–774.

Hovland, C. I., Harvey, O. J., and Sherif, M., 1957. Assimilation and contrast effects in reactions to communications and attitude change. *J. abnorm. soc. Psychol.*, **55**, 244–252.

Hovland, C. I., and Sherif, M., 1952. Judgmental phenomena and scales of attitude measurement: item displacement in Thurstone scales. *J. abnorm. soc. Psychol.*, **47**, 822–832.

Krech, D., Crutchfield, R. S., and Ballachey, E. L., 1962. *Individual in society*. New York: McGraw-Hill.

Osgood, C. E., 1962. Studies on the generality of affective meaning systems. *Amer. Psychologist*, **17**, 10–28.

Osgood, C. E., 1964. Semantic differential technique in the comparative study of cultures. *Amer. Anthrop.*, **66**, No. 3, Part 2, 171–200.

Osgood, C. E., Archer, W. K., and Miron, M. S., 1963. *The cross-cultural generality of meaning systems: A progress report*. Univ. of Ill. Urbana, Ill. (mimeographed).

Osgood, C. E., Suci, G. J., and Tannenbaum, P. H., 1957. *The measurement of meaning*. Urbana, Ill.: Univ. of Ill. Press.

Sherif, C. W., Sherif, M., and Nebergall, R. E., 1965. *Attitude and attitude change*. Philadelphia: Saunders.

Sherif, M., 1960. Some needed concepts in the study of social attitudes. In J. G. Peatman and E. L. Hartley (Eds.), *Festschrift for Gardner Murphy*. New York: Harper.

Sherif, M., 1961. Conformity-deviation, norms and group relations. In I. A. Berg and B. M. Bass (Eds.), *Conformity and deviation*. New York: Harper.

Sherif, M., and Hovland, C. I., 1953. Judgmental phenomena and scales of attitude measurement: placement of items with individual choice of number of categories. *J. abnorm. soc. Psychol.*, **48**, 135–141.

Sherif, M., and Hovland, C. I., 1961. *Social judgment*. New Haven: Yale Univ. Press.

Sherif, M., and Sherif, C. W., 1956. *An outline of social psychology*. New York: Harper.

9. Resolution of the Communication Discrepancy Issue in Attitude Change*

James O. Whittaker

Few issues in the area of attitude change are of such importance or have aroused greater controversy and confusion than that relating to the effects of communication discrepancy. The problem fundamentally involves the question of whether presentation of an extremely divergent stand generates more change than one close to the position of the subject. For example, if we wish to modify the attitude of a staunchly conservative Republican, should we present a communication advocating an extremely liberal view, or should the position presented be only slightly different from that of the subject?

Common sense tells us that if we take a position substantially different from that of our listener, he will reject our position completely. Perhaps he will become even more entrenched or more extreme in his position. He may become more convinced that he is right and we are wrong. There is substantial evidence from psychological warfare efforts to substantiate this common sense notion. For example, many propaganda leaflets were prepared in England during the Second World War as part of a continuing effort to change opinions about the conditions that prevailed in allied POW camps, the treatment prisoners received, and so on. The hope, of course, was that if the attitudes of German soldiers toward probable treatment could be changed, more of them would surrender.

One particular leaflet contained photographs of conditions in a

* Part of the research reported here was supported by a grant from the U.S. Air Force Office of Scientific Research (AF-AFOSR 62-188).

POW camp in Canada. These photographs showed prisoners engaged in playing cards, ping pong, and other activities. The accompanying message included, among other things, a description of meals in the camp—for example, coffee, eggs, and toast for breakfast. An important fact relevant to this particular leaflet is that it represented the unadulterated truth. The photographs were actually taken in the Canadian camp, and the meals described were those actually provided for prisoners.

Before dropping the leaflet behind enemy lines, however, Army personnel decided to "pretest" it with German prisoners already in camps in Italy. These prisoners, it should be emphasized, were already captives and knew something of conditions in allied POW camps. They had discovered that actual conditions and treatment differed considerably from what they had been led to expect. Yet almost without exception, they could not accept the leaflet as truthful. It was too divergent from their own opinions concerning general conditions in allied prison camps, and consequently they regarded it as "propagandistic" (Daugherty and Janowitz, 1958).

Of course we know that common sense notions are often incorrect. Further, it is quite apparent that most psychological warfare activities hardly qualify as scientific experiments, including the one just described. Still, it is surprising that when we look to the psychological literature for an answer to the discrepancy problem, we find a mass of contradictory evidence. Several studies have reported results indicating that more opinion change occurs with *greater* rather than with less discrepancy (Hovland and Pritzker, 1957; French, 1956; Ewing, 1942; Goldberg, 1954; Fisher and Lubin, 1958; Zimbardo, 1960; Fisher, Rubinstein, and Freeman, 1956; Harvey, Kelley and Shapiro, 1957). Festinger (1957) has provided a theoretical interpretation of these findings. He suggests that when individuals are presented with a communication taking an extremely divergent stand, they experience "cognitive dissonance," defined as a tension state with motivational properties.

According to Festinger, a person in such a situation experiencing dissonance may react in one of several ways. He may seek social support for his position, he may derogate the communicator, or he may change his attitude in line with the stand presented in the communication. In several recent publications, Sherif (1965) has taken issue with Festinger's contention. He has pointed out that "the highly committed person exposed to an extremely discrepant communication will *never* react to it by changing his attitude toward the communication. He will feel irritated, derogate the communicator, speak to his friends about it; but he will *never* resort to the alternative of changing toward the communication in order to reduce his irritation, tension, or dissonance." Sherif's contention has been that extremely discrepant communications yield less attitude change than those taking a stand closer to that upheld by the subject. In 1961, for example, Sherif and Hovland presented results showing less frequent change with greater discrepancies between the individual's initial stand on the issue and the position of the communication.

Just as there is evidence supporting the hypothesis that greater discrepancy results in greater change, there is also considerable evidence to support the hypothesis of *smaller* discrepancy, greater change. Hovland, Harvey, and Sherif (1957), Sherif and Hovland (1961), and Whittaker (1957) have all presented such results. In addition, Sherif has provided a theoretical interpretation of these findings, just as Festinger provided a theory to interpret the opposite results.

Sherif's theory is based in part on results of psychophysical studies of judgment in which the discrepancy between the subject's internal anchor and stimulus presented determines either an assimilation or a contrast effect. Applying these observations to communication situations, Sherif has pointed out that the subject's own position serves as an anchor in his perception of other positions. Thus, if the position presented to him is close to his own, he tends to perceive it as being even closer than it objectively is. Conversely, if a substantial discrepancy exists, the subject perceives the position presented as being even more discrepant. The former, of course, is the assimilation effect, and the latter is the contrast effect (Sherif and Hovland, 1961).

There is no question that assimilation-contrast effects do occur in the perception of presented stands. In one of our own experiments, for example, we had farmers holding various attitudes toward government controls in agriculture estimate the position or stand of a pro-control communication (Whittaker, 1965a). These results are presented in Figure 9.1. It will be noted that farmers favoring controls (positions A and B) perceived the position of the communication as much closer to their own than farmers opposed to controls (positions H and I) ($p = < .05$).

Furthermore, as one might expect, subjects tend to perceive positions close to their own more favorably than those that are considerably divergent. When we asked the farmers in the experiment mentioned above to evaluate the communication in terms of fairness and lack of bias, we obtained the results shown in Figure 9.2. Those whose own positions were essentially in line with the communication (positions A and B) judged the communication as fair and unbiased, whereas those opposed tended to judge it as "propagandistic" (Whittaker, 1965a).

These results suggest that when a person is presented with a divergent position, he perceives it as being more in line with his own than it actually is *if* the discrepancy is small. Furthermore, he judges it as essentially fair and unbiased. On the other hand, he perceives extremely divergent positions as even *more* divergent than they are objectively, and he tends to regard such positions as biased and unfair.

If we accept Festinger's formulation, we are forced to conclude that in some cases individuals are more likely to change their opinions when faced with a position that they judge as even more extreme than objectivity dictates and at the same time one they perceive as biased and propagandistic. In other words, Festinger's theory would lead us to predict that under some circumstances the more biased and propagandistic we perceive a communication to be, the more likely we are to be influenced by it. However unreasonable this may sound, in order to resolve our original problem, we still need evidence from studies of the degree of opinion change as a function of the extent of communication discrepancy. Before going into this, however, let me mention one additional aspect of Sherif's theory that is highly relevant to this issue.

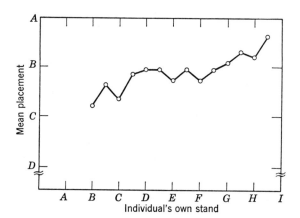

Figure 9.1 Placement of communication favoring farm policy by individuals whose most acceptable positions differed from *A* (favorable) to *I* (opposed). Higher location on figure represents placement as more favorable to policy (Whittaker, 1965a).

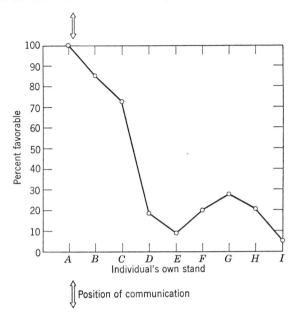

Figure 9.2 Favorable evaluations of communication supporting farm policy (*A*) by persons upholding stands from extremely favorable (*A*) to extremely opposed (*I*) to the policy. Each location represents percentage of persons choosing that position as most acceptable who appraised communication as "fair, unbiased," and so forth (Whittaker, 1965a).

LATITUDES OF ACCEPTANCE AND REJECTION

Traditionally, social psychologists have tended to regard attitudes in terms of the stand or position the individual upholds. Sherif, however, prefers to specify the *range* of positions acceptable (latitude of acceptance), the range of positions rejected (latitude of rejection), and the range of positions toward which the individual feels no commitment (latitude of noncommitment). In terms of predictions about probable reactions to other stands, he has observed that by specifying latitudes of acceptance and rejection we should be able to make more accurate predictions than if we know only the position which the individual chooses as most acceptable. This is because two individuals specifying the same position as their own may differ in the extent to which they tolerate other positions.

In general, it has been demonstrated in several experiments that as the individual's "own position" becomes more extreme, his tolerance for other positions diminishes. In our experiment involving farmers, for example, we asked subjects to choose from among nine statements concerning government controls in agriculture those that were objectionable, those they found unobjectionable, and, in addition, the one statement most closely representing their own stand. The statements ranged from extremely *pro-* to extremely *anti-*control positions.

The data from this part of the experiment is shown in Table 9.1. Note that tolerance for other positions tends to diminish as the subject's own position becomes more extreme. Those subjects either strongly for or strongly against controls rejected almost twice as many items as they accepted. We found one Farm Bureau member, for example, who complained to the experimenter that the most extreme statement he presented was not *extreme* enough. She had checked the most extreme statement as acceptable and had crossed out every other statement on the sheet.

With subjects holding less extreme positions, on the other hand, tolerance for other positions is much greater. They clearly do not tend to see issues in black and white terms, as do those with extreme stands. The extremist, whether on political or other issues, tends to dichotomize in his thinking. He does not discriminate the shades of gray, and more often than not his feeling is that "you're either for us or against us."

We mentioned previously that knowledge of a subject's latitudes of acceptance and rejection should enable us to make accurate predictions about his probable reaction to a communication. In a paper published in 1963, I pointed out that communications taking positions within the subject's latitude of acceptance (which we define as "small"

Table 9.1 *Acceptability of Statements in Relation to Subjects' Position on Issue (Whittaker, 1964a)*

Subjects' Positions	(N)	Mean Number of Items Acceptable	Mean Number of Items Not Checked	Mean Number of Items Rejected
Extreme (1,2,8,9)	(37)	1.97	3.05	3.97
Intermediate (3,4,5,6,7)	(141)	2.86	2.74	3.40
	$t = 3.65$	$p < .01$		

discrepancies), yield smaller shifts than do communications taking positions at the end of or adjacent to the latitude of acceptance (defined as "moderate" discrepancies). We suspect that communications taking positions within the latitude of acceptance and closest to the person's actual stand yield the smallest shifts and that greater shifts occur as the position of the communication is moved progressively further away from the subject's position but still within the latitude of acceptance. Furthermore, it appears warranted to conclude that positive opinion shift diminishes as the position of the communication is moved progressively into the latitude of rejection (defined as "large" discrepancies). Finally, it is apparent that when the communication position is moved far into the latitude of rejection, increasingly larger negative shifts occur. These points were reiterated in a *Public Opinion Quarterly* paper published the following year (Whittaker, 1964a).

Thus, as I pointed out first in 1963, there is a *curvilinear* relationship between opinion change and the degree of discrepancy between the position of the communication and the stand of the subject. Small discrepancies yield small change, moderate discrepancies yield greater change, and large discrepancies yield either negligible positive change, or negative change that becomes more pronounced as the discrepancy increases. This relationship is shown in Figure 9.3.

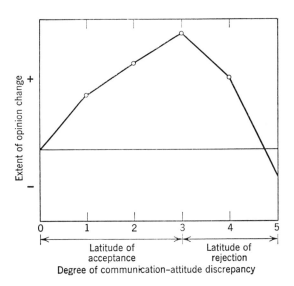

Figure 9.3 Hypothetical curve showing relationship between opinion change and communication-attitude discrepancy (Whittaker, 1963).

If the latitude of acceptance is small, as it is for those holding extreme positions, and the latitude of rejection is large, then the optimal position presented must be very close to the position of the subject. On the other hand, when the latitude of acceptance is large, as it is for those holding moderate positions, the optimal position of the communication is much further away.

There is, as we noted previously, a considerable body of evidence in support of these generalizations. But before presenting it, let us turn our attention to evidence that appears to support the opposite view, namely, greater discrepancy equals greater change.

EVIDENCE SHOWING THAT GREATER
DISCREPANCY EQUALS GREATER CHANGE

In my opinion, investigators have reached the conclusion that greater discrepancy equals greater change either because they were: (1) working with issues about which subjects did not feel strongly, that is, subjects were not ego-involved, or (2) they neglected to employ adequate parameters in their experimental designs, or (3) a combination of these factors was involved.

Sherif has put it very nicely, I think, when he points out that the first question we must consider is

> What is it that is to be changed when a person is exposed to a communication or some other attempt at attitude change? What is it that is resistant to change?
>
> Is it his guesses about the number of beans in a jar, or leaves on a tree, or sand pebbles on a square yard of beach? Or, is it his views on his family, on how he stacks up relative to his contemporaries, on the worth of his religion, his politics, his profession, his country, or his way of life?
>
> It is one thing to change from one brand of soap to another. It is quite another thing to change the person's stand toward persons, objects, groups, and institutions that he accepts or rejects as related to himself (Sherif, 1965).

Far too often, in my opinion, psychologists working in the area of attitude change have tended to use issues about which subjects have little concern. In an experiment designed by Hovland and Pritzker (1957), for example, some of the issues used with college students were: Was Washington or Lincoln the greater President? Will a cure for cancer be discovered in the next five years? Should the executive branch of government be given greater control? They had the students check a position from "agree strongly" to "disagree strongly" in connection with a statement relative to each of the issues employed, that is, "Washington was a greater President than Lincoln." Then they asked the students to check an authority group whose opinion they would most respect on each issue.

Some time later, other questionnaires were returned to the students with a position marked on each issue, and the position checked was attributed to a particular "authority" group. Check marks and authority groups for each issue were determined by the responses of individual students on the first questionnaire. Hence if a student checked "agree strongly" in connection with the statement "Washington was a greater President than Lincoln" and indicated he would most respect the opinions of historians on this issue, he later received a questionnaire with "agree *slightly*" or some other position checked, and this was indicated as the response of historians.

In some cases the fictitious check marks were close to those originally marked by subjects, whereas in other cases they were further away. At any rate, subjects were again asked to indicate their opinions. When the opinions on the second administration were compared with those on the first, the authors noted that greater discrepancy yielded greater change.

There are three factors in this study that appear to account for the results observed by the investigators. *First,* there is little reason to believe that college students are generally ego-involved in issues such as those employed in this study. Consequently, such opinions are easily changed. *Second,* the "communication" presented was attributed to sources marked as highly authoritative by the subjects involved. Hence credibility was maximal. *Third,* the discrepancies employed were relatively small. No check mark was ever more than three positions away from the original position, and no subjects were faced with communications in absolute disagreement with their original positions. In other words, acceptance of the "communication" never required a complete about-face on the part of the subject.

A MODIFICATION OF THE HOVLAND-PRITZKER STUDY

We repeated this experiment in 1963 using the same procedure that Hovland and Pritzker employed. In this case, however, we also utilized issues more likely to arouse involvement in college students, that is, "No athletic scholarships should be awarded"; "There should be curfews for male students"; "Sororities and fraternities should be abolished." We also expanded Hovland and Pritzker's response scale, that is, from "agree strongly, disagree strongly" to "agree absolutely, disagree absolutely." And in addition, when the second questionnaire was given, check marks were as much as eight positions away from those originally marked. Thus we employed greater discrepancies than they had used. Finally, the check mark on the second questionnaire was attributed to "other college students," rather than to highly credible groups of experts.

When the above changes were incorporated into this study, we did not find the linear relationship of greater discrepancy — greater change — as observed by the original authors. Rather, as shown in Table 9.2, the relationship was curvilinear. Small discrepancies yielded small change, moderate discrepancies yielded the maximum change, and the degree of change tended to diminish as the discrepancies became even larger.

Table 9.2   *Mean Change Score with Eight Strengths of Communication* (*Whittaker, 1965b*)

Degree of Change Advocated							
1	2	3	4	5	6	7	8
0.36	1.09	1.21	1.64	1.88	2.36	2.00	1.50

The breakdown of change on each individual issue in the study is shown in Table 9.3. It is interesting to note that in this table, on those issues originally included in the Hovland and Pritzker study, greater discrepancy still yielded greater change. Increasing the discrepancy and decreasing the credibility of the source, as we did in our study, was clearly not enough to alter the results. We suspect that on issues that are low in involvement, the discrepancies would need to be much greater than those we employed before decreasing change would result. This is undoubtedly because the latitudes of acceptance on such issues are so large relative to the latitudes of rejection.

On the other hand, with issues about which subjects feel strongly and where the latitude of acceptance is small and latitude of rejection large, communication discrepancies that appear to be objectively small often result in negligible positive change or in negative change. This latter effect, often referred to as the "boomerang effect," was revealed

Table 9.3 *Changes in Opinion with Eight Degrees of Communication Discrepancy for Each Issue (Whittaker, 1963)*

	1	2	3	4	5	6	7	8
1. President should have power to reduce tariffs	0.50	0.86	1.31	1.05	2.30	3.33	2.50	1.00
2. No athletic scholarships should be awarded	0.13	1.04	0.95	2.11	2.20	2.72	3.25	—
3. Executive branch should have greater control*	0.23	1.08	1.47	2.21	2.50	2.22	2.75	—
4. We should continue supporting the United Nations	0.60	1.05	0.88	1.35	1.42	1.76	1.42	2.42
5. We should purchase $100 million U.N. bonds	1.22	1.72	1.70	1.88	2.71	2.85	2.50	—
6. Sororities and fraternities should be abolished	0.00	1.06	1.05	1.18	1.40	2.90	1.42	0.50
7. Federal aid should be provided to schools	0.52	1.11	1.62	1.33	1.75	1.66	1.50	1.50
8. Medical care for aged under Social Security	0.25	0.94	1.17	1.85	1.38	2.50	2.00	2.00
9. There should be curfews for male students	0.07	1.05	0.76	0.90	0.92	1.10	1.00	0.00
10. No foreign aid should be given to Communist governments	0.65	1.47	1.20	1.57	2.21	3.85	3.00	5.00
11. Likelihood of cancer cure within 5 years*	0.42	0.95	1.27	1.85	2.22	3.00	4.00	—
12. Washington or Lincoln greater President*	0.58	0.73	1.12	0.81	1.66	1.75	2.00	—
Median change	0.46	1.05	1.19	1.46	1.98	2.61	2.25	1.50

* These issues included in the Hovland and Pritzker study.

in our 1963 study of farmers' attitudes toward increased government controls in agriculture.

THE FARM STUDY

In our 1963 farm study we presented a strong argument for increasing government controls in agriculture to members of the Farmers' Union, Farm Bureau, and unselected adults and college students. The Farm Bureau, it should be pointed out, has long taken a public

Table 9.4 *Opinion Change for Subjects with Differing Initial Stands* (*Whittaker, 1964a*)

Group	(N)	Before Communication	Perceived Position of Communication	After Communication	Change in Direction of Communication
Farm group A	(17)	2.60	2.50	2.62	−0.02
Unselected student	(18)	5.50	2.00	4.37	+1.13
Unselected adult	(50)	6.41	2.00	6.43	−0.02
Farm group B	(22)	7.31	1.75	8.00	−0.69

position of strong opposition to what it calls "government meddling in the farmer's business."

Table 9.4 presents the results of this study.

Note that Farm Bureau members (farm group B) moved in the opposite direction from that proposed in the communication. This is the "boomerang effect" so often noted in studies of attitude change. We believe this effect results when communications are presented that take positions well within the subject's latitude of rejection.

ADDITIONAL EVIDENCE SUPPORTING THE HYPOTHESIS OF A CURVILINEAR RELATIONSHIP

In 1964 Freedman tested the hypothesis that more change would occur with greater discrepancy under conditions of *low* involvement but that with high involvement maximum change would occur at the moderate level of discrepancy.

In this experiment a concept formation task was employed as the "issue." A number of concept instances were presented, and the subjects were required to decide what the correct concept was. The first description of the concept was considered as their initial position. Additional concept instances were then presented that essentially constituted discrepant information. Following this information, subjects were asked to give a final description of the concept. Position change was the difference between the subject's initial and final concepts.

Involvement was manipulated before the experiment began by telling members of the high involvement group that the first response was an indication of intelligence and perceptiveness. Members of the low involvement group were told that the first response was relatively unimportant as a personality indicator.

Results of the experiment are shown in Table 9.5 and Figure 9.4. Under conditions of high involvement, the greatest shift occurred with an intermediate discrepancy. But with low involvement, the greatest shift occurred with maximum discrepancy.

Table 9.5 *Amount of Change from Initial to Final Position (Freedman, 1964)*

	Discrepancy		
Condition	Low	Moderate	High
Low involvement	1.85	2.16	3.15
High involvement	1.14	2.12	0.94

Here is another example of a study that yields misleading results because the author neglected to employ adequate parameters, at least under the condition of low involvement. Had he increased the discrepancy still more under this condition, decreased change would doubtless have been the result. Then the monotonic relationship for the low involvement condition (Figure 9.4) would have become curvilinear.

Under conditions of high involvement and when the latitude of acceptance is very narrow, the optimal position yielding maximum

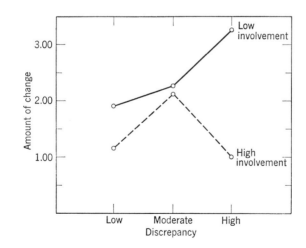

Figure 9.4 Mean amount of change from initial to final response (Freedman, 1964).

change is very close to the subject's own position. Under conditions of low involvement, on the other hand, the optimal position is much further away. Regardless of involvement, however, the relationship between discrepancy and change is nonmonotonic provided that sufficiently large discrepancies are employed. That is, a curvilinear relationship is found between the degree of communication discrepancy and amount of attitude change when the conditions of research are adequate to test the relationship.

Like the blind men attempting to describe an elephant by feeling of its various parts, social psychologists have been confused by the failure on the part of many investigators to employ adequate parameters in their studies of this issue. We ourselves, I should hasten to add, contributed to the confusion in 1957 when we presented results of a study of this problem at the Fifteenth International Congress of Psychology in Belgium (Whittaker, 1957).

In that study we evaluated the effects of various discrepancies upon judgments in the autokinetic situation. It should be noted that this situation is not ordinarily highly ego-involving for subjects.

We first had subjects serve in one session alone, during which they made a series of forty judgments concerning autokinetic movement. Then, in a second session, each subject served with a "plant" or "confederate" who had been instructed to make judgments in accordance with a prearranged scheme. With some subjects the "plant" made judgments centered around a median one inch higher than the subject's largest judgment in the first session. The "plant" always used the same *range* of judgments as that used by the subjects in the first session, but his median differed in the various conditions. With other subjects, the "plant" distributed his judgments about a median and within a range much further away from those originally made by the subject. In fact, in the most extreme condition, the "plant" made judgments ranging upward from a value twelve times the subject's largest judgment in session one.

Our results in this experiment are shown in Figure 9.5. Note that these data show a monotonic relationship between discrepancy and change. Smaller discrepancy equals greater change in this case, which is the reverse of Freedman's findings under conditions of low involvement as shown in Figure 9.4.

As we did additional work on this problem, we became increasingly convinced that the earlier results were not entirely accurate because the smallest discrepancy employed was considerable. In 1962 we again utilized the autokinetic situation and a procedure very similar to that employed earlier. In this later study, however, we included one

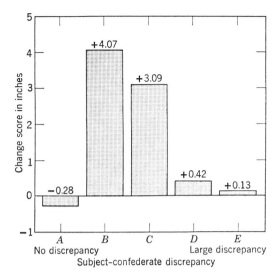

Figure 9.5 Mean change scores as a function of subject-confederate discrepancy in judgments (Whittaker, 1964b).

experimental condition in which the discrepancy employed was *small*er than the smallest we had utilized in the previous study. In other words, in Figure 9.5, this condition would be located between A (control group) and B (the smallest discrepancy employed in the earlier study). In this condition the lowest judgment of the "plant" was set only one inch above the *lowest* judgment of the subject in session one. Hence the range of judgments of the subject and "plant" overlapped considerably.

With this new condition added to the experiment, we found an average change of only +1.06 inches, whereas subjects in group B (smallest discrepancy condition in the 1957 study) showed an average change of +4.07 inches in the direction of the "plant." Thus the monotonic relationship we originally observed was a function of neglecting to include *very small* discrepancies. Conversely, we may conclude now that the monotonic relationship observed by Freedman was a function of his failure to include *very* large discrepancies.

It is clear that investigators have been describing the whole elephant of the discrepancy problem on the basis of examination of its different parts. If, for example, one set of limited discrepancies is employed, the investigator can easily be drawn to the conclusion

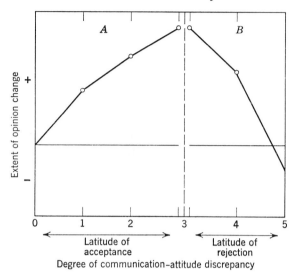

Figure 9.6 Hypothetical curve showing relationship between opinion change and communication-attitude discrepancy. Looking at the *A* part of the curve yields one conclusion, whereas looking only at the *B* part yields the opposite conclusion.

that greater discrepancy equals greater change. This is illustrated in Figure 9.6. If we look only at the "*A*" part of the figure at the left, very obviously the curve shows that greater discrepancy equals greater change. On the other hand, if we look only at the "*B*" part of this figure (as we ourselves did in our 1957 study), we are forced to conclude that *smaller* discrepancy equals greater change.

As mentioned earlier, involvement is important insofar as it determines the relative sizes of the latitudes of acceptance and rejection. Under conditions of higher involvement, the optimal discrepancy (that yielding maximum change) is close to the subject's own position. Under conditions of low involvement, the discrepancy yielding maximum change is much further away. Thus, regardless of degree of involvement on the part of the subject, there is a curvilinear relationship between communication discrepancy and attitude change.

CONCLUSION

In conclusion, let me summarize the main points illustrated in the research results reported here. We have seen that tolerance for various positions on an issue is related to the subject's own stand on the issue and his degree of involvement in that stand. His perception of other positions is influenced by his own stand, causing him to perceive some positions as closer to his own than they actually are and other positions as farther away. His own stand also influences his judgment of other positions: some positions are judged as biased and propagandistic and others as fair and impartial.

The probability that a subject will judge a communication as biased and the probability of assimilation or contrast can be predicted from knowledge of a subject's latitudes of acceptance and rejection.

Regardless of the sizes of the latitudes of acceptance and rejection, however, or degree of involvement in the issue, there is a curvilinear or nonmonotonic relationship between attitude change and communication discrepancy. As discrepancy increases, positive attitude change increases up to a maximum point and then diminishes until, finally, increasingly larger negative changes occur. With narrow latitudes of acceptance, the point of maximum positive change is very close to the subject's own position, whereas with wider latitudes it is further away. If we know the latitudes of acceptance and rejection appropriate to a particular subject or the mean latitudes of acceptance and rejection appropriate to a particular audience, we can predict the optimal discrepancy with considerable accuracy.

Now for those who may think this is an esoteric issue having little to do with the realities of everyday life, let me point out some of the important implications.

First, this research shows that communicators *must* know the positions or stands of individuals with whom they are communicating, at least if they are at all interested in changing attitudes. It is not enough to simply present one's own position. In fact, presentation of one's own position without regard for that of the listener may result in convincing the listener that he is right and the communicator is wrong.

Second, this research shows that the position of the communication must be determined on the basis of latitudes of acceptance and rejection in the audience or at least the principal positions of the individuals who make up the audience. If it is not, the "truth" in many situations may result in "boomerang effects" because it is so discrepant from what the individual already believes. Conversely, it may yield less change than could otherwise be obtained because it is too close to what the individual believes. Clearly then, in many communication situations, presentation of the "truth" is not a guarantee of effectiveness, from the point of view of changing attitudes.

The major implication in these results, it seems to me, is that communicators must know what people believe before they attempt to present any communication. Furthermore, there must be a continuous feedback of information about audience positions or stands. This initial assessment of positions and feedback becomes particularly crucial when the communicator and audience are from very different cultures or social organizations, as is the case today in much international communication. Those responsible for the content of communications must learn to take this information into account. If they desire to be effective, the stands they present should be based on knowledge of the optimal discrepancy existing for specific audiences on specific issues. In addition, when circumstances dictate, they must learn to say nothing. If the truth is damaging, in other words, they need not lie but at least they must keep quiet.

REFERENCES

Daughtery, W., and Janowitz, M. (Eds.), 1958. *A psychological warfare casebook*. Baltimore: Johns Hopkins Univ. Press.

Ewing, T. N., 1942. A study of certain factors involved in changes of opinion. *J. soc. Psychol.*, **16**, 63–88.

Festinger, L., 1957. *A theory of cognitive dissonance*. Evanston, Ill.: Row, Peterson.

Fisher, S., and Lubin, A., 1958. Distance as a determinant of influence in a two-person serial interaction situation. *J. abnorm. soc. Psychol.*, **56**, 230–238.

Fisher, S., Rubinstein, I., and Freeman, R., 1956. Intertrial effects of immediate self-committal in a continuous social influence situation. *J. abnorm. soc. Psychol.*, **52**, 200–207.

Freedman, J., 1964. Involvement discrepancy and change. *J. abnorm. soc. Psychol.*, **69**, 290–295.

French, J. R. P., Jr., 1956. A formal theory of social power. *Psychol. Rev.*, **63**, 181–194.

Goldberg, S. C., 1954. Three situational determinants of conformity to social norms. *J. abnorm. soc. Psychol.*, **49**, 325–329.

Harvey, O. J., Kelley, H., and Shapiro, M., 1957. Reactions to unfavorable evaluations of the self made by other persons. *J. Pers.* **25**, 393–411.

Hovland, C. I., Harvey, O. J., and Sherif, M., 1957. Assimilation and contrast effects in reactions to communication and attitude change. *J. abnorm. soc. Psychol.*, **55**, 244–252.

Hovland, C. I., and Pritzker, H. A., 1957. Extent of opinion change as a function of amount of change advocated. *J. abnorm. soc. Psychol.*, **54**, 257–261.

Sherif, M., 1965. The social judgment-involvement approach vs. the cognitive dissonance approach. Paper presented at the meetings of the Amer. Psychological Ass., Chicago.

Sherif, M., and Hovland, C. I., 1961. *Social judgment*. New Haven: Yale Univ. Press.

Whittaker, J., 1957. The effects of experimentally introduced anchorages upon judgment in the autokinetic situation. Paper presented before the Fifteenth Int. Congr. of Psychol., Brussels, Belgium.

Whittaker, J., 1963. Opinion change as a function of communication—attitude discrepancy. *Psychol. Rep.*, 13, 763–772.

Whittaker, J., 1964a. Cognitive dissonance and the effectiveness of persuasive communications. *Publ. Opin. Quart.*, 28, 547–555.

Whittaker, J., 1964b. Parameters of social influence in the autokinetic situation. *Sociometry*, 27, 88–95.

Whittaker, J., 1965a. In Sherif, C., Sherif, M., and Nebergall, R., *Attitude and attitude change: The social judgment-involvement approach*. Philadelphia: Saunders, p. 155.

Whittaker, J., 1965b. Attitude change and communication—attitude discrepancy. *J. soc. Psychol.*, 65, 141–147.

Zimbardo, P. G., 1960. Involvement and communication discrepancy as determinants of opinion change. *J. abnorm. soc. Psychol.*, 60, 86–94.

10. Attitudes and Arousal: Affect and Cognition In Personality Functioning[*]

James Bieri

The issue discussed in this chapter is so apparently simple to state and so basic to general psychological theory that one would think, in the hundred years of modern psychology, that reliable answers and understanding would surely be at hand. Stated most simply, the problem is: How are the perceptions and judgments we have of events in the world influenced by the feelings, emotions, and affects that we experience in relation to these events?

Man is a creature of strong feelings and affects just as certainly as he is a creature of thought, judgment, and problem-solving. Our typologies in personality theory reiterate this polarity. One version, stemming from the constitutional psychology of somatotypes (Lindzey, 1965), envisions the person with a viscerotonic temperament as one whose system of experiencing the world is his digestive tract: "I know because I feel it in my gut." At the other extreme, the cerebrotonic person experiences the world with his head: "I know because I have thought it out dispassionately." Most of us have neither of the two extremes in body build associated with these two types, and our judgments of the world are neither totally devoid of the influence of our feelings nor entirely subjugated by these feelings.

The theme of this chapter is that the study of attitudes offers a major avenue along which to move toward a more adequate and complete understanding of the interrelations between affects and cog-

[*] Work on this Chapter and some of the research it describes was supported by Grant GS-842 from the National Science Foundation.

nition in general personality theory. In this sense my focus is opposite to that more commonly exposed in attitude research, namely: How might personality theory contribute to the study of attitudes? Rather, I would stress that attitude research and theory have the potential for clarifying at least some of the critical conceptual and methodological problems we continue to run up against in the important area of personality. I propose to consider some of the theoretical and empirical issues of affective-cognitive relations that are common to both personality theory and attitude theory. Concurrently, I would like to indicate some developments in contemporary attitude research that I consider to hold promise for our efforts in building a more solid structure in this field.

ATTITUDES, PERSONALITY, AND JUDGMENT

At the outset, it should be made clear why the study of attitudes offers promise for the student of personality who seeks a clearer grasp of affective-cognitive relations. The reason is simply that an attitude is both an expression of an idea or belief *and* an expression of feeling or affect about this idea or belief (Katz and Stotland, 1959). In short, objects or events toward which we hold strong beliefs are frequently the events toward which we feel most strongly and in which we are most involved. This affect may range along a given attitude continuum from extremely positive to extremely negative such that a person may believe, for example, that immediate disengagement in Vietnam should be our policy and he may support such a belief by intense involvement in activities directed *against* our current posture in Vietnam. Someone else may hold the same belief in terms of our position in Vietnam, but his emotional investment may be considerably less. That is, it can be assumed that given the same position on an attitude dimension, two persons may vary in terms of their affective involvement concerning their position.

When we move to the field of personality, similar conceptions can be advanced. Just as attitudes involve evaluative *dimensions* of a bipolar nature, so our perceptions of our own and others' personalities may be considered dimensional in nature. That is, a person may judge another to be *outgoing* in behavior, the implicit contrast to which might be *shyness* for that same judge. Or, carrying the analogy to attitudes one step closer, two individuals may conceive of themselves as being rather shy persons, but for one this self-belief is accompanied by relatively little feeling or affect whereas the other may consider such a personal characteristic with the utmost distress and anxiety.

One important link, then, between the field of social attitudes and the field of personality is that both can involve dimensions along which judgments are made and that there can be greater or lesser degrees of affective involvement in relation to these judgments (Berkowitz, 1960). Seen in this light, the study of personality, particularly as it involves an emphasis upon our perceptions of others as a major concern, may be considered to be the study of attitudes toward self and towards others. A number of years ago George Kelly (1955) proposed such a conception of personality. Kelly gave the term personal constructs to these personality counterparts of attitudes. Bonarius (1965) has recently reviewed the empirical research generated by this approach. In the past several years, a number of associates and I have been carrying out studies in clinical and social judgment which in turn emphasize the close parallel between attitude formulations and personality formulations and which stress the dimensional basis of judgments in both these realms (Bieri, Atkins, Briar, Leaman, Miller, and Tripodi, 1966).

On a more general level, such an emphasis on the continuity of personality and social attitudes draws upon the formulations of judgment research which, in its psychophysical mode, has been one of the longest theoretical and empirical traditions in psychology. In drawing upon this rich legacy as an aid in formulating principles of personality and attitudes, psychologists have come upon one inescapable fact that may place serious limits on the payoff value of the psychophysical tradition. This is the fact that these principles of judgment were obtained in large measure from our perceptions of the physical world and in particular from rather simple sensory dimensions involving discriminations of weight, loudness, physical size, and the like. Those of us who have tried to borrow from this tradition and who deal with conceptions and judgments of others' behavior as stimuli early call into question the closeness of the parallel between judgments of the social world and the apparently more simple judgments of our physical environment. For one thing, the people about whom we make our most crucial judgments are likely to be those about whom we have the strongest feelings, affect, and personal involvement. At once, the affective variables are introduced more strongly into the judgment conceptions we advance than would be the case in the more traditional psychophysical realm.

There is general recognition, of course, of this greater affective quality of social stimuli in the judgment field. Some believe that the essential regularities occur irrespective of the stimulus domain. Stevens (1966), for example, has reported on a number of investigations of magnitude judgments of social dimensions in which he finds power functions similar to those observed for simple sensory continua. Others, and this is perhaps the course taken by most workers, have attempted to complicate the principles of judgment by incorporating the additional features that seem to be important in dealing with affect-laden stimuli. Here we might mention the work of Helson (1964) on adaptation level and the work of the Sherifs, Hovland, and others in the attitude realm (Sherif and Hovland, 1961; Sherif, Sherif, and Nebergall, 1965; Bieri *et al.*, 1966).

Among those most concerned with contemporary psychophysical approaches, there is increasing recognition that the judge's personality, his feelings, and his emotional reactions to the judgment task may be crucial factors in determining the nature of responses (Galanter, 1962; Atkinson, Carterette, and Kinchla, 1964). In short, psychologists have reacted in a variety of ways to the realization that our judgments about the social world incur feelings and affect that are often less centrally involved in our judgments of the nonsocial world. Affect has entered the once-neutral ground of the experimental laboratory.

To leap from psychophysics to psychoanalysis may seem rather fanciful to some and an example of primary process at best. However, just as psychophysics has been moving more into the realm of affect, so psychoanalysis has been bringing to the fore its long-standing concern with conceptions of the interplay of cognitive processes and affect. Rappaport (1959) has provided an analysis of the primary and secondary models of affect and cognition in psychoanalytic theory, which is central in understanding how strong unconscious feelings channel the direction and form of cognitive processes.

A more recent concern in psychoanalytic ego psychology has been the role and development of *cognitive structures* in personality, structures which may in part have had their roots in the drives and conflicts associated with early social experiences (Rappaport, 1957; 1959). Klein (1958) in particular has emphasized the drive-controlling function of what he has termed cognitive controls. It may well be that the analysis of cognitive structures in personality offers a key to understanding the relation of affective processes to cognitive behavior (Bieri, in press). Although a start has been made to link the development of cognitive structures to attitudes, especially in relation to attitudes toward authority, this effort can only be considered to have barely begun.

This is not to say, of course, that attitude research has ignored affective-cognitive relations. To the contrary, we can cite a number of important areas of work in which the influence of the affective

component in attitudes upon cognition has been a continuing source
of interest. One example is the work on the effects of attitudes on
veridicality of reasoning (Prentice, 1957; Thistlewaite, 1950). Other
examples include the emphasis stemming from dissonance theory on
the influence of such affective variables as commitment and threat
upon attitude change (Aronson and Carlsmith, 1963), and the work
of Schachter (1964) on cognition and emotional arousal.

We see, then, on a variety of fronts in contemporary psychology,
an active concern for bringing affective and cognitive variables into
closer theoretical juxtaposition. Some, of course, have questioned such
efforts by stating that such categories as "cognition" and "affect" belong to an older, outmoded age of faculty psychology. Certainly it
is the happy aspect of the *concept* of attitude that both affect and
cognition are incorporated into a single psychological construct.
Nevertheless, it pays to assay the progress to date in the effort to
initiate new directions for this old problem. Let us turn, then, to
a brief consideration of those fields of prior research which, in my
opinion, come closest to engaging the processes of affective behavior
and cognition in the study of attitudes.

AFFECTIVE PROCESSES IN PERCEPTUAL JUDGMENT

The student of attitudes who would turn to the experimental literature outside the attitude realm for guidance in understanding the
mutual relations of affective processes and judgment will not find
readily at hand the types of generalizations that would make his
research task easier.

Perhaps the most concentrated efforts to conceptualize affective
variables in judgment were the New Look studies of need and perception. However, a major concern in much of this research was the
effect of need arousal upon subthreshold phenomena in perception,
the field of subception. A somewhat related emphasis is the current
work on motivational factors in signal detection (Atkinson, 1963).
The relative lack of systematic analysis of affective factors influencing
the discrimination of suprathreshold stimuli is rather striking. Such
a lack seems especially noteworthy since most events that the individual is called upon to discriminate in social situations involve
above-threshold stimuli, such as issues or positions on an attitude
continuum or the behavior of another person.

It is not surprising, therefore, that the kind of systematic statements
which can be made concerning the impact of affective variables upon
judgment are both few and general in nature and that the evidence

for these generalizations is at best equivocal, when not contradictory. A sampling of some of the general statements includes the following:

1. Affective arousal serves to limit the range of cue utilization (Easterbrook, 1959). This is perhaps the most crucial statement because it relates to such issues in attitude research as the effects of *degree of involvement* upon the judgment of attitude positions and impinges upon such judgmental phenomena as anchoring, latitude of acceptance, and discriminability.

2. Heightened drive decreases the width of cognitive maps (Tolman, 1948). This is essentially a restatement of the first proposition and again finds itself expressed in various guises in attitude research concerned with involvement effects in judgment.

3. The positive or negative *value* of objects influences how they will be perceived by the individual. We have become familiar with this proposition in much of the New Look research concerned with the perception of positively and negatively valued stimuli (Allport, 1955; Postman, 1953). Because attitude dimensions have both a positive and a negative pole, systematic differences in judging positive and negative stimuli should be reflected therefore in attitudinal judgments.

It is apparent that these highly generalized statements need a great deal of specification if they are to be useful propositions in the study of attitudes. Let us take a more definitive view of a number of factors that could lead to such conceptual sharpening, noting as we go along how attitude research relates to the research in personality and allied fields.

LEVEL OF AROUSAL

In general, it is possible to isolate two somewhat different problems concerning the relation between level of arousal and such judgmental phenomena as discrimination. The first of these concerns whether moderate deviation in level of arousal away from some adaptational level is associated with positive affect, such that moderate changes are more pleasurable and extreme changes are less pleasurable. We shall consider this issue more fully in relation to judgments of positive and negative stimuli.

A second problem concerns the effects upon perceptual judgments as increases beyond some basal level of arousal are experienced. Here the question as to the linear or curvilinear relation between level of arousal and discrimination is raised (Easterbrook, 1959). Extremely low levels of affective arousal, as in monotonous tasks or sensory deprivation situations, may be associated with poor discrimination just as extremely high levels of affective arousal might be, for example, in traumatic experiences or crises. In this sense, level of affective arousal and discrimination effectiveness may assume a curvilinear relation consistent with such traditional formulations as that of Yerkes and Dodson.

Thus, for more difficult judgment tasks, a lower level of affective arousal may lead to better performance whereas for higher levels of arousal better performance is found with simple discriminations. Such interaction effects between drive level and performance have been observed in discrimination tasks with animals, in animal learning (Bruner, Matter, and Papanek, 1955), and in human learning (Spence, Taylor, and Ketchel, 1956). However, systematic variation of arousal level and difficulty of the discrimination task has not been reported frequently in the literature dealing with perceptual judgments in humans.

The role of affective disposition arousal has been studied in regard to a number of cognitive functions. Weiner (1966), for example, has recently reviewed research dealing with level of arousal and its influence upon memory. As in work with anxiety arousal and learning, there is some evidence that memory is more affected in complex tasks as arousal is increased than in simple ones.

From such a variety of sources, then, we may formulate the general proposition that the effects of affective arousal will vary as a function of the relative complexity of the stimulus factors with which the person must deal. Strangely, to date, this type of formulation has not been intensively applied to the field of attitude study. One important implication for attitude research is that the effects of level of involvement—for example, upon anchoring effects and latitude of acceptance—may well vary as a function of the relative complexity of the attitude issue at hand.

A number of studies in the attitude realm indicate that a more refined as well as a more meaningful manipulation of *degrees* of involvement is possible. A recent example was the research of Ward (1965), who was interested in the effects of degree of involvement upon judgments of items concerning attitudes towards Negroes. Subjects with the same highly positive own-position attitude towards Negroes were selected as represening two levels of involvement: some of these subjects had been pickets during an integration demonstration and some had not. The third level of involvement was obtained experimentally by heightening the saliency of the picketing behavior for half of the pickets and not for the other half.

Such attempts to vary involvement by at least three degrees seems most noteworthy on several grounds. First, they assure that an estimate can be obtained in attitude research as to linear or nonlinear effects of increasing arousal upon behavior. McGuire (1966), for example, has recently cited several studies in which presumably greater involvement produced *less* attitude change than did a less involving condition. Whether we have here the operation of a curvilinear relation between arousal and behavior change or merely a failure in the effectiveness of more involving manipulation is not clear. Again, it is also possible that until studies are carried out with issues that also vary in their underlying complexity, for example, such differential effects of involvement will be incompletely understood.

Finally, we should note that in pursuing more systematically the effects of varying levels of arousal in attitude research, the issue of the *relevance* of the arousal state should not be overlooked. Although there has at times been a rather cavalier assumption in much experimental personality research that one arousal method was equivalent to another, researchers in the attitude field have of late displayed more caution in this regard. For example, both Millman (1965) and Ward (1965) have used *irrelevant* as well as relevant arousal conditions. Although the latter found greater effects for relevant arousal, there is sufficient evidence for the influence of irrelevant arousal conditions (Rule, 1966) to suggest that this is still an unresolved problem.

Thus, in the problem of the influence of level of arousal, it seems reasonable that, although significant areas of ignorance have yet to be attacked, research in the area of attitudes bodes well toward conceptual clarification of this important issue in general psychological theory. Beginning efforts, such as McGuire's two-factor theory of fear arousal and attitude change (in which a nonmonotonic relation is postulated) are noteworthy in this regard (McGuire, in press).

DISCRIMINABILITY AND AROUSAL

We have noted that a common postulate in general psychological theory is that heightened arousal results in decreased ability to utilize cues in the environment. Such a generalization comes in for some rough going in certain quarters of psychological investigations. Again, it appears to me that attitude research may well provide more sharply etched contours in the currently fuzzy picture.

Two observations about experimental research on discriminability and arousal seem in order in this regard. First, there has been relatively little research with humans on this problem. Second, in those areas in which related issues have been pursued more intensively, such as the effects of increasing drive level on stimulus generalization, the resulting theoretical and empirical picture is far from clear. Storms and Broen (1966) recently reviewed theories and evidence on the effects of increased drive on stimulus generalization, and they strike a sobering note in this regard. Their analysis cautions that any broad formulation dealing with the raising, lowering, sharpness, or flatness of generalization gradients as a function of drive are subject to strong qualification.

Turning to research more relevant to attitudinal judgment, only the slimmest empirical basis exists at present. For example, in a study designed to assess the influence of increasing anxiety upon discrimination, Eriksen and Wechsler (1955) found that discriminations in size judgment were not appreciably changed by increased affective arousal, although response variability was altered. Further, their results seem more congruent with an interpretation that emphasizes *response* effects rather than perceptual-judgmental effects as such. Within the attitude area, several type of research are converging upon this important problem of discriminability and affective arousal, including such time-honored concerns as own-attitude effects on judgment, and relatively more recent conceptions such as latitudes of acceptance and rejection.

Before considering these two areas in detail, it should be noted that ability to discriminate accurately among items on an attitude dimension has been studied in several ways. Sherif, Sherif, and Nebergall (1965) cite several studies in which increased ego-involvement resulted in greater *consistency* in judgment. Such a notion of consistency is germane to the determination of discriminability along an attitude dimension.

For example, in the work my colleagues and I have done (Bieri *et al.*, 1966), informational analysis was used to measure the ability of a subject to discriminate different positions along an attitude dimension. Such informational measures require a determination of the reliability or consistency of a judge's responses as well as their variability. Atkins (in press) obtained measures of discriminability for attitudes toward fraternities and investigated the effects of high versus low discriminability upon anchoring tendencies. It was found that subjects ranged in their ability to discriminate from four perfect positions on this attitude dimension to eight perfect discriminations. The mean value of 2.65 bits represents the largest value of information transmission that we have obtained in studies of a variety of social and clinical stimuli (Bieri *et al.*, 1966).

In these studies, lower discriminability was associated with a tendency toward greater assimilation effects in judgment, that is, systematic shifts toward a standard. These assimilation trends were more marked in relation to size judgments for which discriminability scores were also available on the same subjects. As we shall note shortly, this difference between the two stimulus realms possibly stemmed from the influence of own position on judgment in the anchoring task with attitude items, an affective variable lacking in sensory judgments.

LATITUDE OF ACCEPTANCE AND AROUSAL

The judgment approach to attitudes stresses that a person's ability to discriminate along an attitude continuum is relatively finite and that the number and nature of these discriminations should relate significantly to such phenomena as attitude change, anchoring, and the like. We have seen that discriminability, measured in informational terms, is one approach to this categorization problem which stems from general psychological research. A further approach, and one that seems to me to be especially fruitful, concerns the extensive research in the past years of Sherif and his colleagues upon latitude of acceptance (Sherif and Hovland, 1961; Sherif, Sherif, and Nebergall, 1965).

Here too, we find evidence of the influence of the underlying assumption that affective arousal limits ability to discriminate among stimuli, but perhaps in a form more suited to studying the peculiarly affective qualities of attitude dimensions. For the emphasis here is upon *breadth* or *narrowness* of categorization as a function of acceptability to one's own position. Essentially, the emphasis is upon how we *affectively* discriminate among items rather than upon how capable we are of discriminating the attitude positions reflected in the items themselves. We have, as it were, an affective discrimination measure in the latitude of acceptance concept. Several important consequences flow from this type of measure. First, it allows a more reasonable methodology of studying the influence of affective arousal upon discrimination. Second, it permits a more specific approach to the analysis of anchoring phenomena and attitude change. Finally, it has ramifications for the assessment of personality variables that have yet to be explored intensively.

From the first, it has been postulated that affective arousal would influence latitude of acceptance. The form of this influence is less clearly understood. Sherif and Hovland (1961) reported narrower latitudes of acceptance for subjects with extreme positions, but the more recent work of Sherif, Sherif, and Nebergall (1965) reported significant variations in latitudes of rejection and noncommitment, not in latitude of acceptance, according to extremity of position. Regardless of *extremity* of position, they now postulate that highly involved individuals have a raised threshold for acceptance and a lowered threshold for rejection, resulting in a latitude of acceptance disproportionately narrower than latitude of rejection for highly involved individuals. Further, they suggest the importance of the latitude of noncommitment as an index of the overall involvement of the individual in the issue at hand.

To get a clearer picture of changes in latitude of acceptance as a function of involvement and extremity of own position, a recent study by Atkins and Bieri (1966) is of relevance. On the basis of questionnaire response, 80 subjects were selected who had either extremely *pro* or extremely *con* attitudes toward organized religion and who indicated strong commitment to their own position. To heighten affective arousal or ego-involvement, half of each own-attitude group was engaged in a face-to-face discussion on organized religion in which they defended their positions against contradictory statements. Subjects then judged moderate statements toward religion in contexts of either extreme *pro* or extreme *con* statements. In addition, measures of latitude of acceptance and rejection were obtained by use of the range method described in Atkins, Kujala, and Bieri (1965).

Although the design of this research did not allow us to obtain *before* and *after* measures of latitude of acceptance on the same subjects, an analysis of the latitude of acceptance and rejection scores following the arousal and nonarousal conditions indicated that under high involvement the latitude of acceptance was less for both *pro* and *con* subjects than it was for equally extreme subjects in the noninvolving conditions. Conversely, for both *pro* and *con* subjects, latitude of rejection was *greater* for the aroused subjects than it was for the nonaroused subjects.

Most interesting, perhaps, was the finding that *con* subjects had the greatest disparity between latitudes of acceptance and rejection as a function of involvement. For *pro* subjects, the mean difference in latitude of acceptance for the two conditions was only 0.40, whereas for the *con* subjects the mean difference was 1.90. Despite the lack of statistical significance of these findings, their consistency in direction is noteworthy, particularly in suggesting that latitude of acceptance may *decrease* with increased involvement. A design using *before* and *after* measures of latitude of acceptance and rejection would clarify this situation more fully. Current work in progress is exploring this problem. To date, we continue to find rather consistent effects of decreased latitude of acceptance under conditions of arousal. The fact that a recent study by Singer (1965) reports no effect on latitude of acceptance under conditions of involvement suggests we have not as yet partialed out all of the variables that might be operating and that make comparison of studies difficult.

Whether we focus on latitude of acceptance, rejection, or noncommitment, it is apparent from a wide variety of studies that affective arousal *does* have an effect on this type of discrimination behavior. Given this encouraging start in the attitude realm and considering the paucity of evidence noted earlier in the experimental personality realm, it would seem productive to extend the notion of latitude of acceptance to personality assessment and research. This has been done in a recent study by Kujala and Bieri (1966) using the dimension of masculinity-femininity.

The essential logic behind the application to personality measurement is that one's position on a given personality dimension is most accurately defined not by a fixed position or score but rather by a latitude or range within which the individual can perceive himself as falling. Although further details on this study will be presented later, it is noteworthy that changes in own position as a function of latitude of acceptance on masculinity-femininity were significant, and these effects were comparable in direction to those found in attitude research.

Finally, we should note that measures of discrimination in attitudes, such as latitude of acceptance, may be susceptible to the same affective variables that have received attention in personality research. I refer specifically to the tendency to use extreme response categories as a function of affective dispositions of the individual (O'Donovan, 1965). It is certainly possible, for example, that nonattitudinal dispositions *could* be associated with differences in latitude of acceptance tendencies. On the other hand, on a number of studies we have done, such correlates have *not* been found with such measures as authoritarianism and Pettigrew's Category Width Scale. We have observed a slight but significant correlation between width of latitude of acceptance in attitudes toward fraternities and in masculinity-femininity ($r = .36$, $p < .05$). Latitude of acceptance appears to reflect a more specific affective measure of discrimination not tapped by other cognitive measures.

ANCHORING AND AROUSAL

The study of anchoring phenomena in attitude research is a particularly cogent means of analyzing the influence of affective variables upon cognitive processes. Although the demonstration of anchoring effects in the judgments of social and affective stimuli has a long history (Bieri *et al.*, 1966), until the advent of attitude research in this area the primary efforts were directed toward establishing effects common to the physical and social stimulus realms. To the student of anchoring and attitudes, however, it is apparent that a whole new set of crucial affective variables are introduced that call for either an elaboration or a replacement of our earlier and simpler theories of anchoring. Let me cite a few such variables. They include the judge's involvement in the issue at hand, the extremity of his own position, and the relation of his own position to the context stimuli in the judgment situation.

A number of theoretical developments have appeared to explain the influence of these diverse affective variables in anchoring tasks. The effects of own-position have been perhaps the most intensely studied, starting with the early work of Hinckley (1932, 1963) over thirty years ago up to the present (*e.g.*, Atkins, in press; Ward, 1965; Zavalloni and Cook, 1965).

There seems to be little doubt that one's own position on an attitude dimension can bias his judgments of other positions. The approach within adaptation-level theory, for example, would be to consider one's own position as an internal anchor, a residual stimulus that would need to be incorporated in the calculation of adaptation level. Another approach stemming from the work of Hovland, Harvey, and Sherif (1957) has been to consider the effect of own-position relative to latitude of acceptance. In general, it posits that when moderate stimuli are outside one's latitude of acceptance, they will be displaced in a contrast direction, whereas if they fall within the latitude of acceptance, moderate stimuli will be assimilated toward one's own position. Presumably, increasing the involvement of the subject should increase these tendencies.

In a comprehensive study of the interaction between one's own position and the stimulus context within which judgment occurs, Atkins (in press) has obtained evidence suggesting the importance of own attitude in judging relevant stimuli. Using subjects who had either extremely *pro*, extremely *con*, or neutral attitudes towards fraternities, Atkins had these judges rate moderate statements in alternating contexts of *pro* or *con* items. This procedure of alternating contexts had been found useful in studying assimilation tendencies in earlier research (Bieri, Orcutt, and Leaman, 1963). A major finding of this study was that on the initial judgment trial, when *contrast* effects might have been predicted as a function of the context, no significant anchoring effects produced by context stimuli were found. Rather, a significant effect of *own position* was evident, such that both *pro* and *con judges* assimilated the moderate stimulus toward their own position. Because this assimilation effect worked in opposite directions for subjects with *pro* and *con* own positions, the overall judgments of moderate statements as a function of context were no different.

In short, one's own position influenced judgments to the extent of overcoming, as it were, the influence of the context stimuli. No evidence was found for the suggestion from adaptation-level theory that a pooling of congruent own attitude and context stimuli would occur. On subsequent judgment trials, however, Atkins found that own-position effects were generally minimal, suggesting a dissipation of the influence of own-position over trials. If we assume that extreme positions were also reflective of involvement in the issue, these results would also appear to run counter to the Sherif and Hovland position.

A more stringent test of this position, of course, would involve experimental manipulation of level of arousal concerning one's own position. This was done in a subsequent study (Atkins and Bieri, 1966) that was outlined earlier in relation to the effects of arousal of religious attitudes upon latitude of acceptance. In this study the same alternation of context anchors was used as previously, such that *pro* religious subjects judged moderate items initially either in a *pro* item context or in a *con* item context. Half of each *pro* and *con* own-position group received the involving condition, which consisted of defending their own position in a discussion with another.

The major results of this study for our present discussion were the significant main effect produced by involvement found on the initial trial, as well as a significant interaction between involvement and initial anchor. On this first trial, the differences between the involvement-aroused and the nonaroused groups were quite striking. The groups exposed to the heightened-involvement treatment judged the moderate religious statements in the negative portion of the scale, thus demonstrating strong contrast effects relative to the *pro* context anchor. This contrast tendency was even more pronounced for judges who were themselves *pro* in attitude, thus indicating the pooling effect of congruency of initial context and own-attitude that was absent in the previous study by Atkins (in press). Interestingly, these effects were confined to *pro* context judgments. When we carried the analysis one step further and examined the possible influence of latitude of acceptance, it was found that the most pronounced contrast tendencies are displayed by those *pro* subjects who were in the heightened involvement condition and who had the *narrowest* latitudes of acceptance.

These results clearly offer support for the Sherif and Hovland model, which posits that judges with extreme positions and strong personal involvement will displace attitude statements away from their own positions. It would seem that heightened arousal creates strong affective responses in the judges that are manifested in greater rejection of ambiguous stimuli. The results would also appear to be consistent, for the *pro* judges, with an adaptation level explanation. It should be pointed out, however, that the findings for the antireligious anchors, both context items and own-position, did not yield such definite contrast effects. Although Ward (1965) demonstrated contrast away from own-position in relation to arousal, he studied only *pro* attitude judges. Although no simple reconciliation of these differences as a function of end of the scale can be ascertained, the data do suggest that *pro*-ness and *con*-ness of own attitude may have different properties as extreme attitudes on a dimension. Perhaps one answer to this rather common finding in attitude research is to be found in the differential affective value of positive and negative stimuli, a topic to which we shall now turn.

AFFECTIVE VALUE OF STIMULI AND DISCRIMINATION

It was noted earlier that the concern with how the positive or negative affective value of a stimulus influences its perception has been a major preoccupation in a wide variety of psychological research. It is no less important in the field of attitude research. Extremes of attitude dimensions are by definition extremely positive or negative, especially for the highly involved person. Our judgments of issues close to either pole of an attitude dimension are therefore likely to be influenced by this affective quality or value. For example, we have seen how latitudes of acceptance and rejection may reflect such affective evaluation. In the words of Sherif, Sherif, and Nebergall 1965, p. 109), "The individual who values certain objects in a positive way is highly discriminating when it comes to categorizing them."

In the field of judgment, two perhaps conflicting stances can be taken on this issue. Again the key to the resolution of the inconsistency may lie in the degree of affective arousal involved. The first of these positions stresses that any stimulus that is more salient is likely to increase discrimination in the vicinity of that stimulus on the dimension. Now *end* stimuli are often salient simply as a function of being end stimuli. Further, in the social stimulus realm, end stimuli may also be *natural* end anchors (Bieri *et al.*, 1966). When we consider that extremes of a social continuum, whether they be extremely aggressive behavior or strongly positive attitudes toward religion, have a quality of finality, then we should expect their anchorage value to be high. Studies clearly demonstrate this function of natural end anchors in aiding discrimination in both physical and social stimulus realms (Johnson and King, 1964; Miller and Bieri, 1965b).

Now if we add the second consideration, namely that extremely positive or negative positions are likely to be most affectively involving for the person, we run afoul of the notion that this increasing arousal will *decrease* the relative discriminability of stimuli adjacent to the extreme stimulus. In the effort to reconcile these two apparently contradictory principles of judgment and the results of the studies (Atkins, in press; Atkins and Bieri, 1966), which suggest that arousal activates own-position as an anchor, the following formulation is suggested. Under conditions of increased arousal concerning one's own position, subjects will discriminate *better* near their own position compared to less aroused subjects. At the far end of the scale, discrimination should be *worse* for the more aroused judges, considering their tendency to displace items away from own-position under arousal.

Although data relevant to this problem are not directly available, the results presented by Ward (1965) support the above formulation. He found that displacement away from own (*pro*) position increased with arousal, but we may also consider his results in terms of within-scale discriminations. From such a vantage point, we find that as arousal increased there was progressively greater discrimination between the most positive items and the next most positive items. Similarly, as arousal increases, there was progressively less discrimination between items at the far (negative) end of the attitude scale. It would seem desirable to obtain more information on these types of within-scale discrimination patterns as a function of positive and negative scale extremes. It is interesting in this regard that when arousal level was not considered, Ward found greater discrimination at the *negative* end of the attitude scale than at the positive end.

If we turn again to the general experimental research literature for guidance on this issue of the differences in processing information about negative and positive stimuli, clear messages are difficult to find. In the New Look perceptual studies, for example, a careful review of the existing literature makes it clear that rather equivalent perceptual effects, such as size overestimation, have been found for stimuli with either positive or negative affective value (Allport, 1955; Postman, 1953). It may well be that, at least for conditions of relatively low arousal, the function of negative or positive stimuli is to serve a highlighting function, rendering these stimuli more salient in the perceptual field.

In the field of memory, Weiner (1966) concluded that, although evidence on balance favors the greater recall of positive than negative events, much of the data is contradictory in this regard. Perhaps more significant is the level of arousal or affective intensity. For example, he cites the work of Blum (1961) who found that anxiety may facilitate recall if it is of sufficient intensity.

In the field of social perception, additional evidence for the greater discriminability of negative stimuli is found in studies dealing with cognitive complexity as a function of affective value of the persons being judged (Miller and Bieri, 1965a; Irwin, Tripodi, and Bieri, 1966). In three samples it was found that significantly greater differentiation was observed when subjects were asked to discriminate among negative figures than when they discriminated among figures with either positive or neutral affective value. We have been led to postulate that this greater differentiation among negative persons may arise from the threat they pose to the individual, such that heightened discrimination serves to clarify the nature of this threat. Similarly, in the attitude realm, it could be that greater discriminability among more negative items would represent such an adaptive response to threatening stimuli.

Finally, in relation to affective value and discrimination, it should be pointed out that attitude research presents us with the possibility of studying two approaches to understanding this problem not often found in other areas of social-personality research. First, we can study how well the individual is able to *discriminate* among items as a function of his arousal level and of the affective value of the stimuli for him. Second, we can also determine how he *categorizes* positive and negative stimuli in terms of his own position, as in the latitude of acceptance method. That these processes are not identical, but are related, is seen in the fact that a subject may group items together as most acceptable to him, but this does not tell us whether he has discriminated among the items so grouped. Similarly, the subject may discriminate among items, but he may treat them as functionally related in terms of latitudes of acceptance or rejection. This is, indeed, the unresolved issue in general psychological theory of the relation of discriminability and stimulus generalization (Guttman and Kalish,

1956; Guttman, 1963). We have, in the attitude realm, a significant opportunity to advance understanding of these basic processes that determine our reactions in judging affectively charged stimuli.

AROUSAL AND ATTITUDE CHANGE

The last area to be discussed concerns how affective arousal influences change in one's own position. This problem is a major interest in attitude research and involves such well-known affective variables as fear arousal, coercion, group pressure, rewards, and punishments, among others. In spite of the ambiguities attendant to the interpretation of some of the research in this area, notions stemming from the effects of affective arousal on attitude change seem to offer an interesting approach to studying change in one's own position in more general areas of personality research. One instance of this cited previously is the study by Kujala and Bieri (1966) on changes in own position on the masculinity-femininity continuum.

In that study, following the judgment of a salient communication about a person with whom the subject anticipated that he might have to interact, a subsequent measure of own-position on masculinity-femininity was obtained. It is necessary to realize that such an experimental manipulation in no way implies either a major or lasting change in own-position on a personality dimension such as masculinity-femininity. Fortunately for us, such a change is not likely to occur within the confines of an experimental room. However, by using the concept of latitude of acceptance, one is able to conceptualize own-position as being a *range* within a portion of the scale, such that experimental manipulation can influence self placement within this range.

The major hypothesis of differential change of own position as a function of latitude of acceptance was confirmed. Those subjects who judged another who was *within* their latitude of acceptance shifted their own position *toward* the other, whereas the opposite direction of change was found for subjects judging another who was outside the latitude of acceptance. We find, then, results in the personality realm that are consistent with the attitude formulation of Sherif and Hovland and that are consistent with a comparable study of attitudes (Atkins, Kujala, and Bieri, 1965).

Further analysis of the results of the masculinity-femininity study suggest a more pervasive role of the distance factor in relation to own-position change than is perhaps evident in the work of Sherif, Sherif, and Nebergall (1965). In brief, it was found that distance did exert a significant effect upon own position change. However, when distance effects within categories of close, moderate, and far distance were compared, it was found that *within* each distance category the subjects judging another within their latitude of acceptance shifted own position more toward the other than did the subjects who judged another who was outside the latitude of acceptance.

One additional datum from this study is of interest in relation to latitude of acceptance and own position change. We have found in several studies including this one that, as might be expected, subjects who judge another who is within their latitude of acceptance have significantly *wider* latitudes of acceptance than when the other is outside the latitude of acceptance. Analysis indicates, although the results are not significant, that at close distances one gets increasingly *less* change in the direction of the other as the width of the latitude of acceptance increases and progressively *greater* increase in own position change toward the other at far distances as latitude of acceptance increases. In short, we need closer attention to *width* of latitude of acceptance as an important variable in own position change.

CONCLUSIONS

The impression is inescapable that the research dealing with involvement variables in the attitude realm will continue to make increasingly evident the specific mechanisms by which cognitive and affective systems interact in personality functioning. We can anticipate that formulations stemming from the attitude realm will have increasing impact upon research and theory in personality. Let me underscore three such areas of research that strike me as particularly fruitful.

First, the *levels of arousal* problem offers promise of elucidating how cognitive processes, such as discrimination and anchoring, distort or embellish the efficiency of behavior of the individual under increasing degrees of affective arousal. In particular, attitude research is showing increasing sophistication in relation to such problems of method as manipulating levels of arousal and analyzing the relevancy of the arousal conditions to the task at hand.

Second, *affective categories of judgement,* as in the latitude of acceptance and rejection concept, appear to offer valuable extensions of more traditional measures of discriminability in experimental research. Used in conjunction with informational or other measures of discrimination, we can already see the potential value of such indices to broader areas of personality functioning.

Third, increased attention to the influence of *own-position* under varying levels of involvement and arousal seems a much neglected field in personality research. The potential contribution of attitude studies to such clinical problems as countertransference effects in psychotherapy seems a most obvious and important extension in this regard. Given the amount of emphasis in clinical writing and training on the distorting effects in judgment of countertransference feelings, it may well be that attitude research will move in to fill this void thus far evident in the clinical research literature.

We are, in short, in an era in which attitude research will continue to extend its systematizing influence into realms of more general types of personality functioning, and surely this knowledge can only leave us with positive affect toward the future.

REFERENCES

Allport, F., 1955. *Theories of perception and the concept of structure.* New York: Wiley.

Aronson, E., and Carlsmith, J. M., 1963. Effect of severity of threat on the devaluation of forbidden behavior. *J. abnorm. soc. Psychol.,* **66,** 584–588.

Atkins, A. L., In press. Own attitude and discriminability in relation to anchoring effects in judgment. *J. person. soc. Psychol.*

Atkins, A. L., and Bieri, J., 1966. Ego involvement and anchoring of social stimuli. Unpublished manuscript.

Atkins, A. L., Kujala, K., and Bieri, J., 1965. Latitude of acceptance and attitude change: Empirical evidence for a reformulation. Unpublished manuscript.

Atkinson, R., 1963. A variable sensitivity theory of signal detection. *Psychol. Rev.,* **70,** 91–106.

Atkinson, R., Carterette, E., and Kinchla, R., 1964. The effect of information feedback upon psychological judgments. *Psychonomic Sci.,* **1,** 83–84.

Berkowitz, L., 1960. The judgmental process in personality functioning. *Psychol. Rev.,* **67,** 130–142.

Bieri, J., In press. Cognitive structures in personality. In H. M. Schroder and P. Suedfeld (Eds.), *Information processing: A new perspective in personality theory.* New York: Ronald.

Bieri, J., Atkins, A. L., Briar, S., Leaman, R. L., Miller, H., and Tripodi, T., 1966. *Clinical and social judgment: the discrimination of behavioral information.* New York: Wiley.

Bieri, J., Orcutt, B. A., and Leaman, R., 1963. Anchoring effects in sequential clinical judgments. *J. abnorm. soc. Psychol.,* **67,** 616–623.

Blum, G. S., 1961. *A model of the mind.* New York: Wiley.

Bonarius, J. C. J., 1965. Research in the personal construct theory of George A. Kelly: Role construct repertory test and basic theory. In B. A. Maher (Ed.), *Progress in experimental personality research.* Vol. 2. New York: Academic.

Bruner, J. S., Matter, J., and Papanek, M. L., 1955. Breadth of learning as a function of drive level and mechanization. *Psychol. Rev.,* **62,** 1–10.

Easterbrook, J. A., 1959. The effect of emotion on cue utilization and the organization of behavior. *Psychol. Rev.,* **66,** 183–201.

Eriksen, C. W., and Wechsler, H., 1955. Some effects of experimentally induced anxiety upon discrimination behavior. *J. abnorm. soc. Psychol.,* **51,** 458–463.

Galanter, E., 1962. Contemporary psychophysics. In R. Brown, E. Galanter, E. H. Hess, and G. Mandler, *New directions in psychology.* New York: Holt, Rinehart, and Winston, pp. 87–156.

Guttman, N., 1963. Laws of behavior and facts of perception. In S. Koch (Ed.), *Psychology: A study of a science.* Vol. V. New York: McGraw-Hill.

Guttman, N., and Kalish, H. I., 1956. Discriminability and stimulus generalization. *J. exp. Psychol.,* **51,** 79–88.

Helson, H., 1964. *Adaptation-level theory.* New York: Harper.

Hinckley, E. D., 1932. The influence of individual opinion on construction of an attitude scale. *J. soc. Psychol.,* **3,** 283–296.

Hinckley, E. D., 1963. A follow-up on the influence of individual opinion on the construction of an attitude scale. *J. abnorm. soc. Psychol.,* **67,** 290–292.

Hovland, C. I., Harvey, O. J., and Sherif, M., 1957. Assimilation and contrast effects in reactions to communication and attitude change. *J. abnorm. soc. Psychology,* 1957, **55,** 244–252.

Irwin, M., Tripodi, T., and Bieri, J., 1966. Affective stimulus value and cognitive complexity. Unpublished manuscript.

Johnson, D. M., and King, C. R., 1964. Systematic study of end anchoring and central tendency of judgment. *J. exp. Psychol.,* **67,** 501–506.

Katz, D., and Stotland, E., 1959. A preliminary statement to a theory of attitude structure and change. In S. Koch (Ed.), *Psychology: A study of a science.* Vol. III. New York: McGraw-Hill.

Kelly, G. A., 1955. *The psychology of personal constructs.* New York: Norton.

Klein, G. S., 1958. Cognitive control and motivation. In G. Lindzey (Ed.), *Assessment of human motives.* New York: Holt, Rinehart and Winston.

Kujala, K., and Bieri, J., 1966. Latitude of acceptance in judgments of masculinity-femininity. Unpublished manuscript.

Lindzey, G., 1965. Morphology and behavior. In G. Lindzey and C. S. Hall (Eds.), *Theories of personality: Primary sources and research.* New York: Wiley.

McGuire, W. J., 1966. Attitudes and opinions. In *Annual review of psychology*. Vol. 17. Palo Alto: Annual Reviews.

McGuire, W. J., In press. Personality and susceptibility to social influence. In E. F. Borgatta and W. W. Lambert (Eds.), *Handbook of personality theory and research*. Chicago: Rand McNally.

Miller, H., and Bieri, J., 1965a. Cognitive complexity as a function of the significance of the stimulus objects being judged. *Psychol. Rep.,* **16,** 1203–1204.

Miller, H., and Bieri, J., 1965b. End anchor effects in the discriminability of physical and social stimuli. *Psychonomic Sci.,* **3,** 339–340.

Millman, S., 1965. The relationship between anxiety, learning and opinion change. Unpublished doctoral dissertation, Columbia University.

O'Donovan, D., 1965. Rating extremity: Pathology or meaningfulness? *Psychol. Rev.,* **72,** 358–372.

Postman, L., 1953. The experimental analysis of motivational factors in perception. In *Current theory and research in motivation*. Lincoln, Nebr.: Univ. of Nebr. Press.

Prentice, N. M., 1957. The influence of ethnic attitudes on reasoning about ethnic groups. *J. abnorm. soc. Psychol.,* **55,** 270–272.

Rappaport, D., 1957. Cognitive structures. In *Contemporary approaches to cognition*. Cambridge, Mass.: Harvard Univ. Press.

Rappaport, D., 1959. The structure of psychoanalytic theory: A systematizing attempt. In S. Koch (Ed.), *Psychology: A study of a science*. Vol. III. New York: McGraw-Hill.

Rule, B. R., 1966. Anti-semitism, stress, and judgments of strangers. *J. Pers. soc. Psychol.,* **3,** 132–134.

Schachter, S. S., 1964. The interaction of cognitive and physiological determinants of emotional state. In L. Berkowitz (Ed.), *Advances in experimental social psychology*. Vol. 1. New York: Academic.

Sherif, C. W., Sherif, M., and Nebergall, R. E., 1965. *Attitude and attitude change: The social judgment-involvement approach*. Philadelphia: Saunders.

Sherif, M., and Hovland, C. I., 1961. *Social judgment: assimilation and contrast effects in communication and attitude change*. New Haven: Yale Univ. Press.

Singer, A., 1965. Anchor effects on mean judgments and latitudes of acceptance under varying conditions of involvement and discrepancy. Unpublished doctoral dissertation, Columbia University.

Spence, K. W., Taylor, J. A., and Ketchel, R., 1956. Anxiety (drive) level and degree of competition in paired-associates learning. *J. exp. Psychol.,* **52,** 306–310.

Stevens, S. S., 1966. A metric for social consensus. *Science,* **151,** 530–541.

Storms, L. H., and Broen, W. E., 1966. Drive theories and stimulus generalization. *Psychol. Rev.,* **73,** 113–127.

Thisthlewaite, D., 1950. Attitude and structure as factors in the distortion of reasoning. *J. abnorm. soc. Psychol.,* **45,** 442–458.

Tolman, E. C., 1948. Cognitive maps in rats and men. *Psychol. Rev.*, **55**, 189–208.

Ward, C. D., 1965. Ego involvement and the absolute judgment of attitude statements. *J. Pers. soc. Psychol.*, **2**, 202–208.

Weiner, B., 1966. Effects of motivation on the availability and retrieval of memory traces. *Psychol. Bull.*, **65**, 24–37.

Zavalloni, M., and Cook, S. W., 1965. Influence of judges' attitudes on ratings of favorableness of statements about a social group. *J. Pers. soc. Psychol.*, **1**, 43–54.

11. Conceptual Systems and Attitude Change*

O. J. Harvey

Among their many effects, an individual's more central concepts direct him toward efforts at making and keeping his world consonant with these concepts. Serving as a kind of evaluative prism or yardstick in terms of which the impinging world is rendered relevant, coded and processed into psychological significance (Sherif and Cantril, 1947; Harvey, 1965; Harvey, Hunt, and Schroder, 1961), they dispose the individual not only toward selective, channelized, and often distorted perception and thought but also, wittingly and unwittingly, toward attempts at shaping or modifying the social environment to accord with them.

The degree of subjective correspondence between an individual's central concepts and his personally relevant environment is a major determinant of the quality and intensity of motivational arousal he experiences. Confirmation of one's self-relevant concepts, the perception of congruity between them and related aspects of his environment, tends to result in positive affect, including feelings of success, positive regard toward the self and toward other persons and objects included in the congruous relationship. Refutation of the same concepts, on the other hand, tends to produce the opposite hedonic and behavioral effects (Harvey, 1962, 1965; Harvey, Hunt, and Schroder, 1961; Harvey, Kelley and Shapiro, 1957; Hunt, 1963).

* Most of the research discussed in this chapter has been supported by the Group Psychology Branch, Office of Naval Research, under Contract Nonr 2149(02) with Vanderbilt University initially and since 1958 under Contract Nonr 1147(07) with the University of Colorado. My sincere thanks are extended to ONR for its support.

Individuals vary, of course, in the nature of the concept-standards to which they strive to match the world, in the amount of correspondence they seek, in both the overt and covert styles of establishing and maintaining such concept-environment accord and hence in their affective and behavioral response to refuting events and situations. Patterned variation among individuals in the *referents* of their central concepts (that is, objects to which they are most strongly committed) and in the *ways they relate to or anchor themselves to these* referents may be taken as key dimensions of, if not synonymous with, the self.

Elsewhere we have referred to the variation among individuals in the referents to which they conceptually link themselves as *content* differences in self-systems and variation in *how* they tie to or relate to these objects as *structural* or *organizational* differences (*e.g.*, Harvey, Hunt, and Schroder, 1961). The purpose of this chapter is to suggest how certain structural and content differences in the more central concepts or self-systems of individuals produce a selectivity and directionality of functioning, which, in turn, determines the kinds of events persons are psychologically opened and closed toward, the kinds of sources and the kinds of approaches that are effective in producing acceptance and rejection of incongruous and aversive events, and the kinds of reactions, including change and related responses, individuals are likely to make to conceptual refutation.

Only a small number of the several studies we have carried out during the past eight years on the effects of variation in content and structural attributes of self-systems have been concerned directly with attitude change and reactions to incongruities. Their relevance can be made more apparent by considering them against the backdrop of the general theory from which we have been working and other results we have obtained.

BASIC ASSUMPTIONS

When facing a situation of personal relevance, an individual will differentiate and integrate it, will somehow structure it and make sense out of it in ways compatible with his motives and subjective ends. Moreover, once in being, an individual's way(s) of ordering, or concept(s), seem to possess as a salient characteristic resistance to change and the tendency to be perpetuated across time and subsequent situations. The tendency toward evolving a way of reading the world and of maintaining it in the face of often discrepant inputs disposes toward a kind cognitive paradox involving conflict between the costs and credits of having the world too highly structured or not having it ordered enough.

Although the environing world would remain a blooming, buzzing confusion, to borrow from James (1890), or probably even in a state of irrelevance and nothingness without concepts (*e.g.*, Harvey, 1965), once a mode of construal becomes established it tends to preclude seeking or acceptance of other definitional possibilities.

> Perceiving, thinking, judging and related activities are profoundly affected by—perhaps even wholly dependent upon—a pre-established system of ordering or conceptual placement. . . . And yet this very dependence on a system of categories leads to a kind of conceptual closedness, reflected in a functional blindness to alternative evaluations that are not embodied in the conceptual framework employed at the moment (Harvey and Beverly, 1961, p. 25).

James expressed a related notion in his "law of inhibition of instincts by habits": "When objects of a certain class elicit from an animal a certain sort of reaction, it often happens that the animal becomes partial to the first specimen of the class on which it has reacted, and will not afterward react on any other specimen" (James, 1890, Vol. 2, p. 394).

Such "tunnel vision" and resistance to all but a limited band of environmental impingements by both man and infrahuman animal have been "explained" by several somewhat related but considerably different theories. Four of these, which I have described in some detail elsewhere (Harvey, 1965), are (1) field theory and thermodynamics, (2) homeostasis and wisdom of the body, (3) cortical stimulation, and (4) maintenance of self and a system of meaning.

The tenet from field theory of greatest relevance to the present question is that all systems are endowed with inherent organizational tendencies which dispose toward the evolution of stable parts and toward the establishment and maintenance of a state of equilibrium or synchrony among them. Incursion from external sources or malfunctioning of some intrasystem element upsets the balanced state and produces states of tension and mobilization toward restoration of equilibrium and harmony. Based on the notion of inherency and closed systems, this physicalistic assumption makes no allowance for the possibility of systems differences, of individuals or social entities, in either the conditions that produce imbalance and disequilibrium or in the responses systems make to such states. Nor, because it is considered by its adherents to start at the irreducible level, does this assumption consider the instrumental utility of the tendency toward equilibrium other than by implication that disequilibrium is uncomfortable and motivates the system toward its reduction.

Closely related to field theory is the notion of homeostasis introduced by Claude Bernard and popularized by Cannon and Richter. Cannon quotes Bernard as having said: "It is the fixity of the *milieu interieur* which is the condition of the free and independent life. . . . all the vital mechanisms, however varied they may be, have only one object, that of preserving conditions of life in the internal environment" (Cannon, 1932, p. 38). On the basis of his own impressive and extensive work (*e.g.*, Richter, 1927; 1936; 1942; Richter and Eckert, 1939) and that of Cannon (1932) and others, Richter concluded that ". . . in human beings and animals the effort to maintain a constant internal environment or homeostasis constitutes one of the most universal and powerful of all behavior urges or drives" (Richter as quoted in P. T. Young, 1961, p. 113). As this drive came to be construed, its operation meant that, because of some innate "wisdom of the body", to borrow from Cannon, the organism always acted in ways most compatible with his welfare and survival, an assumption that is not in accord with the maladaptive behavior of man and lower animals under certain conditions.

Since Hebb's *Organization of Behavior* (1949) it has become more prevalent to view organisms as disposed toward maintenance of habituated tendencies through the maintenance of some more or less standardized and optimal level of cortical activity (Fiske and Maddi, 1961; Berlyne, 1960; Hebb, 1955; Glanzer, 1958). Too much deviation from the optimal level of cortical arousal and too marked a departure from what the organism is accustomed to and has come to expect, toward either too much or too little stimulation, is assumed to result in negative reaction to the input and avoidance of the conditions that produced the affect or with which it has become associated.

A fourth "explanation" of the tendency to maintain habitual modes of construing certain bands or domains of stimulus events centers around the concept of self and the relationship of such maintenance to it. It is this last rationale which I find more relevant to such questions as those involved in attitude change and negative responses to deviant events.

An individual's conceptual system(s), the totality of his ties to and definitions of the world, may be equated with the self (Harvey, 1963b; Harvey, Hunt, and Schroder, 1961). Thus refutation of or threat to one's definitional matrix would be equivalent to threat to the self, would portend negation of the personal instrument through which an individual predicts recurrences and consistencies in his environment and, if severe enough, would impair the ability to "read" the situation with the necessary degree of veridicality for need satisfaction and survival.

To do no more than equate self and totality of concepts, however, would be simply a game in labeling and would lead to no more specific statements than can be generated from the notions of inherency embodied in thermodynamics and homeostasis. The problem of such generality and simplicity is overcome, on the other hand, if such a superordinate construct as the self is characterized and dimensionalized in ways such that variation in these dimensions vary appropriately with the end product to which prediction is being made. This is a requirement that neither psychoanalysis nor dissonance theory, both of which represent offshoots of thermodynamics and field theory, has adequately satisfied. The occurrence of either the positive or "mirror image" of certain responses is sufficient to confirm psychoanalytic notions; "reaction formation," the negative version of a response, provides as much theoretical "proof" as the positive version. For dissonance theorists, the occurrence of a certain response is interpreted as evidence for theoretically proper resolution of dissonance whereas the absence of such a response is interpreted as dissonance not having been induced in the first place.

STRUCTURAL VARIATION: DIFFERENCES
IN CONCRETENESS-ABSTRACTNESS

Of the many structural attributes of conceptual systems, our concentration has been on concreteness-abstractness, a quality of *how* the individual articulates and organizes his concepts of relevant aspects of his environment (Harvey, Hunt, and Schroder, 1961; Harvey and Schroder, 1963). Concreteness-abstractness, as we have characterized and validated the construct, refers to a superordinate conceptual dimension encompassing such more molecular organizational properties as the degree of differentiation, articulation, integration, and centrality of the cognitive elements. Being more generic and qualitative, variation in concreteness-abstractness rests upon differences in patterning or organization and not in differences in algebraic quantity of these subordinate characteristics. Different syndromes of interpretive, affective, and behavioral tendencies accompany or underlie concrete and abstract functioning.

More concrete functioning is expressed at the behavioral level by high stimulus-response requiredness, the extreme of which could be illustrated by such one-to-one correspondence as that between the stimulus of a light and the taxic response of a moth. More abstract functioning, on the other hand, because of a more enriched and complex mediational system and a greater ability to transcend and depart from the immediate and perceptual characteristics of the impingements, results in less absolutism, that is, greater relativism in thought and action.

From a series of studies we have found greater concreteness, in contrast to greater abstractness, to be manifested in several ways, including:

1. A simpler cognitive structure, comprised of fewer differentiations and more incomplete integrations within more central and ego-involving domains *but not within domains of low involvement* (Harvey, 1966; Harvey, Wyer, and Hautaluoma, 1963; Harvey, Reich, and Wyer, 1966).

2. A greater tendency toward more extreme and more polarized evaluations, namely, good-bad, right-wrong, black-white (Adams, Harvey, and Heslin, 1966; Campbell, 1960; Ware and Harvey, 1966; White and Harvey, 1965).

3. A greater dependence on status and authority-related cues as guidelines to belief and action (Crockett, 1958; Harvey, 1964; Harvey and Beverly, 1961; Tiemann, 1965; Kritzberg, 1965; Harvey, 1966).

4. A greater intolerance of ambiguity expressed in higher scores on such measures as the F Scale and Dogmatism Scale and in the tendency to form judgments of novel situations more quickly (Harvey, 1966; Reich, 1966).

5. A greater need for or tendency toward cognitive consistency and greater arousal and change from the experience of cognitive dissonance (Harvey, 1965; Ware and Harvey, 1967; Harvey and Ware, 1966).

6. A greater inability to change set and hence greater stereotypy in the solution of more complex and changing problems (Felknor and Harvey, 1963; Harvey, 1966; Reich, 1966; Harvey and Ware, 1966).

7. A poorer delineation between means and ends and hence a paucity of different methods of solving a problem or achieving a goal (Harvey, 1966).

8. A greater insensitivity to subtle and minimal cues and hence a greater susceptibility to false but obtrusive cues (Harvey, 1966).

9. A poorer capacity to "act as if," to assume the role of the other, or to think and act in terms of a hypothetical situation (Harvey, 1963a; Harvey and Kline, 1965).

10. The holding of opinions with greater strength and certainty that the opinions will not change with time (Hoffmeister, 1965).

11. A higher score on the factor of dictatorialness reflected in such behavioral characteristics as high need for structure, low flexibility, high rule orientation, high dictation of procedure, high frequency of the usage of unexplained rules, high punitiveness, low diversity of activities and low encouragement of individual responsibility (Harvey, White, Prather, Alter, and Hoffmeister, 1966).

12. A lower score on the factor of task orientation (Harvey, White, Prather, Alter, and Hoffmeister, 1966).

13. A greater tendency to form and generalize impressions of other people from highly incomplete information (Ware and Harvey, 1967).

Greater abstractness has been found to accompany reverse quantities on the above dimensions.

CONTENT DIFFERENCES IN CONCEPTUAL SYSTEMS

In the process of achieving its goals, evolving and transmitting its values, each society comes to delineate and formally or informally codify the referents or social objects of greatest significance to it. Differences in such referents, through their reciprocal influence upon and influence from social norms, are among the attributes that differentiate most sharply among societies.

Although membership in a given society disposes toward a common content in the conceptual or self-systems of the members (this being fairly synonymous with what has traditionally been referred to as the social self), variation exists among individual members in their *personal ordering of significance* of these referents. Some referents of socially designated significance are thus more central to some individuals whereas other individuals commit themselves more strongly to other social objects.

Although the content and structure of self-systems are theoretically independent, we have generated a set of developmental assumptions that led to our positing a high relationship between an individual's level of abstractness and the content of his *more central* concepts. It should be stressed that such a relationship is assumed *not to obtain for concept referents of low centrality and involvement.* In support of this assumption, the results of several of our experiments in which involvement was varied have made it clear that system differences such as those to be noted later *hold for the higher but not the lower levels of involvement or centrality.*

Specific Self-Systems

From the interaction between conceptual content and structure several patterns may be theoretically deduced in which the tendency to make certain objects central is accompanied by a particular level of concreteness-abstractness. Although in our earlier work (Harvey, Hunt, and Schroder, 1961), several such patterns or self-systems were deduced, my major theoretical and research interest has centered around the four summarized below.

System 1. This most concrete mode of relating to and construing the world best fits the description of concrete functioning described earlier. It is assumed to evolve from a developmental history in which the individual has been restricted in the exploration of that part of his world concerned with values, power relations, and social causality. Along with minimal exposure to diversity in these domains, the rewards and punishments of the developing individual and his feelings of acceptance as a "good person" have been contingent upon his ideas and approaches to problems conforming catechismically to the omnipotently and omnisciently imposed standards of the parent or controlling authority. More than any other method of inculcation, the socialization techniques surrounding system 1 development follows the conditioning model of S-R psychology, generating concepts through trial and error and fostering the internalization of values without insight and the ritualistic adherence to rules without understanding. System 1 functioning consequently manifests itself in such characteristics as high superstition, high religiosity, high absolutism and closedness of beliefs, high evaluativeness, high *positive* ties with and dependence on representatives of institutional authority—especially those of more nearly unimpeachable validity, such as God and religion—high identification with social roles and status positions, high conventionality, and high ethnocentrism or strong beliefs that American values should be adopted as a model by the rest of the world.

System 2. This self-system, somewhat more abstract than system 1, is thought to result from experience with an authority who, in addition to acting omnipotently and omnisciently, is also capricious in the control of rewards and punishments, administering these in such unpredictable fashions that the child (or any other recipient for that matter) is always unsure of the course of action that will enhance positive feedback and minimize the chances of punishment and rejection. Owing to their failure to provide any stable or predictable guidelines in an unstructured world, such vacilating practices present the developing child with diversity far in excess of the optimal. Although such variation in treatment tends to result in higher abstractness than in system 1 because of rejection of authority and consequent forced independence, it also produces deep feelings of uncertainty, distrust of authority, and rebellion against the more socially approved guides of behavior. System 2 representatives, more than persons of any of the other self-systems, seem to be in a psychological vacuum, guided more by rejection of social prescriptions and avoidance of dependency on God and other representations of institutional authority that serve as positive guides for system 1 than by positive adherence to personally derived standards.

System 3. This mode of functioning is next to the highest level of abstractness treated by Harvey, Hunt, and Schroder (1961). It is assumed to be the consequence of overindulgence by one or both parents, which, by preventing exploration of the physical world and by encouraging manipulation of the parents, produces in the developing child inflated notions of esteem and social power alongside the feeling of inability to cope with problems except by the control of others through dependency. Because of their domination of their parent(s), representatives of this system are much less oriented toward institutional power and authority than either persons from system 1, with their attitudes of deference and acquiescence, or individuals from system 2, with their orientation of negative independence and social rebellion. System 3 representatives, more than representatives of any of the other systems, are concerned with establishing friendships, intragroup consensus and dependency relations in order to avert the feeling of helplessness and social isolation that would result from being forced to be on their own. Through the use of highly developed skills of manipulation, particularly through exploitation of dependencies, system 3 functioning tends to favor success in effecting desired outcomes in the social sphere.

System 4. The most abstract of the four systems, this mode of construal and behaving is viewed as the consequence of childhood freedom to explore both the social and physical aspects of one's own experience and thought and to solve problems and evolve solutions without fear of punishment for deviating from established truth and the social imperatives. This developmental history eventuates in a high task orientation, information seeking, exploratory behavior, risk taking, and independence.

In summary, system 1 is characterized by the lowest level of abstractness and a positive orientation toward extrapersonal referents, such as God and institutional authority. System 2 is slightly more abstract and negatively oriented toward the same social objects. System 3 is next to the highest in abstractness and is oriented toward establishing and maintaining intragroup consensus as a step toward dependency and control of others. And system 4 is the most abstract, more impersonal, and more oriented toward information seeking and problem solving for intrinsic rather than extrinsic rewards.

An understanding of the specific functioning of the four systems may be enhanced by a description of the method by which we have assessed them.

MEASURES OF CONCEPTUAL OR SELF-SYSTEMS

Several scales exist which, singly or in some combination, can be used as a measure of a facet of one or more of the systems.

For example, the F Scale, as well as other measures of authoritarianism, provides a fairly reliable measure of system 1 functioning but not of the other systems. Although F scores correlate highly with the system 1 orientation, a low F score does not correlate very highly with the orientation of system 4 because low scorers on F are comprised of both system 4 and system 2 representatives. Before developing a more appropriate measure of conceptual systems, we did employ the F Scale, however, as one measure of concrete functioning. Some of the results to be discussed later were obtained through use of this instrument.

Rokeach's Dogmatism (D) Scale (1960) correlates significantly with the dimension of abstractness but does not sufficiently distinguish effectively between systems. A combination of the F and D Scales discriminates more accurately among systems than does either instrument alone. With scores from both scales split into high, middle, and low thirds, system 1 subjects tend to fall in the cell of high authoritarianism-high dogmatism, system 2 individuals to be in the cell of low authoritarianism-high dogmatism, system 3 representatives to fall in the middle authoritarianism-middle dogmatism group, and system 4 persons to fall in the cell of low authoritarianism-low dogmatism.

We have developed two instruments specifically as measures of conceptual systems. The "This I Believe" Test, a semiprojective sentence completion test, has been used most extensively and successfully. The Conceptual Systems Test is an objective scale only recently developed and still being perfected and validated.

The This I Believe (TIB) Test

This instrument aims at providing a basis of dimensionalizing an individual's more central concepts or beliefs according to the criteria implicit in the characterization of the four systems. Thus the sentences to be completed have to do with significant personal and social referents. Subjects are asked to indicate their beliefs about these referents by completing in two or three sentences the phrase; "This I believe about ———," the blank being replaced successively by one of the following referents: friendship, the American way of life, guilt, marriage, myself, religion, sin, majority opinion, people, compromise, the future, and the past. As can be seen, some of these referents are relevant mainly to one system whereas the relevance of others is more general.

As detailed in earlier publications (Harvey, 1964; 1965; 1966; Ware and Harvey, 1966; White and Harvey, 1965), the completions are scored both in terms of their positive and their negative orientations toward the referents and their absolutism evaluativeness, multiplicity of alternatives, triteness, and normativeness. In the more than 30 studies in which it has been used at the University of Colorado and other universities, the TIB has been found to predict accurately and reliably to a wide range of both paper and pencil tests and experimentally induced behavior. Many of these between-systems differences from tests and behavioral situations have been described elsewhere (Harvey, 1966).

The Conceptual Systems Test (CST)

The items in the CST were derived form statements made by subjects in their completions of the TIB and from certain other tests purporting to measure personality aspects related to dimensions of conceptual systems. Factor analysis of each of the five revisions of the CST by Tryon's method of cluster analysis (Tryon and Bailey, 1965; 1966) has yielded seven theoretically meaningful and replicated factors from the five independent samples of respondents. These factors, as we have tentatively labeled them, together with some of their representative items, are:

1. *Divine Fate Control (DFC)* is assessed by such items as, "There are some things which God will never permit man to know," "In

the final analysis, events in the world will be in line with the master plan of God," and "I believe that to attain my goals it is only necessary for me to live as God would have me live."

2. *Need for Simplicity-Consistency* (*NS-C*) is inferred from response to such statements as "I dislike having to change my plans in the middle of a task," "It is annoying to listen to a lecturer who cannot seem to make up his mind as to what he really believes," and "A group which tolerates extreme differences of opinion among its own members cannot exist for long."

3. *Need for Structure-Order* (*NS-O*) is derived from such items as "I don't like to work on a problem unless there is a possibility of coming out with a clear-cut, definite answer," "I don't like for things to be uncertain and unpredictable," and "I like to have a place for everything and everything in its place."

4. *Distrust of Social Authority* (*DSO*) is tapped by such items as "Most public officials are really interested in the poor man's problems" (negatively loaded), "Government officials are as interested in serving the poor as others" (negatively loaded), and "A lot of people in positions of respect don't deserve as much respect as they receive."

5. *Friendship Absolutism* (*FA*) is assessed by such statements as "I do not enjoy arguing with my friends," "I cannot believe that a friend of mine could be guilty of stealing," and "Sometimes I don't like any of my friends" (negatively loaded).

6. *Moral Absolutism* (*MA*) is revealed through answer to such items as "I think I am stricter about right and wrong than most people," "Friendship is of greater value than adhering to a morally righteous cause" (negatively loaded), and "It is less important to get along with others than to follow a code of conduct."

7. *General Pessimism* (*GP*) is measured by such items as "The world is run by a few people in power and there isn't much one can do about it," "Most people don't really care what happens to the other fellow," and "You sometimes can't help wondering whether anything is worthwhile anymore."

The mean score of each of the four systems, as measured by the TIB, on each of these CST factors is presented in Figure 11.1. It can be seen that these system profiles conform closely to the theoretical attributes described earlier.

Self Systems and Attitude Change

With the self systems depicted, we can now turn briefly to the question of how their variation relates to each of two related facets

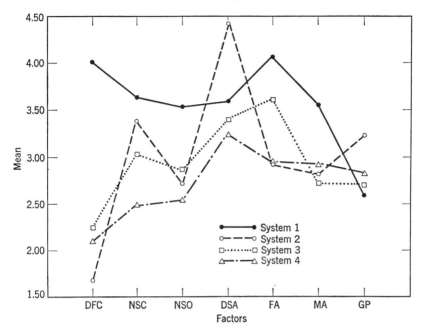

Figure 11.1 Mean score of each system as determined by TIB on the Conceptual Systems Test. °DFC is divine fate control; NSC is need for simplicity-consistency; NSO is need for structure-order; DSA is distrust of social authority; FA is friendship absolutism; MA is moral absolutism; GP is general pessimism.

of attitude change: (1) source characteristics and behavior that foster change, and (2) responses in addition to or in lieu of change evoked by conceptual refutation and/or attempts at change.

Characteristics of an effective source. The descriptions of system 1 imply that if a source is to be a "significant other" in the eyes of system 1 representatives and if he can influence them in a direction counter to their own beliefs, he must be of high formal status, behave in accordance with clear-cut role definitions and issue highly structured and rule-oriented messages.

In line with this hypothesis, Crockett (1958) found more authoritarian soldiers to prefer more autocratic leaders. And in an unreported study, Harvey found that college students representing system 1, to a greater extent than representatives of the other systems, preferred instructors who were high in academic rank, gave precise and highly structured assignments, made the criteria for grading very explicit, and gave lectures of greater absolutism and simplicity, that is, of fewer contingencies, more "facts," and fewer theoretical interrelationships.

In further accord with this reasoning are the findings from several experiments that authoritarianism tends to be positively correlated with attitude change (*e.g.*, Crutchfield, 1955; Wagman, 1955; Christie and Cook, 1958; Titus and Hollander, 1957; Harvey, 1963c; Harvey and Beverly, 1961, Wright and Harvey, 1965). Significantly, the relationship between authoritarianism and attitude change holds only for a high status source. As we have suggested, "Authoritarianism is positively related to opinion change when the source of the incongruous input is of high status and the target concept is of low involvement. But it is negatively related to change when the source is of low status, and the target concept is of high involvement" (Wright and Harvey, 1965, p. 180). Presumably for the same reason—that is, warding off conflicting inputs from all but a high status source—authoritarianism relates negatively to change in concepts of heaviness of weights and distance between lights produced by discrepant anchor weights and lights (Harvey, 1963c).

Evidence that an autocratic approach is more effective than its counterpart in producing concept change among more authoritarian individuals is provided in an experiment by Wright and Harvey (1965). Subjects varying in authoritarianism were tested on their attitudes toward several referents, following which they were criticized to the point of derogation by a high status source (their instructor) and retested.

> With the exception of the ratings of professions, upon which derogation occurred, persons high on authoritarianism were high on pretreatment dependent variable scores and became still higher after treatment. Persons low in authoritarianism remained low on the dependent variable or became still lower. . . . Instead of a displacement theory, as suggested by Adorno, et al. (1950), these results suggest that high authoritarianism disposes one toward expecting (and accepting as proper) extreme treatment from authority. Rather than frustration and negative affect, it appears such treatment may result in the opposite effects for more authoritarian individuals (Wright and Harvey, 1965, p. 180).

In a somewhat related experiment, Harvey and Rutherford (1958) found that more authoritarian individuals changed their concepts of light movement more from an absolute than a gradual approach, that is, from an approach in which the source made all of his judgments differ a fixed amount from those of the subject instead of first making his judgments match those of the subject and then gradually deviating from them.

That authoritarianism sensitizes an individual toward formal status and power rather than information may be inferred from the study by Harvey and Beverly (1961). Following refutation of their preassessed attitudes toward alcohol by a high status and powerful source, subjects varying in authoritarianism were asked to reproduce the main arguments the speaker (who was both their instructor and minister of their church) had made in favor of alcohol. Despite changing their opinion more in the direction of the communication, the more authoritarian subjects were able to reproduce fewer of the speaker's points than were the persons lower in authoritarianism. Thus the more authoritarian individuals appear to have changed their opinions more because of the status of the source than from their grasp of the reasons he advanced for change.

Although four of our experiments have shown that formal status is a characteristic of differential significance to individuals of the four systems (Harvey, 1963a; 1964; Kritzberg, 1965; Tiemann, 1965), only one study has been concerned directly with systems' influence on source effectiveness. In that study (Harvey, 1964) representatives of each of the four self systems, among other tasks, judged the contents of 16 projected slides of varying clarity following exposure to a prerecorded narration that described the contents of each slide in a general way. The contents of the *nine more ambiguous* slides were incorrectly depicted whereas the contents of the seven slides of *greater clarity* were correctly described. The narration accompanying the projection of the slides was attributed to either an undergraduate student interested in photography (*low status* source) or to a professor of psychology interested in the slides as experimental stimuli (*high status* source). As hypothesized, the number of incorrect descriptions accepted in identification of the slides under the high status condition was greater for system 1 than any other system.

The assumed history of concept acquisition by system 1 representatives, especially of those concepts representing more central values and beliefs, suggests several important leads as to the most effective approach for modifying the more central concepts of these individuals. If indeed these concepts have been acquired through ways that approximate the S-R conditioning model, as we proposed earlier, then this basic behavioristic assumption may be applied to deduce notions of conceptual, or at least behavioral, modification. One obvious implication is that—since individuals of system 1 have only rudimentary mediational linkages between stimulus impingements and response, their connections between S and R are more of classical conditioning than of insight learning, and they are more autonomic and affective than central—such persons would not be receptive to an informational approach to change of their central concepts. On the other hand, they should be more receptive to an approach that relies on deconditioning or some other application of S-R theory aimed at lessening the affective strength of the S-R bond. This could be done, theoretically, by repeated pairing of the emotion producing stimulus with the response under conditions in which the autonomic system was not aroused. Repeated presentation of the stimulus unaccompanied by the reinforcement of negative affect could lead the individual to more freely explore the formerly negative object and to accept different definitions of it. Role playing and the use of tranquilizer-type drugs may provide ways of bypassing or neutralizing the autonomic system of the more concrete individual and through so doing of allowing him to engage central processes and become more receptive to an informational approach. One vein of our research hopes to pursue these possibilities.

Systems 2, 3, and 4 will be considered together because of the paucity of data specifically relevant to the question of what kind of source characteristics are most effective for each of these systems. Since, as noted earlier, both systems 2 and 4 score low on authoritarianism scales, the responses of the low authoritarians, in contrast to the high authoritarians considered in the preceding section, cast little light on either system 2 or 4.

The earlier depiction of system 2 would indicate a negative orientation toward authority sources by its representatives and presumably a negative weighting by them of cues emanating from authority. In line with this and presumably reflective of the fear and distrust of authority, system 2 individuals performed the most poorly of the four systems on a role-playing task under the instruction that their performance was to be evaluated by a curriculum committee from the university (Harvey, 1963a); but when led to believe no one, including the experimenter, would ever hear how they played the role, these same individuals out-performed individuals of both systems 1 and 3. In the study noted earlier (Harvey, 1964), in which no mention was made of the possibility of their performance being evaluated by an authority person, system 2 representatives were significantly more influenced by a low status than by a high status source in the number of incorrect descriptions of the slides they accepted, the opposite of system 1. As will be noted later, whether the system 2 individual adheres to or rejects suggestions from authority depends to a great extent upon the degree of fate control the authority has over him and whether the response occurs in the presence or absence of authority surveillance.

The study that found representatives of systems 1 and 2 to be strongly influenced by the status of the source in their acceptance of falsely depicted slides found individuals from systems 3 and 4 to be only slightly influenced.

> The acceptance of false descriptions by System 3 individuals, high under the low authority condition, was only slightly increased under the high authority variation; and System 4 representatives, who accepted a relatively low number of false depictions under the low authority condition, accepted only a fraction more under the high authority treatment (Harvey, 1964, p. 220).

Another part of the same study suggests that system 3 individuals are more susceptible to peer groups than to authority influences. Representatives of each of the four systems, in addition to being asked to identify the contents of the 16 slides, judged the distance between 12 pairs of dots, first in the presence of a falsely calibrated but authentic appearing ruler, and then in the absence of the ruler but with knowledge of the judgments of two other members of a temporary triad. Judgments in the social context were made under instructions that either made no reference to conformity or specifically depicted the experiment as one in conformity. As predicted, the degree of social influence, as measured by the difference between an individual's judgment before and after group discussion, was greatest for system 3 in the condition that made no reference to conformity. This finding is consistent with other findings that system 3 individuals score higher than representatives of the other systems on need for affiliation, as assessed both by French's scale and Edward's Personal Preference Schedule.

As a partial aside, it may be noted that specific reference to the experiment as a study in conformity reduced the social influence only slightly on systems 1, 3, and 4 but lessened it markedly on representatives of system 2, implying a greater tendency toward negative independence on the part of these last individuals.

A second experiment relevant to the interaction of source characteristics and self systems is that of Adams, Harvey, and Heslin (1966). In a study aimed at telescoping developmental histories, representatives of each of the four systems were hypnotized, their own pasts removed through suggestion, and one of the four childhood pasts assumed to accompany each system of functioning was hypnotically implanted. Subjects performed the same tasks under each of the four hypnotic sets or pasts. The one task aimed at measuring social influenceability required each subject, as in Sherif's early experiment (1935), to form a personal norm of autokinetic movement by first judging the phenomenon alone, then to judge the movements in the presence of discrepant judgments by Dr. Brainard, a source of both formal status and expertise, and lastly to judge again the movement of the light alone.

Because of their assumed experience of controlling authority more than being controlled by it, representatives of system 3 were the least influenced of the four systems when judging in the presence of Dr. Brainard; and because of their assumed positive orientation toward expertise, system 4 individuals were the most influenced by Brainard's judgments. We conjectured that if the source

> had been depicted as a policeman, minister, judge, or a representative of an institutionalized position, it is likely that subjects would have been significantly more influenced by his judgments under the System 1 than under the System 2 induction. Moreover, it is also likely that had the source been of the latter variety, without special accomplishments or expertise in the particular area, subjects under the System 4 set would have been influenced appreciably less by his judgment (Adams, *et al.*, 1966, p. 232).

CHANGE AND OTHER RESPONSES
TO CONCEPTUAL REFUTATION

Until fairly recently, the tendency among researchers in attitude change was to concentrate on the effects of their treatment on the one dependent variable of change in the target concept. Increased movement toward the use of a multivariate rather than a single-variable approach has made it clear, however, that significant effects other than or in addition to change may occur as the result of a concept-event incongruity. This, the last section of this chapter will concentrate on systems differences in such reactions.

"Warding off" Behavior and Other Instances of Selectivity

Presumably any system—biological, conceptual or social—will attempt to ward off or in some way transform events and impingements that are too incompatible with it in the direction of greater system-event accord. However, systems of the same order differ in their tolerance of deviant events and hence in their thresholds for warding off such impingements as well as in the particular response they make when the threshold is surpassed. The empirical evidence we have on this general question relates primarily to more concrete and more abstract functioning. Therefore, comparisons will be made only between systems 1 and 4 throughout the remainder of this chapter.

One of the more reliable indices of an individual's threshold for warding-off behavior is the extent to which he notes the disparity or distorts it to fit some other category. In several studies we have found greater concreteness, as measured both by scales of authoritarianism and the TIB Test, to correlate positively with the tendency to keep negative inputs out of the self system through minimizing the discrepancy between the subject's target concept and the evaluation from the source, *if* the source is of high status in the eyes of the subject and the concept is of high involvement. Thus, although scores from the F Scale correlated positively with change in concept of autokinetic movement produced by discrepant judgments from a planted source, they correlated positively with the tendency to minimize the discrepancy by underestimating the difference between own and source's judgments. Similarly, scores from the scale of Webster, Sanford and Freedman (1955) correlated positively with change in concept toward alcohol produced by a contradictory communication from an unimpeachable authority source and positively with minimization of the distance between own position and source's assertions. Additionally, scores from the scale of Webster *et al.* (1955) correlated negatively with changes in concepts both toward self and toward source but positively with the tendency to minimize the self-source discrepancy by favorable distortion in recall of the negative evaluations of the self. Moreover, higher authoritarianism was found to dispose the individual toward other behaviors aimed at neutralizing or minimizing the effects of negation of concepts about the self: (*a*) toward lowering his estimates of how well the source of the negative evaluations actually knew him; (*b*) toward denying the source had any reason to be angry at him; and (*c*) toward expressing certainty that the source actually had not made the negative evaluations he had received of himself (Harvey, 1962; 1963c).

When the "source" of a concept-input discrepancy is an inanimate psychophysical anchor instead of a conflicting judgment or evaluation from another person of high status, authoritarianism correlates with the tendency to maximize rather than minimize the concept-event difference. Thus, although scores from the F Scale correlated negatively with changes in the concepts of distance between lights and heaviness of weights produced by discrepant anchor lights and weights, they correlated positively with overestimation of the magnitude of both kinds of anchors.

In another study, concerned mainly with systems differences in dependency on external cues (Harvey, 1964), representatives of the four self systems, as measured by the TIB Test, judged the distance between pairs of dots in the presence of an authentic appearing but falsely scaled ruler (a 15-inch ruler that was made to appear as a typical 12-inch ruler). Of the 124 subjects, all but two, both system 4 individuals, relied upon the ruler to some extent in making their judgments. The magnitude of this reliance differed markedly, however, across systems. System 4 representatives were influenced significantly less than any other system whereas System 1 individuals were influenced next to the least.

The bases for lessened influence on systems 1 and 4, however, appear to be very different. After completing their judgments, subjects were administered a short questionnaire which asked: "In making your estimates of the distance between the dots, how did you react to the ruler? (a) Tried not to look at it; (b) looked at it and consciously used it; and (c) looked at it but did not consciously use it." Sixty-one percent of System 1 subjects reported trying to exclude the ruler from their vision while only 16 percent of System 4 individuals so reported. At the same time, only 11 percent of System 1 representatives indicated that they were aware of the ruler but did not rely on it, while 73 percent of System 4 subjects so reported. These results were interpreted as "suggesting that System 1 functioning disposes toward system or belief maintenance through the exclusion of potentially conflicting inputs, while System 4 functioning disposes toward system maintenance through admission of incongruous events and consideration of them without undue influence by them" (Harvey, 1966, p. 60).

One further, indirect, index of a system's receptivity to alien and discrepant inputs is its tolerance of inconsistency among its elements. The more abstract system, presumably because of greater internal differentiation and integration, should be more able to withstand more conflict and inconsistency than the concrete system before beginning to ward off and transform the impingements. Three of our experiments have found this to be so. Harvey (1963a) and Harvey and Kline (1965) found system 1 individuals exposed themselves to less cognitive conflict than system 4 persons through a poorer performance of a role that involved arguing against their own beliefs on involving issues. At the same time, however, despite their exposure to less dissonance, the system 1 individuals changed their opinions more than representatives of system 4. Along the same lines, Harvey and Ware (1966) found that while system 1 subjects were more unwilling than system 4 individuals to attribute positive and negative characteristics to the same person simultaneously, they were also more negatively aroused at evidence that the same person could possess both socially desirable and undesirable attributes.

The evidence seems quite clear that concreteness disposes toward conceptual closedness and a tendency to ward off deviant inputs through minimization, denial, distortion, and reevaluation of the discrepant events. Failing in keeping such conflict out of the system, this same characteristic disposes toward resolving the internal conflict or dissonance through change.

Response under Surveillance and Nonsurveillance Conditions

A factor of obvious theoretical significance to the issue of the influence of one person on another is the degree of fate control that one individual holds over another, that is, the extent to which he can control the rewards and punishments or successes and failures of the other along lines relevant to the other. How variation in the fate control of a source over the recipient of his suggestions or evaluations affects his effectiveness is largely an unexplored question. Yet it is very likely that the tendency of some individuals to adhere to a source's judgments under surveillance conditions, that is, when the source is either present or likely later to have the opportunity to evaluate the subject's performance, and to depart from the source's judgments under nonsurveillance conditions is at least partially attributable to the source's fate control over the subject.

According to our theorizing throughout this chapter, individuals of systems 1 and 2 have been the recipients of high fate control by representatives of authority. Thus they, more than persons of systems 3 and 4, should show a disparity between their behavior in a surveillance and nonsurveillance situation. In line with this possibility are the findings that subjects of system 1 and especially of system 2 were impaired in their role-playing performance when they believed their arguments would later be evaluated by a university curriculum committee, whereas representatives of systems 3 and 4 were minimally affected by the likelihood of later authority evaluation (Harvey, 1963a). Of even more direct relevance is the results of a facet of the study of hypnotically induced pasts, mentioned above (Adams, et al. 1966), which was addressed directly to this question. Subjects under hypnotically induced systems 1 and 2 reverted back toward the norm of their pre-influence judgments of the autokinetic phenomenon following the departure of the authority source, Dr. Brainard, from the judgmental situation, whereas under the system 3 and system 4 hypnotic sets subjects were as much or more influenced by Brainard's discrepant judgments in his absence as they had been in his presence. That is, there was a disparity between judgments under surveillance and nonsurveillance conditions for systems 1 and 2 but little disparity for systems 3 and 4.

These results suggest, to use a combination of Kelman's (1958) and Festinger's (1953) terminology, that functioning in terms of either system 1 or system 2 disposes the individual toward compliance (that is, conformity to the source's judgments without acceptance of them), and system 3 and system 4 functioning, particularly the latter, disposes toward internalization (that is, adherence to the source's judgments with acceptance) once influence has occurred in the first place.

Continuous versus Discontinuous Response to System-Event Disparities

Without its having been made explicit, theories of attitude change are based on either of two assumptions: that if change occurs it may do so in any gradation, that is, change is continuous; or that change, if it occurs, will be in an either-or, discontinuous fashion.

Most theories of change and reaction to concept refutation are based upon the assumption of response continuity. Those that are not are theories that have sprung directly from notions of field theory and thermodynamics, alluded to in an earlier section of this chapter. Even some of the theories that have evolved from thermodynamics do not assume complete discontinuity in the response repertory of the individual; among these are such theories of balance and consistency as those of Heider (1946; 1958), Newcomb (1961), and others, all of whom allow for the restoration of balance through a kind of fusion of or compromise between the conflicting cognitive elements, such as change toward both the target concept and the source of the disparate event.

The theory based most heavily on the assumption of response discontinuity is Festinger's notion of dissonance (e.g., Festinger, 1957; Brehm and Cohen, 1962). Dissonance exists, according to these theorists, when the existence of one cognitive element implies the obverse of the other. Faced with this polarity of opposites, the respondent is forced to choose one extreme or the other. And once having chosen, the subject is supposed to act in ways to further increase the psychological distance between the former response alternatives by extolling one and derogating the other. Based on notions of inherency and a closed system, dissonance theory makes no allowances for individual differences in response to conceptual conflict.

However, whether an individual responds continuously or discontinuously to conflict in cognitive elements depends, among other things, upon the conceptual system that mediates between input and output and underlies the quality and frequency of response alternatives. Undifferentiated and bifurcated conceptual systems, such as those possessed by more concretely functioning individuals, are likely to eventuate in polarized and discontinuous responses, such as those stressed by dissonance theorists. At the same time, more differentiated conceptual systems, like those of more abstractly functioning persons, provide the bases for fine discriminations and accompanying continuities in response. Thus, it appears that although the assumptions of dissonance theory have some validity for concretely functioning individuals, they are considerably less valid for the more abstractly functioning persons.

REFERENCES

Adams, D. K., Harvey, O. J., and Heslin, R. E., 1966. Variation of flexibility and creativity as a function of hypnotically induced past histories. In O. J. Harvey (Ed.), *Experience, structure and adaptability.* New York: Springer, pp. 217–234.

Adorno, T. W., Frenkel-Brunswik, Else, Levinson, D. J., and Sanford, R. N., 1950. *The authoritarian personality.* New York: Harper.

Berlyne, D. E., 1960. *Conflict, arousal and curiosity.* New York: McGraw-Hill.

Brehm, J. W., and Cohen, A. R., 1962. *Explorations in cognitive dissonance.* New York: Wiley.

Campbell, V. N., 1960. *Assumed similarity, perceived sociometric balance, and social influence.* Doctoral dissertation, Univ. of Col.

Cannon, W. B., 1932. *The wisdom of the body.* New York: Norton.

Christie, R., and Cook, Peggy, 1958. A guide to published literature relating to authoritarian personality through 1956. *J. Psychol.,* **45,** 171–199.

Crockett, E. P., 1958. Authoritarianism and leader acceptance. ONR tech. Rep. No. 5, Vanderbilt Univ.

Crutchfield, R. S., 1955. Conformity and character. *Amer. Psychologist,* **10,** 191–199.

Felknor, Catherine, and Harvey, O. J., 1963. Cognitive determinants of concept formation and attainment. Tech. Rep. No. 10, Contract Nonr 1147(07), Univ. of Col.

Festinger, L., 1953. An analysis of compliant behavior. In M. Sherif and M. O. Wilson (Eds.), *Group relations at the crossroads.* New York: Harper, pp. 232–256.

Festinger, L., 1957. *A theory of cognitive dissonance*. Evanston Ill.: Row, Peterson.

Fiske, D. W., and Maddi, S. R. (Eds.), 1961. *Functions of varied experience*. Homewood, Ill.: Dorsey.

Glanzer, M., 1958. Curiosity, exploratory drive and stimulus satiation. *Psychol. Bull.*, **55**, 302–315.

Harvey, O. J., 1962. Personality factors in resolution of conceptual incongruities. *Sociometry*, **25**, 336–352.

Harvey, O. J., 1963a. Cognitive determinants of role playing. Tech. Rep. No. 3, Contract Nonr 1147(07), Univ. of Col.

Harvey, O. J., 1963b. Current status of the incongruity hypothesis. In O. J. Harvey (Ed.), *Motivation and social interaction*. New York: Ronald pp. 289–300.

Harvey, O. J., 1963c. Authoritarianism and conceptual function in varied conditions. *J. Pers.*, **31**, 462–470.

Harvey, O. J., 1964. Some cognitive determinants of influenceability. *Sociometry*, **27**, 208–221.

Harvey, O. J., 1965. Cognitive aspects of affective arousal. In S. S. Tomkins and C. E. Izard (Eds.), *Affect, Cognition and Personality*. New York: Springer, pp. 242–262.

Harvey, O. J., 1966. System structure, flexibility, and creativity. In O. J. Harvey (Ed.), *Experience, structure and adaptability*. New York: Springer, pp. 39–65.

Harvey, O. J., and Beverly, G. D., 1961. Some personality correlates of concept change through role playing. *J. abnorm. soc. Psychol.*, **63**, 125–130.

Harvey, O. J., Hunt, D. E., and Schroder, H. M., 1961. *Conceptual systems and personality organization*. New York: Wiley.

Harvey, O. J., Kelley, H. H., and Shapiro, M., 1957. Reactions to unfavorable evaluations of the self made by other persons. *J. Pers.*, **25**, 393–411.

Harvey, O. J., and Kline, J. A., 1965. Some situational and cognitive determinants of role playing: A replication and extension. Tech. Rep. No. 15, Contract Nonr 1147(07), Univ. of Col.

Harvey, O. J., Reich, J., and Wyer, R. S., 1966. Affective and personality determinants of differentiation. Unpublished manuscript, Univ. of Col.

Harvey, O. J., and Rutherford, Jeanne, 1958. Gradual and absolute approaches to attitude change. *Sociometry*, **21**, 61–68.

Harvey, O. J., and Schroder, H. M., 1963. Cognitive aspects of self and motivation. In O. J. Harvey (Ed.), *Motivation and social interaction*. New York: Ronald, pp. 95–133.

Harvey, O. J., and Ware, R., 1966. Personality differences in dissonance reduction. Tech. Report No. 18, Contract Nonr 1147(07), Univ. of Colorado, 1966.

Harvey, O. J., White, B. J., Prather, Misha, Alter, R., and Hoffmeister, J. K., 1966. Teachers' beliefs and preschool atmospheres. *J. educ. Psychol.*, **57**, 373–381.

Harvey, O. J., Wyer, R. S., and Hautaluoma, J. E., 1963. Some cognitive and affective determinants of differentiation and integration. Tech. Rep. No. 8, Contract Nonr 1147(07), Univ. of Col.

Hebb, D. O., 1949. *The organization of behavior.* New York: Wiley.

Hebb, D. O., 1955. Drives and the C.N.S. (conceptual nervous system). *Psychol. Rev.,* **62,** 243–254.

Heider, F., 1946. Attitudes and cognitive organization. *J. Psychol.,* **21,** 107–112.

Heider, F., 1958. *The psychology of interpersonal relations.* New York: Wiley.

Hoffmeister, J. K., 1965. Conceptual determinants of strength and certainty of beliefs. Unpublished manuscript, Univ. of Col.

Hunt, J. McV., 1963. Motivation inherent in information processing. In O. J. Harvey (Ed.), *Motivation and social interaction.* New York: Ronald, pp. 35–94.

James, W., 1890. *Principles of psychology.* Vol. 2. New York: Holt.

Kelman, H. C., 1958. Compliance, identification and internalization: three processes of attitude change. *J. Confl. Resolut.,* **2,** 51–60.

Kritzberg, S. F., 1965. Conceptual systems and behavior styles. Tech. Rep. No. 13, Contract Nonr 1147(07), Univ. of Col.

Newcomb, T. M., 1961. *The acquaintance process.* New York: Holt, Rinehart and Winston.

Richter, C. P., 1927. Animal behavior and internal drives. *Quart. Rev. Biol.,* **2,** 307–343.

Richter, C. P., 1936. Increased salt appetite in adrenalectomized rats. *Amer. J. Physiol.,* **115,** 155–167.

Richter, C. P., 1942. Total self-regulatory functions in animals and human beings. *Harvey Lecture Series,* **38,** 63–103.

Richter, C. P., and Eckert, J. F., 1939. Mineral appetite of parathyroidectomized rats. *Amer. J. med. Sci.* **198,** 9–16.

Reich, J., 1966. Conceptual systems and group performance. Unpublished manuscript, Univ. of Col.

Rokeach, M., 1960. *The open and closed mind.* New York: Basic Books.

Scott, W. A., 1959. Empirical assessment of values and ideologies. *Amer. sociol. Rev.,* **24,** 299–310.

Scott, W. A., 1964. *Values and organizations: a study of fraternities and sororities.* Chicago: Rand McNally.

Sherif, M., 1935. Some social factors in perception. *Arch. Psychol., N.Y.,* **27** (Whole No. 187).

Sherif, M., and Cantril, H., 1947. *The psychology of ego-involvements.* New York: Wiley.

Tiemann, H. A., 1965. Some social and personality determinants of reaction to sensory deprivation. Tech. Rep. No. 14, Contract Nonr 1147(07), Univ. of Col.

Titus, H. E., and Hollander, E. P., 1957. The California F Scale in psychological research. *Psychol. Bull.,* **54,** 61–68.

Tryon, R. C., and Bailey, D. E., 1965. *Try User's Manual.* Boulder, Cal.: Univ. of Col. Computing Center.

Tryon, R. C., and Bailey, D. E., 1966. The B. C. Try system of cluster and factor analysis. Univ. of Col.

Wagman, M., 1955. Attitude change and authoritarian personality. *J. Psychol.,* **40,** 3–24.

Ware, R., and Harvey, O. J., 1967. A congnitive determinant of impression formation. *J. Pers. soc. Psychol.,* 5, 38–44.

White, B. J., and Harvey, O. J., 1965. Effects of personality and own stand on judgment and production of statements about a central issue. *J. exp. soc. Psychol.,* 1, 334–347.

Webster, H. Sanford, N., and Freedman, M. A., 1955. A new instrument for studying authoritarianism. *J. Psychol.,* **40,** 73–84.

Wright, J. M., and Harvey, O. J., 1965. Attitude change as a function of authoritarianism and punitiveness. *J. Pers. soc. Psychol.,* 1, 177–181.

Young, P. T., 1961. *Motivation and emotion.* New York: Wiley.

12.   Toward an Analysis of the Components
of Interpersonal Attitudes*

Harry C. Triandis

When social psychology became a distinctive discipline, the concept
of attitude already had a distinguished history in experimental psychology. At that time it meant a *set* to respond in a particular way
to particular situations. In the last 60 years the term *attitude* has
been used in a variety of contexts, and there are many definitions
for it. Common to most of these definitions, however, is the notion
that an attitude is a predisposition toward action.

One of the most significant events in the history of social psychology
was the publication of Thurstone and Chave's volume (1929) on
the measurement of attitudes. It suddenly opened the way toward
measurement of an aspect of this nebulous concept. Soon followed
a variety of other techniques, such as the approach of Likert and
later those of Guttman, Lazersfeld, and others (Edwards, 1957; Green,
1954).

The advances made in the measurement of attitudes as a result
of these contributions were considerable. However, these advances
were accompanied by oversimplifications in theoretical treatment. Attitudes became "that which is measurable by my attitude scale." In

* Most of the studies reviewed in this chapter were supported by the contract
to study Communication, Cooperation, and Negotiation in Culturally Heterogeneous Groups between the University of Illinois and the Advanced Research
Projects Agency and the Office of Naval Research [Contract NR 177-472, Nonr
1834(36), Fred E. Fiedler, Lawrence M. Stolurow, and Harry C. Triandis,
principal investigators]. E. E. Davis, M. Fishbein, U. Foa, and T. Ostrom made
valuable critical comments, which improved an earlier version of this manuscript.

recent times many writers have used very simple measurement, for example, the sum of the scores on a set of evaluative scales in Osgood's Semantic Differential, as the complete and adequate measurement of attitudes.

Those who were not concerned with measurement alone did continue to argue that attitudes have several dimensions, such as clarity, intensity, and so on. Among such authors are Smith, Bruner, and White (1956), who mention seven dimensions along which attitudes may vary: differentiation, saliency, time perspective, informational support, object value, orientation, and policy stand. In other words, the individual may differentiate among many parts of the attitude object; he may experience the attitude object with differing degrees of salience, may employ a temporal frame of reference in thinking about it, may have much or little information about it, may experience differing degrees of affect, may be oriented to approach, avoid or be hostile toward it, and may have a preference for certain proposals for collective action toward it.

Katz and Stotland (1959) summarize their arguments under the usual distinction of the affective, cognitive, and behavioral components. Under each of these labels they discuss further differentiations. For example, under the cognitive component they discuss beliefs about the attitude object, its characteristics, its relation to other objects, the degree of differentiation, the degree of integration into a hierarchical pattern of cognitions, and the specificity or generality of the beliefs.

Thus, it is fair to say that there is a gap between those who are primarily concerned with the *measurement* of attitudes and those who have written *theoretically* about attitudes. The former frequently rest their case after providing us with a single score, whereas the latter make a large number of theoretical distinctions but do not provide us with precise and standard procedures for measurement.

This gap is beginning to be filled. For example, Zajonc (1960) operationalized four dimensions of the cognitive component. Sherif, Sherif, and Nebergall (1965) provided a review of work in which the individual's *involvement* with the attitude issue is measured by a precise procedure. They showed that the number of statements on an attitude scale to which the subject responds with indifference is clearly related to subsequent attitude change.

Here, a further attempt will be made to close the gap between measurement and theory by describing a number of new approaches for the measurement of the various components of attitude. It should be made clear, however, that we do not claim to have eliminated the gap between attitude measurement and attitude theory. All that we can claim is to have provided a shaky scaffold that leads from one to the other.

ON THE MULTIDIMENSIONAL APPROACH
TO ATTITUDE MEASUREMENT

The typical approach in Thurstone scaling is to collect a large number of items that have some relevance to an attitude object and to ask judges to indicate the degree of favorableness toward the object implied by agreement with each item. Thus, the statements "My church has 10 million members" (cognitive), "My church provides me with delightful experiences" (affective), and "I always give one tenth of what I earn to my church" (behavioral) are treated as equivalent, in the sense that each of these statements is supposed to provide information about the same theoretical construct, namely the subject's attitude toward his church. Yet there is strong evidence that a person may have positive or negative positions on each of these three components, in all possible combinations. For example, Triandis and Triandis (1962) found that some white Americans will indicate they consider a Negro physician *clean, honest,* and *good,* but at the same time they would *not accept* him in their neighborhood or as a member of their club. This is an example where the affective and behavioral components are inconsistent. If we construct scales paying no attention to this distinction, we are bound to limit our measurement only to that portion of the variance that is common among the components.

The distinction between the three components is clearly seen in a recent study by Ostrom (1966). He developed a procedure for generating items relevant to the three components. He constructed several attitude scales for each of the components, using different procedures of attitude scale construction. Then, he employed the Campbell and Fiske (1959) approach to test the construct validity of the conceptualization of attitudes as having three distinct components. The criteria set by this procedure require that the correlations among the scales measuring the *same* component by *different* scale methods be higher than the intercorrelations among the scales *across* components. Ostrom's data tend to support the three-partite conceptualization of attitudes. He found that the first set of correlations (among scales for the same components) was significantly higher than the second set of correlations (among scales for different components).

Not only are three components of attitude distinct, but within the behavioral component it is possible to isolate different kinds of "behavioral intentions" (Triandis, 1964a) that are independent of each other. Thus, through factor analysis Triandis (1964b) found a factor of behavioral intentions described by the items *to admire, to invite, to cooperate with, to obey* that may be labeled RESPECT. Another factor, orthogonal to the previous one, included the behaviors *to marry, to love, to date* and was labeled MARITAL ACCEPTANCE. A third included *to gossip with, to accept as a partner in an athletic game, to eat with* and was labeled FRIENDSHIP ACCEPTANCE. A fourth included the behaviors to *exclude from the neighborhood, to prohibit from voting,* and *not accept as a close kin by marriage* and was called SOCIAL DISTANCE. Finally, a fifth factor included the behaviors *to be commanded by, to obey, not treat as a subordinate* and was called SUBORDINATION.

The distinction between RESPECT and FRIENDSHIP was also found in two other studies employing different samples and procedures. Triandis, Vassiliou, and Thomanek (1966) found similar factors in 400 individuals who constituted a representative sample of the population of greater Athens, Greece. Kiesler and Goldberg (1966) exposed their subjects to a tape recording of an interview and asked them to respond to a 24-item questionnaire on interpersonal attraction. Factor analyses of the judgments resulted in two orthogonal factors. The first was a social-emotional factor characterized by high loadings on *liking* for the interviewee, willingness to *spend free time* with him, willingness to *have lunch* with him, and so forth. The second factor was related to task relevant attraction with high loadings on the scales *believe, admire, respect,* and *vote for.* The authors noted the similarity of these two factors to Triandis' FRIENDSHIP and RESPECT factors.

To summarize to this point: The classic approaches to attitude measurement usually result in a single score. The theoretical analysis of attitudes usually specify the existence of a variety of components. Some recent studies demonstrate that it is possible to measure these components independently. Furthermore, the behavioral component is itself multidimensional.

In the sections that follow, a number of new approaches to the measurement of the components are reviewed. The multidimensionality of the behavioral component is then discussed in detail. Next, the evidence concerning the relationships between the components is reviewed. The final section summarizes the relationships between different characteristics of stimulus persons, on the one hand, and the responses on various dimensions representing the components of attitude on the other.

EXAMPLES OF APPROACHES TO ATTITUDE MEASUREMENT

The basic approach advocated by the present author is the adequate sampling of attitude *variables*. In psychological theorizing and empirical research, we have generally been concerned much more with the sampling of subjects, or the social situations in which we place them for purposes of study, than with the sampling of the variables or the response alternatives that we allow our subjects to utilize. The present position requires a preliminary "mapping" of the individual's universe of meaning when he responds to a representative sample of social objects. This "mapping" is here seen as a preliminary step before a rigorous hypothetico-deductive theory can be developed.

Explorations of the Cognitive Component

The first question to establish is exactly what instances, events, or people are included by a sample of persons in a particular category. For example, if we are interested in studying attitudes towards FREE-DOM, we might seek to determine how the subjects classify a variety of stimulus events. "Does this event imply that the person involved is 'free' or not?" We will have to be ingenious in constructing events, so that we will sample the relevant attributes. In principle, however, this procedure should define for us what events are categorized under the label FREEDOM.

Next, we might inquire as to the relationship between the cognitive category and other categories. Here a procedure developed by Triandis, as shown in Exhibit 1, can be helpful. He presented to a group of subjects an opportunity to give free-response *antecedents* of the concept FREEDOM, as well as free-response *consequences* of this concept. The instrument shown in the exhibit presents the most frequently given *antecedents* and most frequently given *consequents* by American, Greek, Indian, and Japanese subjects. The subjects are asked to pick one out of the five antecedents or the five consequences in each set. This procedure can tap the relationships between a cognitive category and other categories and thus give information about the cognitive component of attitudes. A cross-cultural study using this approach is now in progress (Triandis, Davis, Shanmugam, Tanaka, and Vassiliou, in preparation).

Exhibit 1

If one has _____, then one has FREEDOM.

1.		2.		3.	
peace	_____	love	_____	democracy	_____
rights	_____	freedom of speech	_____	America	_____
love of freedom	_____	combat	_____	servitude	_____
unity	_____	war	_____	tact	_____
equality	_____	respect for human beings	_____	respect for individual	_____

4.		5.		6.	
courage	_____	strength	_____	power	_____
peace of mind	_____	the Constitution	_____	discipline	_____
instinct	_____	money	_____	faith	_____
quarrel	_____	patriotism	_____	God	_____
liberation	_____	restriction	_____	suppression	_____

If one has FREEDOM, then one has _____.

1.		2.		3.	
peace	_____	responsibility	_____	rights	_____
love	_____	knowledge	_____	democracy	_____
progress	_____	free speech	_____	growth of civilization	_____
no restrictions	_____	unity	_____	industrial production	_____
disorderly society	_____	degradation	_____	satisfaction	_____

4.		5.		6.	
happiness	_____	public disorder	_____	joy	_____
respect	_____	life	_____	courage	_____
well-being	_____	abuse	_____	civilization	_____
misuse	_____	educational facilities	_____	crime	_____
duty	_____	irresponsibility	_____	wealth	_____

In a recent study, Davis and Triandis (1965) employed the second half of this procedure with civil rights issues. The subjects were given items of the following format:

If you have SEGREGATED SCHOOLS then you have JUSTICE.

improbable ′__′__′__′__′__′__′ probable

Large differences were observed between prejudiced and unprejudiced subjects in the kinds of responses they made to this instrument, which was designed to measure the *implicative meaning* of concepts.

Furthermore, these differences predicted the subjects' behavior towards Negroes.

In addition to these new procedures for the measurement of the cognitive component of attitudes, a number of the standard procedures may be used. Some of these—such as componential analysis, Kelly's personal constructs approach (1955), and others—were reviewed by Triandis (1964a). Factor analysis of descriptions of the attitude object (Osgood, Suci, and Tannenbaum, 1957) and multidimensional scaling of domains of similar attitude objects may also be used. A number of dimensions—such as cognitive complexity (Scott, 1962), salience, and time perspective—may be used to characterize a person's cognitive component. Zajonc (1960) has operationalized the dimensions of *differentiation, complexity, unity,* and *organization* of this component.

Explorations of the Affective Component

The first factor of Osgood's Semantic Differential (Osgood, Suci, and Tannenbaum, 1957) permits a most suitable measurement of the affective component of attitudes. Most of the variance on this instrument is accounted for by the affective factor. The basic format looks like this:

Negro Physician

good   '__'__'__'__'__'__'   bad
dirty '__'__'__'__'__'__'   clean

In detailed studies of person perception with this instrument, there is often a distinction between "pure evaluation" (good, sensitive) and "moral correctness" (moral, clean) of the stimulus person (Davis, 1966). In some cases, the classic factors of *potency* and *activity* are also likely to tap affective rather than denotative (cognitive) dimensions of an attitude object.

Explorations of the Behavioral Component of Interpersonal Attitudes

Triandis (1964b) developed an instrument called the Behavioral Differential, which is an adaptation of the Semantic Differential format. It employs items of the following form:

Negro physician

would   '__'__'__'__'__'__'   would not
admire the ideas of

would not   '__'__'__'__'__'__'   would
cooperate in a political campaign with

The five factors that emerged from the factor analysis of the behavioral scales of this instrument have already been discussed above.

A NOTATION FOR A THEORY OF
INTERPERSONAL ATTITUDES

Before attempting a formal statement of a theory of interpersonal attitudes, a definition of attitudes is in order: An attitude is a (enduring) syndrome of response consistency with regard to (a set of) social objects (Campbell, 1950). This definition implies that the psychologist observes some regularities in the relationship between a set of similar social situations and a set of similar social responses made by a particular individual. Thus, in order to determine that a person P has an attitude toward another person O, it is necessary to observe more than one occasion in which O (or the symbolic representation of O) and P are present in similar social situations, and P makes social responses that show some regularity.

The attitude is not directly observable. It is inferred from the above mentioned regularities. Attitude measurement depends on the observation of regularities in the person's behavior when he is presented with symbols that represent the social situations. These regularities in behavior are not describable by a single dimension; rather a structure of interrelated dimensions is necessary in order to describe these regularities. It is for this reason that we stated above that attitude measurement is multidimensional.

Person O has a great variety of characteristics. The attitudes of P toward O are determined in part by O's characteristics; however, a number of other variables are also important. The characteristics of P and the way they relate to O's characteristics, the culture in which the interaction is taking place, and the social context of the interaction (Sherif, 1966) are all important determinants of P's attitudes toward O.

Since O has many characteristics, the observation that P has a certain attitude toward him gives only idiographic information. What is needed are the observations of P's behaviors toward people who have or do not have the various characteristics. Regularities in these behaviors would lead to conclusions, such as "P avoids Negroes," "P prefers blondes," and so forth. Then, P's attitude toward O can be understood. Of course, complete understanding would require answers to such questions as "Why does P prefer blondes?" For the present analysis, however, we will limit ourselves to the superficial explanation of why P prefers O, given the characteristics of P and O and the context of their interaction.

To reach even this point of understanding of P's attitudes, we should as a minimum learn something about his personal constructs (Kelly, 1955) concerning the characteristics that are likely to be important *for him* in viewing other people. To exactly what characteristics does he attend?

Table 12.1 shows the classes of variables that determine interpersonal attitudes and interpersonal behavior. To the left, the first column includes the criterial attributes (cues) that a person uses to "conclude" that another person has certain characteristics. For example, one P might use O's *skin color* as the sole determinant of whether or not O is a Negro, so that this P would classify albino Negroes as whites. Another person may use several attributes as criteria in order to classify O into the Negro or white category. Some persons may break down the listed criterial attributes into finer attributes. For example, dress designers may subdivide the criterial attribute

Table 12.1   *Basic Concepts of a Theory of Interpersonal Attitudes*

Criterial Attributes for Characteristics of O	Inferred (by P) Characteristics of O	Relationship between Characteristics of O and P (as perceived by P)	Context
O's behavior			Culture
	Inferred personality Characteristics		
O's clothes			
	Sex	Same/different	P's reference groups
O's accent			
	Religion	Same/different	
O's rate of speech			
	Status	Same/different	
O's loudness of speech			
			Role relationship between
O's type of hair			O and P
	Race	Same/different	
O's color			
.	.	.	.
.	.	.	.
.	.	.	.

clothes into finer attributes such as "expensive versus inexpensive clothes," "Parisian versus local clothes," "good versus poor color balance," "good versus poor balance of textures." Accent may imply a variety of personal characteristics for certain kinds of people (Lambert, 1964). Jones and Davis (1965) have provided a theory that ties *O*'s behaviors and *P*'s perception of *O*'s characteristics. They suggest that only the behaviors of *O* which are "unusual" are likely to lead to inferences that *O* has certain characteristics.

The second column shows some of the characteristics of *O* that *P* infers from *O*'s attributes. The next column shows the possible relationships between the characteristics of *O* and the characteristics of *P*. The last column shows the context of the interaction, that is, the culture, *P*'s reference groups, and their role relationship.

Table 12.2 shows the norms, previous reinforcements and punishments, and habits of *P* with respect to persons such as *O*. The direction of the arrows represents causal links between variables. We distinguish cognitive norms (that is, ideas derived from family and friends of a particular *P* on the characteristics of such a person as *O*) from behavioral norms (that is, concepts about appropriate behavior derived from the family and friends of a particular *P* concerning people such as *O*). We assume that the cognitive norms will have an effect on the cognitive component and that the behavioral norms will have an effect on the behavioral component. Previous reinforcements and punishments received by *P* in the presence of *O* will have an influence on the affective component. (For example, *O*'s who have reinforced *P* will appear to him to be *good, honest, clean.*)

Next in Table 12.2, we assume that the inferred characteristics of *O* will also have an influence on *P*'s cognitive component and that the relationship between the characteristics of *O* and *P* will have an effect on the behavioral component. However, this latter causal link, we assume, is moderated by the social context (represented at the far right).

In Table 12.2 we show a number of influences on the behavioral component, including *P*'s habits of behavior toward persons like *O*. As a final link, we assume that *P*'s habits, expected consequences of behavior, and behavioral intentions jointly determine his interpersonal behavior.

Thus, Tables 12.1 and 12.2 present a preliminary statement of a theory of interpersonal attitudes and interpersonal behavior. This theory, it is hoped, will mature to connect all the variables listed in the tables, thus explaining *P*'s attitudes and behavior toward *O*.

Table 12.2

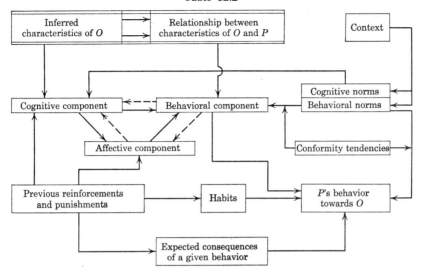

The research that we have completed so far touches only on some of the variables in the tables. It is most complete in the connection between the variables of column three of Table 12.1 and the behavioral intentions of P as measured by the Behavioral Differential. Future work, it is hoped, will fill in the many gaps that still remain before the theory can become a solid contribution to social psychology.

DESCRIPTION OF SOME OF THE EMPIRICAL STUDIES

In order to study the relationships among some of the variables affecting interpersonal attitude and behavior, as shown in Tables 12.1 and 12.2, we have employed a variety of approaches. In one study, the manipulation of the criterion attributes was accomplished by: presenting slides of persons who looked either well-dressed or poorly dressed; or tape recorded statements in a heavy (poor) accent or in a "correct" accent; or the opinions of the stimulus persons. In other studies, these opinions were varied either by presentation of different kinds of statements for or against different issues, or by presentation of complex stimuli to be appraised by P, such as "a Negro college student who is in favor of the new civil rights law." In several studies, we varied different characteristics of the stimuli by systematically presenting all possible combinations of characteristics, such as race (for example, white-Negro), religion (for example, Roman Catholic-Protestant-Jewish), age, sex, nationality, competence in doing a job, and sociability. In some studies the stimulus persons were described as having physical disabilities (for example, being deaf), a prison record, a recent discharge from a mental hospital, and so on. For a representative set of these studies see Triandis and Triandis (1960; 1962); Triandis (1963); Rickard, Triandis, and Patterson (1963); Triandis (1964b); Triandis, Loh, and Levin (1966).

In most of the research, the characteristics of O (see the second column of Table 12.1) were varied by the experimenter, but in some cases the criterion attributes (behavior, speech, skin color, etc.) were manipulated, leaving it up to P to infer O's characteristics. The subjects were Americans, Greeks, Germans, Japanese, or Indians, depending on the study. For a representative set of cross-cultural studies, see Triandis, Davis, and Takezawa (1965); Triandis and Triandis (1965), Triandis, Tanaka, and Shanmugam (1966).

A typical item employed in many of these studies will clarify the basic format of the questionnaires:

A Negro female physician, 50 years old

would '__'__'__'__'__'__'__'__' would not
                  let go first through a door

The standard technique was to present all possible combinations of these characteristics. Thus, it was possible, through analysis of variance, to determine whether the subject was responding to the race, sex, occupation, or age of the stimulus person.

Our studies suggest that there are *regularities* in the relationships between the characteristics of O and the cognitive and affective components of the attitude of P. Further there are regularities in the relationship between the characteristics of O and P and the behavioral component of P, between the *context* of the interaction and the behavioral component of P, and between the three attitudinal components and the behavior of P toward O.

The complexity of the theory presented in Table 12.2 has prevented its test in a single study. However, Davis and Triandis (1965) have employed a situation in which white naïve subjects interacted with Negro confederates of the experimenters. The attitudes of the white subjects toward whites and toward Negroes who "are in favor" or "opposed to civil rights legislation" were studied by measuring all the components of attitude (cognitive, affective, and behavioral). The behavior of the white subjects in an experimental session in which

they negotiated different civil rights issues with the Negro confederates was observed.

The civil rights issues were presented in the form of ten positions
from Thurstone successive-interval scales, ranging from complete opposition to a civil rights law (position 1) to enactment of a sweeping
civil rights law (position 10). The typical white subject in this experiment favored a position between positions 5 and 6. The Negro confederates were told to demand position 10 and to yield to the white
subjects by shifting but no further than position 8. The dependent
variable (P's behavior toward O) was the extent to which the white
subjects yielded to the Negroes, thereby reaching agreement at position 8 or 9, or indicated that they were unwilling to go beyond a
given position (say, position 7).

The behavior of the white subjects in the negotiation sessions was
predictable from the pretest measurements of their attitudes. Approximately 31 percent of the variance of this behavior was predictable
from their responses to the attitude instruments. About 5 percent
was predictable from the affective component (Semantic Differential
evaluation), about 19 percent from the cognitive component (implicative meaning instrument described above), and 11 percent from the
behavioral component (the Behavioral Differential social-distance factor). There was some overlap in the variance between the three components; therefore, the variance predicted from the instruments was
not the sum of the variances predicted from the three components
(35 percent) but only 31 percent.

SOME REPRESENTATIVE FINDINGS IN DETAIL

The Multidimensionality of the Behavioral Component

Triandis (1964b) extracted a large sample of social interactions
from a random sample of American novels as a basis for constructing
situations and stimulus persons in all possible combinations of the
following characteristics: race (Negro-white), occupation (physician-
soda fountain clerk), sex (male-female), age (25 and 50 years old),
and religion (Roman Catholic-Protestant-Jewish). Samples of white
American subjects indicated whether they would or would not behave
as indicated under the scale with the particular persons described.
Factor analyses of the behaviors showed the results described previously. The factors extracted were RESPECT, FRIENDSHIP AC-
CEPTANCE, MARITAL ACCEPTANCE, SOCIAL DISTANCE, and
SUBORDINATION.

With white American subjects, it was found that RESPECT was highest in the case of stimulus persons of the same age, religion, and race as the subjects. However, the most important determinant of respect was the stimulus person's *occupation,* with high-level occupations receiving maximal respect. FRIENDSHIP was highest in the case of stimulus persons of the same age, sex, race, and religion as the subjects. MARITAL ACCEPTANCE was highest toward persons of the same age, race, religion, and, of course, the most important was the opposite sex from that of the subject. SOCIAL DISTANCE was determined mostly by race, with maximal distance toward persons of the Negro race. Finally, SUBORDINATION was determined almost completely by occupation.

Do these results hold cross-culturally? To examine this problem three scales with the highest loadings on each of the basic five factors of the Behavioral Differential were employed by Triandis, Tanaka, and Shanmugam. The scales were presented to American, Japanese, and Indian subjects. The scales were translations of the scales used by Triandis (1964b) in the study just summarized. The stimulus persons varied in age, sex, occupation, and religion. The results showed that in all three cultures there were RESPECT, MARITAL, and FRIENDSHIP factors. However, the Japanese RESPECT factor included a very strong *subordination* element (would obey, would be commanded by). Similarly, the FRIENDSHIP factor of the Japanese also had a subordination element, although this is not true in the other cultures.

The MARITAL factors of the three cultures were also somewhat different. The Japanese males had a high loading on the scale *would treat as a subordinate* on their MARITAL factor. The Japanese females had a high loading on *would be commanded by* on the same factor. Neither of these loadings were found in the other two cultures. In the United States, *would admire the ideas* typically appears together with the RESPECT factor, but in Japan it was associated with the FRIENDSHIP factor. Thus, we may conclude that although three of the factors hold up cross-culturally, the specific *content* of each factor is influenced by culture.

What happens if we change the sample of behaviors used in the Behavioral Differential? As noted above, the behaviors in the differential developed by Triandis (1964b) were obtained from a content analysis of American novels. In a more recent study we began with one hundred roles and asked the subjects themselves to supply the behaviors that they believed were typical in interactions within such roles. We obtained about 10,000 such behaviors. The total was then reduced to a smaller number through facet analysis (Foa, 1965). The new smaller sample of behaviors was factor analyzed. Six factors were found that resemble very closely the factors obtained in the previous study.

1. RESPECT: *enjoy meeting, praise, admire, learn with help of, depend upon.*
2. HOSTILITY: *argue with, dislike, disagree with* (a factor that is reminiscent of the social distance factor).
3. MARITAL ACCEPTANCE: *love, marry.*
4. FRIENDSHIP: *help, protect, wish good luck to.*
5. SUPERORDINATION: *treat as a subordinate, command.*
6. DEEP EMOTIONAL INVOLVEMENT: *confess sins to, idolize, cry for.* This factor is new, but the other factors appear to replicate the Triandis (1964b) study.

Can these results be replicated in another culture? In the Triandis, Tanaka, and Shanmugam (1966) study comparing American, Japanese, and Indian subjects, the behavior scales were *translations* of the scales used in the United States. If the behavior scales are obtained by *direct elicitation* from persons in different cultures, then the subjects would be responding to their own culturally defined set of social behaviors. In such a case, the likelihood would seem much greater that there might not be any correspondence across cultures. Triandis, Vassiliou, and Nassiakou (1966) tested this by repeating the study of free elicitation of behaviors in Greece. Indeed, the factor structures were now different. Six orthogonal factors were obtained. The first factor might be named ASSOCIATION versus DISSOCIATION. The associative pole includes *help, love,* and *thank for goods;* the dissociative includes *cheat, exploit,* and *be enemy of.* The second factor appears to be a FRIENDSHIP factor (*study with, apologize to,* and *cooperate with*). The third factor is HOSTILITY (*hate, fear,* and *feel inferior to*). The fourth is SUPERORDINATION (*reprimand, scold,* and *not have difficulty understanding*). The fifth is ACTIVE AVOIDANCE (*have difficulty understanding, show abhorence of,* and *detest*). The final factor was ATTEMPTS AT ACCEPTANCE BY HIGH STATUS PERSONS (*complain, boast,* and *boast of success to*).

Examination of the *content* of the American and Greek factors shows substantial differences. Even the factors that were given the same names in the two studies are really rather different. For example, consider the two FRIENDSHIP factors: the American (*help, protect,* and *wish good luck to*) and the Greek (*study with, cooperate with,*

and *apologize to*) have little in common. The two SUPERODINA-
TION factors are also different.

Some factors are unique. For example, The Greek ATTEMPTS
AT ACCEPTANCE BY HIGH STATUS PERSONS factor is nowhere
to be found in the American work. In fact, *boasts* did not even
appear in the list of 60 American behaviors, whereas it appeared
twice in the Greek list. My own naturalistic observations of the two
cultures suggest that such a difference does reflect a true difference
in the frequency of behavior in the two cultures. Greeks *do* boast
more than is typical of Americans, and it is "culturally correct" to
boast in Greece whereas it is somewhat offensive to do so in America.

In conclusion, it may be stated that when we translate instruments
that are factorially pure for American subjects into the languages
of other cultures, we obtain results that replicate the American results.
However, *when we allow members of the other cultures to develop
their own Behavioral Differentials, the resulting factor structures are
different.* This is because those behaviors that are most frequent in
a given culture determine the factor structures.

The implication that we have to construct a new set of instruments
for each culture we study complicates our task enormously. However,
there is one helpful finding: the first three *unrotated* factors obtained
from Americans and Greeks are the same. Since they *are* the first
three, they are also the most important. Furthermore, they bear resemblance to the classic three factors of the Semantic Differential:
evaluation, potency and activity.

The first factor includes ASSOCIATIVE or DISSOCIATIVE behaviors and corresponds to EVALUATION. In America it includes:
praises, admires, enjoys and, conversely, *dislikes, is prejudiced against.*
In Greece it includes *shows love to, enjoys* and, conversely, *is enemy
of, feels antipathy for.* The second factor includes SUPERORDINATE
behaviors, thereby resembling the POTENCY factor. It includes *cor-
rects, reprimands* in America and *scolds, teaches* in Greece. The third
factor includes mostly ACTIVITY behaviors. In America it includes
argues with, asks for help of, and *throws rocks at;* in Greece it includes
annoys, quarrels with, and *flatters.* These three "common" factors
account for 65 percent and 57 percent of the variance in the two
cultures respectively.

In conclusion, our studies show, without qualifications, that the
behavioral component of attitudes is itself multidimensional. The stability of the structure is limited by the sampling of the stimulus
persons, behavior scales, and the subjects making the judgments. Over
a wide range of studies, we found that changes in the *behavior scales,*
while keeping the stimuli and subjects constant (Triandis, 1964b),

produce almost identical factor structures for the two samples of behavior scales. Changes in subjects, while keeping stimuli and scales
constant (Triandis, Tanaka, and Shanmugam, 1966), result in minor
changes in the factors. Changes in the *stimuli*, while keeping the
subjects and the behaviors constant (Triandis, Vassiliou, and Nas-
siakow, 1966) result in major changes in the factor structure. Of
course, when more than one of the basic elements of Behavioral
Differentials are changed simultaneously, the resulting factor structures differ from each other even more.

Correspondence with Studies of Emotion and Personality

It is interesting to note the similarity between the results obtained
with the Behavioral Differential, the Semantic Differential, and studies
of emotional expression. Here again we find the three dimensions
discussed above. Schlosberg (1954) called them *pleasant-un-
pleasant, attention-rejection,* and activation (*tension-sleep*). Triandis
and Lambert (1958) found that the judgments of facial expressions made by subjects in rural Greece or by sophisticated urban
dwellers in Athens were very similar to the judgments made
by American students and were well accounted by Schlosberg's
theory. They further noted the similarity of Schlosberg's dimensions
and Osgood's factors. More recently, Osgood (1966) reanalyzed several studies of emotional expression and further supported these
conclusions.

Another correspondence can be found in studies of personality.
For example, the LaForge and Suczek (1955) theory of interpersonal
personality postulates three orthogonal factors: love-hate; dominance-
submission; and intensity, as indicated by the number of items
checked. More recently, Lorr and McNair (1965) presented a theory
in which dominance-submission and affection-hostility appear to be
orthogonal components. They in turn relate their system to those
proposed by LaForge and Suczek, Stern, Schaefer, Cattell, and others.

It appears that we are dealing here with rather fundamental dimensions of human responses that involve human judgments entangled
with emotional experiences. Much of social behavior is entangled
with emotional experience. It is not surprising, then, that the first
three factors of our unrotated factor analyses of social behaviors and
of personality are reflecting the basic dimensions of emotion.

The Relationship between the Components of Attitude

There is good evidence that some close relationships are found
among the three components of attitude. Fishbein (1965), Rosenberg
(1965), and others have shown this to be the case. When all the

information obtained from Semantic and Behavioral Differentials is pooled and *combined* factor analyses are performed, we find that EVALUATION and RESPECT merge into a single factor (Davis and Grobstein, 1966). In other words, people *admire* and *obey* those whom they see as *good, honest*, and *clean*. However, the correlations of the remaining factors are much lower over a large sample of stimulus persons (Triandis, Fishbein, and Hall, 1964). The weights given by subjects to various characteristics or criterial attributes for appraising another person (such as the ones listed in Table 12.1) are essentially identical for the EVALUATION and RESPECT factors, but they are quite different for the other factors. Triandis, Loh, and Levin (1966), working with Americans of different degrees of prejudice toward Negroes, and Triandis, Tanaka, and Shanmugam (1966), working with Americans, Indians, and Japanese, found similar weights given to person characteristics on the EVALUATION and RESPECT factors but not for the other factors.

Triandis and Davis (1965) presented subjects with stimulus persons varying in race (Negro-white), sex (male-female), and belief (favors strong civil rights legislation-opposes major changes in the *status quo* on civil rights). A factor analysis of subjects revealed two types. One was a "conventionally prejudiced" person who responded primarily to the race of the stimulus persons; the other was a "belief prejudiced" person who responded primarily to the beliefs of the stimulus persons. The belief characteristic controlled most of the variance for judgments on the EVALUATION factor of the Semantic Differential. The same was true, broadly speaking, for the RESPECT factor, with the exception of the conventionally prejudiced subjects who attended primarily to the race characteristic.

Conversely, the SOCIAL DISTANCE factor was almost completely determined by the race characteristics of the stimuli. Only in the case of the *belief*-prejudiced subjects was social distance influenced perceptibly by the beliefs of the stimulus persons. The MARITAL factor was determined by the sex and the race of the stimulus persons. These findings held broadly for most of the subjects. But individual differences between subjects occurred on the SUBORDINATION and FRIENDSHIP factors. Here the responses of prejudiced and unprejudiced persons showed completely different patterns. The prejudiced were concerned with race but not with the beliefs of the stimulus persons when they made their subordination and friendship judgments. The unprejudiced were concerned with the beliefs and unconcerned with race of the stimulus person when they made their judgments. This study, then, showed that individual differences exist in responses to the various subcomponents of the behavioral component of attitudes.

The most direct study of the relationship between the components of interpersonal attitudes is that by Triandis, Tanaka, and Shanmugam (1966). The data were collected from American, Indian, and Japanese subjects. These data are shown in Table 12.3. The correlations in this table were obtained from approximately 50 subjects of the same sex from each of the three cultures. They responded to 35 stimulus persons. The number of observations (N) is approximately equal to 1750, although the exact N depends on the number of subjects tested and is shown in the table.

Table 12.3 reveals a definite pattern of correlations among the components of interpersonal attitudes that often holds well across the three cultures. It is notable that the sign of 114 of these 126 correlations is similar. Thus, the *pattern* of correlations is similar across cultures: the tendency is for *good* people to be *potent* and *active* and *young;* such people also receive *respect, friendship,* and *marital acceptance.*

On the other hand, it is clear in Table 12.3 that the correlations are rarely high. The median correlation in the table is only .22. This means that the shared variance between the subcomponents of interpersonal attitudes does not exceed 5 percent. Furthermore, in some instances, the results obtained from the three cultures are quite different, as can be seen, for example, with the potency factor for the Indian sample. Some of the results across sexes are also quite different.

Thus, it is naïve to attempt to study interpersonal attitudes with only one instrument, especially cross-culturally. A single instrument would tap only one of the components and any single component shares very little variance with other components of attitude.

Ostrom's (1966) study also provided information about the relationship between the components of attitude. His attitude object was the church. The correlations between the components ranged between .43 to .81, but some of the larger correlations undoubtedly reflected common response sets for particular attitude measurement methods that were used to assess the various components.

Relationship between Stimulus Characteristics and Interpersonal Attitudes

This section summarizes some of the findings that relate the variables in the first three columns of Table 12.1, with the behavioral component of interpersonal attitudes.

Table 12.3 *The Correlations between the Subcomponents of Interpersonal Attitudes*

			Semantic Differential			Behavioral Differential		
Factor	Sample	N	Subcomponents					
			Potency	Activity	Age	Respect	Friendship	Marital
Evaluation	American males	1715	.25	.56	−.14	.42	.38	.18
	American females	1680	.31	.64	−.16	.48	.31	.39
	Indian I	1750	−.14	.42	−.08	.23	.18	.13
	Indian II	1715	.03	.68	−.12	.31	.09	.11
	Japanese males	1925	.65	.24	−.24	.24	.31	.27
	Japanese females	1995	.02	.04	−.05	.08	.16	.16
Potency	American males	1715		.33	−.21	.11	.22	−.16
	American females	1680		.48	−.30	.13	.05	.35
	Indian I	1750		−.15	.17	−.02	−.06	−.01
	Indian II	1715		.01	.13	.16	.04	−.07
	Japanese males	1925		.26	−.25	.16	.29	.15
	Japanese females	1995		.60	−.27	.24	.19	.26
Activity	American males	1715			−.39	.18	.31	.23
	American females	1680			−.41	.34	.28	.36
	Indian I	1750			−.16	.22	.17	.06
	Indian II	1715			−.18	.20	.07	.11
	Japanese males	1925			−.39	−.05	−.06	.18
	Japanese females	1995			−.42	.02	.15	.16
Age	American males	1715				.08	−.37	−.43
	American females	1680				−.01	−.31	−.43
	Indian I	1750				.03	−.07	−.02
	Indian II	1715				.03	−.06	−.08
	Japanese males	1925				.01	−.06	−.39
	Japanese females	1995				.12	−.11	−.36
Respect	American males	1715					.40	.04
	American females	1680					.36	.29
	Indian I	1750					.35	.20
	Indian II	1715					.22	.15
	Japanese males	1925					.36	.24
	Japanese females	1995					.43	.30
Friendship	American males	1715						.32
	American females	1680						.32
	Indian I	1750						.26
	Indian II	1715						.04
	Japanese males	1925						.21
	Japanese females	1995						.37

Note. These data were obtained by Triandis, Tanaka, and Shanmugam (1966). They are correlations obtained from approximately 50 same sex subjects from each culture. The Indian sample has two samples of males. The subjects responded to 35 stimulus persons, and the N of the correlations is based on approximately $35 \times 50 = 1750$ observations. The exact number is shown under the N column.

A correlation of .07 is significant at $p < .01$
.09 $p < .001$
.11 $p < .0001$

Table 12.4 summarizes the results of various analyses of variance performed on the composite scores of complex stimulus persons for the various subcomponent factors of interpersonal attitudes that contribute most and least to the total variance. Consistency is high in the results of studies done with different samples of subjects, stimuli, and scales.

Although Table 12.4 is quite long and comprehensive of the available studies, it may be read easily, as follows: The first column (left) lists the *factors* obtained (for example, RESPECT), then beneath each factor, the composition of the subject samples in each study of the factor (for example, American males . . . females . . . Indian males, etc.). The second column lists illustrative *items* that were closely associated with the factor, hence representative of it in the study in question (reading across the row).

The central portion of Table 12.4 is divided into three columns that list the person characteristics accounting for the *most* to the *least* variance (reading each row from left to right). For example, in row 1, we read that in Triandis' study of American males, the characteristic contributing the *most* variance for the RESPECT factor was *race,* followed by *occupation* (middle subcolumn). In that study, religion contributed *least* to the total variance. The entire table may be read in this manner, the identification of the study being found in the column at the extreme right.

Certain generalizations are possible on the basis of Table 12.4.

RESPECT Factor. The characteristics of same race, same religion, same beliefs, light skin color (for white subjects), English fluency (for English speakers), and a highlevel occupation lead to high scores on RESPECT consistently in more than one study. What appears common among the person attributes that lead to high-respect responses is "high status as defined by my in-group," which is accompanied by positive affect. We can guess that any highly desirable instrumental characteristic—such as competence, intelligence, high education, scholarship, erudition, expertise, leadership ability—would produce high respect responses. Cognitive similarity should do the same, for example, Communists would show respect to Communists, fascists to fascists, and so forth. As the in-group changes, from one person to the next, we should expect changes on what is considered to be a high-status person, and hence different characteristics would elicit the RESPECT response.

MARITAL Factor. The characteristics of same race, same age, same religion, light skin color (white subjects), different sex, fluent

Table 12.4 *Person Characteristics as Determinants of Interpersonal Attitudes*

Attitude Factor (Sample)	Scales Loading Highly on Factor	Statistically Significant Characteristics in Order of Importance			Studies (Characteristics Studied)
		Controlling Most Variance I	II	Controlling Least Variance III	
RESPECT American males	(Admire ideas of) (Admire character) (Obey) (Ask for opinion of) (Believe)	Same race	High-level occupation	Same religion	Triandis (1964b) (race, religion, occupation, age, sex)
American conventionally prejudiced males	"	Same race	Same beliefs (opinions)		Triandis and Davis (1965) (race, belief, sex)
American conventionally unprejudiced males	"	Same beliefs			"
American belief unprejudiced males	"	Same beliefs	Same race		"

American males	(Admire character) (Be commanded by) (Believe) (Admire ideas of) (Obey)	High-level occupation	Same religion	Same sex	Triandis, Tanaka, and Shanmugam (1966) (age, religion, occupation, sex)
American females	"	High-level occupation	Same religion	Opposite sex	"
American males (graduate students)	(Admire character) (Invite to club) (Admire ideas of)	High-level occupation	English fluency	Light skin color	Triandis, Fishbein, and Hall (1964) (Occupation, nationality, sex, age, skin color, English fluency)
Indian males (graduate students)	"	English fluency	High-level occupation		"
Japanese males	(Be commanded by) (Obey) (Admire character) (Believe)	High-level occupation	Same religion (that is, no religion)	Same sex	Triandis, Tanaka, and Shanmugam (1966) (age, religion, occupation, sex)
Japanese females	(Not treat as subordinate) (Admire character) (Be commanded by) (Believe) (Obey)	High-level occupation	Same religion (that is, no religion)	Older age	Triandis, Tanaka, and Shanmugam (1966) (age, religion, occupation, sex)

Table 12.4 (*Continued*)

Attitude Factor (Sample)	Scales Loading Highly on Factor	Statistically Significant Characteristics in Order of Importance			Studies (Characteristics Studied)
		Controlling Most Variance I	II	Controlling Least Variance III	
RESPECT Indian males	(Admire character) (Be commanded by) (Believe) (Obey) (Admire ideas of)	Same religion	Same sex	High-level occupation	Triandis, Tanaka, and Shanmugam (1966) (age, religion, occupation, sex)
Americans (both sexes)	(Admire character) (Admire ideas of)	Speaks good English	Same belief		Triandis, Loh, and Levin (1966) (race, beliefs, English, dress)
American males	(Go to meeting with) (Learn with help of) (Depend upon) (Enjoy meeting) (Admire character) (Praise) (Admire)	High-level occupation	Speaks English fluently		Triandis, Vassiliou, and Nassiakou (1966) (occupation, English, age, race, sex, religion)
Americans	(Admire character)	High-level occupation	Same religion	Same race	Davis and Grobstein (1966) (race, occupation, religion, sex,

Group	Behavior				Reference
Negro females	(Admire ideas)	High-level occupation	Same religion	Same race	skin color)
Negro males	(Elect to political office)	High-level occupation	Same religion	Same race	"
White females		High-level occupation	Same religion	Same race	"
White males	(Plus SD evaluation)	High-level occupation	Same religion	Same race	"
					Triandis (1964b) (race, religion, occupation, age, sex)
MARITAL ACCEPTANCE American males	(May fall in love with) (Go on date with) (Physically love) (Kiss hand of) (Love even after her death)	Same race	Different sex	Same age	
Conventionally prejudiced	"	Same race	Different sex		Triandis and Davis (1965) (race, beliefs, sex)
Conventionally unprejudiced	"	Different sex	Same race		"
Belief prejudiced	"	Different sex	Same race		"
Belief unprejudiced	"	Different sex	Same race		
American males	(Fall in love with) (Marry)	Different sex	Same race	Same religion	Triandis, Tanaka, and Shanmugam (1966) (age, religion, occupation, sex)

Table 12.4 (*Continued*)

Attitude Factor (Sample)	Scales Loading Highly on Factor	Statistically Significant Characteristics in Order of Importance			Studies (Characteristics Studied)
		Controlling Most Variance I	Controlling II	Controlling Least Variance III	
MARITAL ACCEPTANCE American females	(Fall in love with) (Marry)	Different sex	Same race	Same religion	Triandis, Tanaka, and Shanmugam (1966) (age, religion, occupation, sex)
Japanese males	"	Different sex	Same age	High-level occupation	"
Japanese females	"	Different sex	Same age	High-level occupation	"
Indian males	"	Same religion	Same age	Different sex	"
American males	(Marry, love)	Same race	Same age	Fluent English	Triandis, Vassiliou, and Nassiakou (1966) (occupation, English, age, race, sex, religion)
American males (graduate students)	(Marry, love, date)	Opposite sex	Light skin color	Fluent English	Triandis, Fishbein, and Hall (1964) (occupation, nationality, sex, age, skin color, English)
Indian males (graduate students)	"	Opposite sex	High-level occupation	Light skin color	"

Americans					
Negro males	(Marry, love, date)	Different sex	Same race	High-level occupation	Davis and Grobstein (1966) (race, sex, religion, occupation, skin color)
Negro females	"	Different sex	Same race	Same religion	
White males	"	Different sex	Same race	Same religion	
White females	"	Different sex	Same race	Same religion	
FRIENDSHIP American males	(Be partners with) (Eat with) (Gossip with)	Same sex	Same age	Same religion	Triandis (1964b) (race, religion, occupation, age, sex)
American conventionally prejudiced males		Same race			Triandis and Davis (1965) (race, beliefs, sex)
American conventionally unprejudiced males		Same belief			"
American belief prejudiced males		Same race	Same belief		"
American belief unprejudiced males		Same belief	Same race		"

Table 12.4 (*Continued*)

Attitude Factor (Sample)	Scales Loading Highly on Factor	Statistically Significant Characteristics in Order of Importance			Studies (Characteristics Studied)
		Controlling Most Variance I	II	Controlling Least Variance III	
FRIENDSHIP (*Cont'd*) American mixed sexes	(Accept as intimate friend) (Eat with)	Good English	Same race	Good dress	Triandis, Loh, and Levin (1966) (race, beliefs, English, dress)
American males	(Gossip with) (Be partners in athletic game) (Permit to do me favor) (Teach) (Accept as intimate friend)	Same age	Same sex	Same religion	Triandis, Tanaka, and Shanmugam (1966) (age, religion, occupation, sex)
American females	"	Same age	Same religion	High-level occupation	"
Japanese males	(Admire character) (Gossip with) (Admire ideas)	Same religion	Same age	High-status occupation	"

Group	Behaviors				Reference
Japanese females	(Accept as intimate friend)	Same religion	High-status occupation	Same age	"
Indian males	(Love) (Gossip with) (Partners in athletic games) (Permit favor) (Accept as intimate friend)	Same sex	Same age	Same religion	Triandis, Tanaka, and Shanmugam (1966)
American males Indian males (graduate students)	(Partners in athletic game) (Eat with) (Teach) (Be on first-name basis)	High-level occupation	English fluency		Triandis, Fishbein, and Hall (1964) (occupation, nationality, sex, age, skin color, English)
SOCIAL DISTANCE American males	(Exclude from neighborhood) (Prohibit from voting)	Different race	Low occupation	Different religion	Triandis and Triandis (1960) (race, occupation, nationality, religion)
American males	"	Different race	Different religion	Low occupation	Triandis and Triandis (1962) (race, occupation, nationality, religion)

Table 12.4 *(Continued)*

Attitude Factor (Sample)	Scales Loading Highly on Factor	Statistically Significant Characteristics in Order of Importance			Studies (Characteristics Studied)
		Controlling Most Variance I	Controlling II	Controlling Least Variance III	
SOCIAL DISTANCE Greek males	(Exclude from neighborhood) (Prohibit from voting)	Different religion	Different race	Different nationality	Triandis and Triandis (1962) (race, occupation, nationality, religion)
American conventionally prejudiced males	"	Different race	Different belief		Triandis and Davis (1965) (race, belief, sex)
American conventionally unprejudiced males	"	Different race			"
American belief prejudiced males	"	Different race	Different belief		"
American belief unprejudiced males	"	Different race	Different belief		"

American males	"	Different race	Low occupation	Different religion	Triandis, Davis, and Takezawa (1965) (race, religion, occupation, nationality)
German males	"	Low occupation	Different religion	Different race	"
Japanese males	"	Low occupation	Different race	Different nationality	"
American mixed	"	Different race	Low occupation	Different beliefs	Triandis (1961) (race, beliefs, occupation, religion)
American mixed	(Exclude from neighborhood) (Prohibit from voting)	Different race	Poor English		Triandis, Loh, and Levin (1966) (race, beliefs, English, dress)
Americans White males	(Invite to club [—])	Different race	Different religion	Low occupation	Davis and Grobstein (1966) (race, religion, sex, occupation, skin color)
White females	(Exclude from neighborhood)	Different race	Different religion	Low occupation	
Negro males		Different religion	Different race	Low occupation	
Negro females	(Accept as close kin [—])	Different religion	Different race	Low occupation	
SUPERORDINATION American males	(Treat as subordinate)	Low occupation	Different religion		Triandis (1964b) (race, religion, occupation, age, sex)

Table 12.4 (*Continued*)

Attitude Factor (Sample)	Scales Loading Highly on Factor	Statistically Significant Characteristics in Order of Importance			Studies (Characteristics Studied)
		Controlling Most Variance I	II	Controlling Least Variance III	
SUPERORDINATION (*Cont'd*) American conventionally prejudiced males	(Treat as subordinate)	Different race			Triandis and Davis (1965) (race, beliefs, sex)
American conventionally unprejudiced males	"	Different belief			"
American belief prejudiced	"				"
American belief unprejudiced	"	Different belief			"
American males	"	Low-level occupation	Poor English fluency	Different race	Triandis, Vassiliou, and Nassiakou (1966) (occupation, English, age, sex, religion)

POTENCY					
American males	(Big, powerful strong)	Same sex	Same age	Same religion	Triandis, Tanaka, and Shanmugam (1966) (age, religion, occupation, sex)
American females	"	Same age	Opposite sex	Same religion	"
Indian males	(Huge, great, big)	High-level occupation	Same sex		"
Japanese males	(Strong, brave, active, democratic)	Same age	Same religion	Same sex	"
Japanese females	(Heavy)	Older	High-level occupation	Same religion	"
EVALUATION					
American males (graduate students)	(Good, clean, healthy)	High-level occupation	English fluency		Triandis, Fishbein, and Hall (1964) (occupation, nationality, sex, skin color, English)
American mixed	(Good, wise)	Fluent English	Same belief		Triandis, Loh, and Levin (1966) (race, beliefs, English, dress)
American conventionally prejudiced males	"	Same belief			Triandis and Davis (1965) (beliefs, race, sex)
American conventionally unprejudiced males	"	Same belief			"

Table 12.4 (Continued)

Attitude Factor (Sample)	Scales Loading Highly on Factor	Statistically Significant Characteristics in Order of Importance			Studies (Characteristics Studied)
		Controlling Most Variance I	Controlling II	Controlling Least Variance III	
EVALUATION (Cont'd) American belief prejudiced males	(Good, wise)	Same belief			Triandis and Davis (1965) (beliefs, race, sex)
American belief unprejudiced males	"	Same belief			"
American males	(Familiar, nice, good)	Same religion	High-level occupation	Same sex	Triandis, Tanaka, and Shanmugam (1966) (age, religion, occupation, sex)
American females	(Familiar, nice, good, sweet)	Opposite sex	Same religion	High-level occupation	"
Indian males	(Good, active, delicate, calm)	Same religion	Same sex		"
Japanese males	(Happy, good, comfortable, familiar)	Same religion	Same age	Same sex	"

Japanese females	"	Same religion	Same age	High-level occupation	"
ACTIVITY American males	(Fast, dour, alive)	Same age	High-level occupation	Same religion	Triandis, Tanaka, and Shanmugam (1966) (age, religion, occupation, sex)
American females	(Fast, alive)	Same age	High-level occupation	Same religion	"
Indian males	(Active, fast)	Same religion	High-level occupation		"
Japanese males	(Cheerful, active, light, colorful)	Same age	Opposite sex	Low-level occupation	"
Japanese females	"	Same age	Same religion	Low-level occupation	"
EMPLOY-ABILITY American personnel directors	(Strongly recommend hiring of)	High competence	High sociability	Same race	Triandis (1963) (Competence, religion, sociability, race, sex, age, family wealth)
Greek personnel directors	"	Youth	High competence	Same race	"
American students	"	High competence	High sociability	Same race	"

Table 12.4 (*Continued*)

Attitude Factor (Sample)	Scales Loading Highly on Factor	Statistically Significant Characteristics in Order of Importance			Studies (Characteristics Studied)
		Controlling Most Variance I	II	Controlling Least Variance III	
EMPLOY-ABILITY (*Cont'd*) Greek students	(Strongly recommend hiring of)	High competence	High sociability	Same religion	Triandis (1963) (competence, religion, sociability, race, sex, age, family wealth)
American personnel directors				No disability (ex-tubercular wheel chair)	Rickard, Triandis, and Patterson (1963) (competence, disability, sociability, sex)
American personnel directors	(Strongly recommend hiring of)	High competence	No disability (deaf, epileptic)	High sociability	Rickard, Triandis, and Patterson (1963)
American personnel directors	"	High competence	Not ex-mental patient	High sociability	"
American personnel directors	"	High competence	Not prison parolee	High sociability	"

English (for English speakers), and a high occupation are related to high scores on this factor.

FRIENDSHIP Factor. This factor is very much like the marital factor, except for the obvious difference in the sex characteristic. The maximum friendship responses are made toward "same sex" individuals. But, the other characteristics (same race, same age, same religion, fluent English, good dress, and high level of occupation) appear to make the two factors very similar.

SOCIAL DISTANCE. This factor is maximal when the other person is of *different* race, religion, nationality, and belief, speaks poor English, and is engaged in a low-level occupation. These characteristics define "low status according to my in-group" accompanied by negative affect. Note, therefore, that the characteristics contributing the most variance do differ with samples from different cultures.

SUPERORDINATION. This factor is relevant for people having a low-level occupation. Differences in race, belief, and religion may also lead to high superordination.

If we compare the affective-cognitive components, we find that EVALUATION is very much like RESPECT. The same characteristics associated with one are associated with the other. POTENCY is associated with maleness, youth, high-level occupations, but also with the same religion.

ACTIVITY is associated with youth, high-level occupations, and same religion, although in Japan people in low-level occupations are seen as more active. It is possible that in Japan the dignity associated with high status is also associated with low rates of activity.

Finally, the studies of EMPLOYABILITY show that high competence, high sociability, same race, and same religion are significant determinants of employability.

Although these regularities in the characteristics that are important determinants of judgments on a given component are quite impressive, the *differences* in the emphasis on various characteristics should also be kept in mind. We note, for example, that *same belief* is more important than *same race* for the RESPECT factor judgments of many samples of white American males but that conventionally prejudiced males emphasize *race* more than *belief* in their respect judgments. In examining differences between samples we must, of course, consider the stimuli employed in the particular study. These are shown in the right-hand column of Table 12.4. We note that when *race* is not experimentally manipulated in the characteristics of the stimulus person, *occupation* and *English fluency* become particularly important.

On the MARITAL ACCEPTANCE factor, we note that *same* race is an important characteristic for American white males and females, as well as for Negro females, but it is much less important for Negro males. *Same religion* is important for Indians and for American white males and females, but high occupation is important for Negro females and for the Japanese. Thus, we note differences in emphasis between samples.

On FRIENDSHIP ACCEPTANCE, we note again the importance of the *same race* characteristic for the prejudiced but not for the unprejudiced Americans. A *high-level occupation* appears important for females in all samples, but for males it is of major importance only for the Japanese males and for American and Indian male graduate students. The latter emphasize both a *high-level occupation* and *English fluency* as bases of friendship.

SOCIAL DISTANCE is determined predominantly by *race* among white Americans, by *religion* among Greeks and American Negroes, and by occupation among the samples of Germans and Japanese that were studied. SUPERORDINATION is determined by *race* only among prejudiced American white males, but a *difference in beliefs, religion,* or a *low-level of occupation* is likely to be important among other samples of Americans in the determination of SUPERORDINATION responses.

On the Semantic Differential *evaluation* factor, all samples tend to evaluate highly persons of *similar beliefs* (for example, religion). Presumably, similarity in beliefs leads to positive reinforcements of one person by another and thus to positive affect. This finding is consistent with the assumptions that led to the construction of Table 12.2.

How can these results be cast in a more abstract, theoretical framework?

Table 12.5 shows a simple classification of the behavioral component of the factors governing interpersonal attitude adapted from Foa (1964). Two basic facets (Foa, 1965) are postulated: *status* and *affect*. Status (see columns) can be higher, similar, or lower. Affect (see rows) can be positive or negative. The five factors obtained from the American subjects (Respect, Marital Acceptance, Friendship Acceptance, Social Distance, and Superordination) are classified in different cells, with the exception of the Marital and Friendship Acceptance factors. However, we do know that these two factors are separated by the *sex* facet. Same sex maximinizes the responses on the friendship factor and different sex the responses on the marital. The sex facet, on the other hand, is not particularly relevant in the

Table 12.5 *The Basic Dimensions of Interaction as Determinants of the Behavioral Subcomponents of Interpersonal Attitudes*

Affect (between P and O)	Status of P with Respect to O		
	Higher	Similar	Lower
Positive	PROTECTION SUPERORDINATION	MARITAL AC-CEPTANCE FRIENDSHIP ACCEPTANCE	RESPECT SUBORDINATION
Negative	SOCIAL DISTANCE EXPLOITATION	HOSTILITY	REBELLION

other parts of the table. Therefore, to avoid complications, we did not enter it as an additional facet in Table 12.5.

The absence of the factors of HOSTILITY and the REBELLION factors in the large amount of research presented earlier in Table 12.4 reflects the inadequate sampling of such behaviors in most of the earlier American work. On the other hand, it should be recalled that the study using free elicitation of behaviors did result in HOS-TILITY factors from both Americans and Greeks. In one study with Greeks, a factor suggesting REBELLION (*not reprimand, be indignant with, be jealous of*) was obtained. In Table 12.5, we also entered the words Protection and Exploitation to suggest the possible existence of several factors, undiscovered as yet, that may logically exist and that might be obtained with sampling of behaviors in cultures where such factors are more salient.

Table 12.5 suggests some reasons why the behavioral component of attitudes is multidimensional. The various subcomponents (factors) are determined by different combinations of the *affect* and *status* facets. Another determinant of the separation of the factors in the behavioral component of attitudes is the differential application of *sanctions* for breaking group norms. Sanctions appear to be clearer in the case of the MARITAL and SOCIAL DISTANCE factors; intermediate for FRIENDSHIP and SUBORDINATION; minimal in the case of RESPECT. Most social groups would ridicule but would not reject a group member who respects a member of the out-group.

On the other hand, they are likely to reject him if he marries a member of this out-group. For example, among prejudiced whites, if a person votes for a Negro (a behavior loaded on the RESPECT factor) he will receive less punishment than if he marries a Negro.

One implication of the conceptual model illustrated in Table 12.5 concerns the behaviors of the FRIENDSHIP ACCEPTANCE and RESPECT factor. When we consider the characteristics of P with respect to O, we should find that the *greater the similarity in the status* of P and O, the greater the FRIENDSHIP ACCEPTANCE. On the other hand, the greater the difference in the status of P and O, the greater should be the RESPECT. These hypotheses were tested by Triandis, Vassiliou, and Thomanek (1966) with a representative sample from Athens, Greece. The status of O was varied by presenting stimulus persons described as (a) physicians, (b) bank clerks, and (c) unskilled workers. The status of P was determined from responses concerning his education, occupation, income, and from an inspection of his house and neighborhood. The two hypotheses were strongly confirmed. Thus, it was shown that RESPECT is a positive function of the status of the stimulus person (O) and a negative function of the status of the respondent (P). FRIENDSHIP ACCEPTANCE was highest in those cases where the difference in the status of O and P was minimal. It was also shown that *same sex* is an important determinant of FRIENDSHIP ACCEPTANCE responses, with the males giving significantly more positive responses on this factor toward other males and females toward other females.

In summary, there is considerable stability in the finding that the components of interpersonal attitudes are distinct but are related in lawful ways to characteristics of O and P and to the relationship between these characteristics. The cross-cultural invariance of these findings is not always as great as would be ideal for convenience; however, in a very *general* way, these findings do hold for the cultures tested so far.

IMPLICATIONS FOR PREDICTING
INTERPERSONAL BEHAVIOR

In view of the multidimensional nature of attitudes, it would appear naïve to attempt to predict social behavior from the measurement of attitudes, utilizing only one attitude score. In fact, it appears necessary to obtain a *number* of scores to describe *each of the components* of attitude. There is evidence (Ostrom, 1966) that the behavioral component of attitudes provides the best set of attitude scores for the prediction of behavior. Thus, the theory sketched at the beginning in Tables 12.1 and 12.2 appears to have some utility. Nevertheless, it is not fully developed, and much more work is required before we can be sure that it is an adequate theory. The operation of habits, norms, previous rewards and punishments, and personality factors in the determination of behavior is as yet unexplored in the context of investigations such as those presented here. Yet the results obtained so far are promising and suggest that the present approach may be fruitful.

SUMMARY

I have presented evidence that interpersonal attitudes are multidimensional. In addition to the distinctions between the affective cognitive, and behavioral components, it was shown that these components *themselves* are multidimensional. A number of studies dealing with the dimensionality of the behavioral component were reviewed. Operational procedures for the measurement of each of the components and subcomponents were presented. The stability of such measurements across different samples of *social stimuli* and obtained from samples of *individuals from several cultures* was reviewed. The relationships between the characteristics of individuals and responses to the various components and subcomponents of attitudes were reviewed. Finally, a theory was presented that relates the individual's attitudes to his behavior.

REFERENCES

Campbell, D. T., 1950. The indirect assessment of social attitudes. *Psychol. Bull.*, **47**, 15–38.

Campbell, D. T., and Fiske, D. W., 1959. Convergent and discriminant validation by the multitrait-multimethod matrix. *Psychol. Bull.*, **56**, 81–105.

Crowne, D. P., and Marlowe, D., 1964. *The approval motive.* New York: Wiley.

Davis, E. E., 1966. A methodological study of behavioral and semantic differential scales relevant to intercultural negotiations. Tech. Rep. No. 32, Group Effectiveness Research Laboratory, Univ. of Ill.

Davis, E. E., and Grobstein, Nadine, 1966. Multimode factor analysis of interpersonal perceptions. Tech. Rep. No. 36, Group Effectiveness Research Laboratory, Univ. of Ill.

Davis, E. E., and Triandis, H. C., 1965. An exploratory study of intercultural negotiations. Tech. Rep. No. 26, Group Effectiveness Research Laboratory, Univ. of Ill.

Edwards, A. L., 1957. *Techniques of attitude scale construction.* New York: Appleton-Century-Crofts.

Fishbein, M., 1965. A consideration of beliefs, attitudes and their relationship. In I. Steiner and M. Fishbein (Eds.), *Current studies in social psychology.* New York: Holt, Rinehart and Winston, pp. 107–120.

Foa, U. G., 1964. Cross-cultural similarity and differences in interpersonal behavior. *J. abnorm. soc. Psychol.*, **68**, 517–522.

Foa, U. G., 1965. New developments in facet analysis and design. *Psychol. Rev.*, **72**, 262–274.

Green, B. F., 1954. Attitude measurement. In G. Lindzey (Ed.), *Handbook of social psychology.* Reading, Mass.: Addison-Wesley, **1**, pp. 335–369.

Jones, E. E., and Davis, K. E., 1965. From acts to dispositions. In L. Berkowitz (Ed.). *Advances in experimental social psychology.* Vol. 2. New York: Academic, pp. 220–266.

Katz, D., and Stotland, E., 1959. A preliminary statement to a theory of attitude structure and change. In S. Koch (Ed.), *Psychology: A study of a science.* Vol. 3. New York: McGraw-Hill, pp. 423–475.

Kelly, G. A., 1955. *The psychology of personal constructs.* New York: Norton.

Kiesler, C. A., and Goldberg, G., 1966. A multi-dimensional approach to the experimental study of interpersonal attraction: the effect of a blunder on the attractiveness of a competent other. (Mimeographed draft, Yale Univ.)

LaForge, R., and Suczek, R., 1955. The interpersonal dimension of personality: III. An interpersonal checklist. *J. Pers.*, **24**, 94–112.

Lambert, W. E., 1964. The role of language and accent variations in person perception. *Acta Psychologica*, **23**, 190–191.

LaPiere, R. T., 1934. Attitudes *vs.* actions. *Special Forces*, **14**, 230–237.

Lorr, M., and McNair, D. M., 1965. Expansion of the interpersonal behavior circle. *J. Pers. soc. Psychol.*, **2**, 823–830.

Osgood, C. E., 1966. Dimensionality of the semantic space for communication via facial expressions. *Scandinavian J. Psychol.*, **7**, 1–30.

Osgood, C. E., Suci, G. J. and Tannenbaum, P. H., 1957. *The measurement of meaning.* Urbana: Univ. of Ill. Press.

Ostrom, T. M., 1966. A tripartite study of attitudes. Research proposal, Ohio State Univ.

Rickard, T. E., Triandis, H. C., and Patterson, C. H., 1963. Indices of employer prejudice toward disabled applicants. *J. appl. Psychol.*, **47**, 52–55.

Rosenberg, M. J., 1965. Inconsistency arousal and reduction in attitude change. In I. D. Steiner and M. Fishbein (Eds.), *Current studies in social psychology.* New York: Holt, Rinehart and Winston, pp. 121–134.

Schlosberg, H., 1954. Three dimensions of emotion. *Psychol. Rev.*, **61**, 81–88.

Scott, W. A., 1962. Cognitive complexity and cognitive flexibility. *Sociometry*, **25**, 405–414.

Sherif, Carolyn, Sherif, M., and Nebergall, R. E., 1965. *Attitude and attitude change*. Philadelphia: Saunders.

Sherif, M., 1966. Theoretical analysis of the individual-group relationship in a social situation. In G. DiRenzo (Ed.), *Problems of Conceptual Definition in the Behavioral Sciences*. New York: Random House.

Smith, M. B., Bruner, J. S., and White, R. W., 1956. *Opinions and personality*. New York: Wiley.

Thurstone, L. L., and Chave, E. J., 1929. *The measurement of attitude*. Chicago: The Univ. of Chicago Press.

Triandis, H. C., 1961. A note on Rokeach's theory of prejudice. *J. abnorm. soc. Psychol.*, **62**, 184–186.

Triandis, H. C., 1963. Factors affecting employee selection in two cultures. *J. appl. Psychol.*, **47**, 89–96.

Triandis, H. C., 1964a. Cultural influences upon cognitive processes. In L. Berkowitz (Ed.), *Advances in experimental social psychology*. New York: Academic, pp. 1–48.

Triandis, H. C., 1964b. Exploratory factor analyses of the behavioral component of social attitudes. *J. abnorm. soc. Psychol.*, **68**, 420–430.

Triandis, H. C., and Davis, E. E., 1965. Race and belief as determinants of behavioral intentions. *J. Pers. soc. Psychol.*, **2**, 715–725.

Triandis, H. C., Davis, E. E., and Takesawa, S. I., 1965. Some determinants of social distance among American, German and Japanese students. *J. Pers. soc. Psychol.*, **2**, 540–551.

Triandis, H. C., Fishbein, M., and Hall, Eleanor R., 1964. Person perception among American and Indian students. Tech. Rep. No. 15, Group Effectiveness Research Laboratory.

Triandis, H. C., and Lambert, W. W., 1958. A restatement and test of Schlosberg's theory of emotion with two kinds of subjects from Greece. *J. abnorm. soc. Psychol.*, **57**, 187–196.

Triandis, H. C., Loh, W. D., and Levin, Leslie A., 1966. Race, status, quality of spoken English and opinions about civil rights as determinants of interpersonal attitudes. *J. Pers. soc. Psychol.*, **3**, 468–472.

Triandis, H. C., Tanaka, A. V., and Shanmugam, V. T., 1966. Interpersonal attitudes among American, Japanese and Indian students. *International J. Psychol.*, **1**, 177–206.

Triandis, H. C., and Triandis, Leigh M., 1960. Race, social class, religion and nationality as determinants of social distance. *J. abnorm. soc. Psychol.*, **61**, 110–118.

Triandis, H. C., and Triandis, Leigh M., 1962. A cross-cultural study of social distance. *Psychol. Monogr.*, **76**, No. 21 (Whole No. 540).

Triandis, H. C., and Triandis, Leigh M., 1965. Some studies of social distance. In I. D. Steiner and M. Fishbein (Eds.), *Recent studies in social psychology.* New York: Holt, Rinehart and Winston, pp. 207–217.

Triandis, H. C., Vassiliou, Vasso, and Nassiakou, Maria, 1966. A cross-cultural study of role perceptions. In preparation.

Triandis, H. C., Vassiliou, Vasso, and Thomanek, E. K., 1966. Social status as a determinant of social acceptance and friendship acceptance. *Sociometry,* **29,** 396–405.

Zajonc, R. B., 1960. The process of cognitive tuning in communication. *J. abnorm. soc. Psychol.,* **61,** 159–167.

Part IV

13. Political Attitudes in New Nations: Examples from the British Caribbean*

Charles C. Moskos, Jr., and Wendell Bell

INTRODUCTION

Among the new men of power are today's leaders of the many new nations that have come into existence since the Second World War. Such men, entering the world stage at a time when human mastery is higher than ever before in history, generally have set for themselves the tasks of rewriting the past, altering the present, and creating a new future through their historical actions. They face, of course, enormous practical obstacles in carrying out these ambitions, ranging from lack of capital and natural resources to impoverished and un-

* This is a revised version of "Some Implications of Equality for Political, Economic, and Social Development," which was previously published in *International Review of Community Development*, n. 13–14, 1965, pp. 219–246. The data reported are part of the results of the former West Indies Study Program of the University of California, Los Angeles. The program was financed by the Carnegie Corporation of New York, whose assistance we gratefully acknowledge. We also thank the UCLA Political Change Committee, which, under another Carnegie grant, aided the writing of this chapter. Additionally, Charles Moskos, wishes to thank the Social Science Research Council for a Pre-Doctoral Research Fellowship, 1961 to 1963, and Wendell Bell thanks the Center for Advanced Study in the Behavioral Sciences for a Fellowship, 1963 to 1964. The authors alone accept responsibility for the interpretations and conclusions.

educated populations. Nonetheless, they are change leaders. Though their achievements may fall short of their marks, they have set their countries in motion on courses toward political independence, economic progress, and social reform.

It is now clear that a key element in the images of the future that are shaping the new nations is to be found in the attitudes toward equality held by different elite groups. In the transition from colony to nation-state, some men have been changing, or attempting to change, the boundaries, membership, degree of autonomy, external coalitions, organizational structure, internal relationships, history, and personal character of an emergent large-scale organization, the nation-state. Reasons that they have generally advanced for doing so have prominently included a desire to create a more egalitarian society. Thus, attitudes toward equality constitute an important part of the ideology that has given rise to nationalist movements, and also they significantly influence the value premises of decision-making after the nationalist leaders come to power.

Our thesis is as follows: *Within the conditions characteristic of colonial political, economic, social, and cultural settings, if egalitarian attitudes exist, then the desire for political independence will exist.* There are, of course, obvious exceptions. White South African and white Rhodesian nationalism, based as they are on sectional interests and socially exclusive principles, come immediately to mind. But for the vast majority of the new nations of the twentieth century, the generalization appears to hold. It holds as well for many of the nations formed in the nineteenth century and also for those of the eighteenth, where domination of some social classes over others in some instances provided conditions similar to the colonial subordination.

Despite many excellent studies of the new states, we still know relatively little about the attitudes that make up the value context of decision-making. Although we are coming to recognize equality as a master value, we know little about its implications for directions of political, economic, social, and cultural change. Our purpose here is macrosociological, since we deal with the forming and the shaping of whole nations and with the perceptions and evaluations of social reality that help account for both. Our orientation is substantive rather than methodological, since we stress the content and implications of egalitarian attitudes rather than details of logic or technique. It is focused on a "natural" rather than a laboratory experiment, since we study attitudes that are distinctively related to the larger social setting and to the cleavages in opinions that reflect the ongoing struggle among people who are part of that struggle to control the future of the whole society.

Using as an example empirical data from a study of attitudes in four emergent nations in the British Caribbean, we first describe and analyze attitudes toward equality held by top leaders on the eve of political independence. Such attitudes represent, as we shall demonstrate, an important part of the ideology of such leaders, persons with the power to formulate and implement policy in the British West Indies. The analysis of these data is of practical significance because it reveals some of the sources of support or opposition to the spread of equality. It is of theoretical significance because it shows the ways in which the distribution of attitudes toward equality are related systematically to the social differentiation of West Indian leaders.

Second, and most important, we examine the relationship between egalitarian attitudes and political, economic, social, and cultural development. We ask, What are the implications of attitudes toward equality for images of the future? What are the implications for the emergent polity, economy, society, and culture that West Indian leaders are in the process of creating? The answers to these questions permit us to make some preliminary observations on the meaning and character of these emergent Caribbean nations and, by cautious generalization, perhaps on the future prospects of some other new states as well.

EMERGENT CARIBBEAN NATIONS

Two of the Caribbean nations studied have already become fully independent: Jamaica, which is 90 miles south of Cuba and 100 miles west of Haiti, with a population of about 1.7 million; and Trinidad and Tobago with a population of over 800,000 in the Eastern Caribbean near the coast of Venezuela. Others are still, at the time of writing, on the road to complete self-government: British Guiana on the continent of South America with 83,000 square miles of land, by far the largest territory in area of those discussed here, but with only about 600,000 people, and which is scheduled for nationhood in May 1966; and the so-called "Little-Eight" consisting of Barbados and the Lilliputian islands of the Leeward and Windward island chains in the Eastern Caribbean that are inhabited by a total of 700,000 people.[1]

[1] It should be noted that at least one of the Little-Eight, Grenada, may decide to join with Trinidad and Tobago in a unitary state, and another, Barbados, may become independent in its own right in the near future. Others, such as Antigua, may be content with a political status somewhat short of full independence. Since this chapter was written, British Guiana became independent Guyana on May 26, 1966 and Barbados became independent on November 30, 1966.

The modern political history of the British West Indies began in the late 1930's when outbreaks of poverty-induced strikes and riots engulfed most of the area. The economic discontent of the populace, which was soon given voice by new leaders, led to a series of constitutional advances that began in the mid-1940's. Although delayed by the outbreak of the Second World War, the transformation of the old crown colony system into a modified ministerial form of government with local leaders was started at that time, and by the early 1950's, each of the territories had achieved large measures of local autonomy under a democratic system based on universal adult suffrage. Although there have been several attempts to unify the area, the most recent being the West Indies Federation, the various territories have followed different roads toward political independence.

Nearly all West Indians are descended from people brought over in previous times to meet the demands of an economy based on the sugar plantation, the bulk of the population being persons of African descent whose forebearers were slaves. After the emancipation of the slaves in the 1830's, indentured laborers were brought over for agricultural labor. Of these later arrivals, the most numerous were from India (East Indians), who today represent the largest ethnic group in British Guiana and constitute a sizable minority in Trinidad. Also contributing to the West Indies' demographic mosaic are small numbers of English, Irish, Scots, Welsh, Portuguese, Levantines, Chinese, and Amerindians. Although the West Indies are still heavily dependent upon sugar exports, such tropical products as bananas, coconuts, spices, rice, and citrus fruits are also marketed abroad. The major extractive industries (all foreign owned) are bauxite in Jamaica and British Guiana and petroleum in Trinidad. Some small-scale manufacturing is done locally in Jamaica and Trinidad, and tourism has also become an important source of income.

BASIC DATA

The data reported here are from interviews with 112 top leaders in Jamaica, Trinidad and Tobago, British Guiana, and in Barbados, Grenada, and Dominica, these last three giving a sample from the Little-Eight. These leaders were interviewed from August 1961 through April 1962 and included in each territory: the premier, the most influential cabinet members, top leaders of the opposition party(ies), heads of labor unions, wealthy merchants, large plantation owners, and newspaper editors. Also interviewed were leading members of the clergy, ethnic leaders, top educationalists, leaders of voluntary organizations, prominent professionals, and high-ranking civil servants. In each of the territories, the leaders who were interviewed constituted, with a few exceptions, a systematically defined universe of the top national decision-makers.[2]

To locate such national leaders, a modified "snowball" technique was used. Initially, from a cross-section of institutional sectors persons were selected who, on the basis of their formal roles or institutional positions, were likely to be top leaders. They were asked to identify individuals whom they considered to wield national influence. As the nominations of the national leaders accumulated, the most frequently mentioned persons were in turn asked to identify other influentials. In this way the original positional approach gave way to a reputational approach, and the list of reputed leaders was increasingly refined. The same procedure was used in each of the territories so that comparability between the units was insured. No leaders so selected refused to be interviewed, and when the field research had been completed, each leader had been questioned at some length about the issues presented in this chapter.

Although the data formally presented here are limited to the interviews with the 112 top leaders, our thinking has been informed by observation, discussions with informants, additional and less systematic interviews, and reading a wide range of local newspapers and periodicals throughout several periods of fieldwork and shorter trips to the West Indies from as early as 1956 (for one of the writers) to 1966.

AN INDICATOR OF EGALITARIAN ATTITUDES

In the view of West Indian leaders, equality means primarily equality of opportunity. Egalitarians want a situation in which ascribed barriers to individual advancement will be practically nonexistent. Some leaders thought in terms of minimum sets of human rights applied equally to all persons in the society, and others went so far as to stress equal rewards for all individuals in a society. A classic and succinct definition of the philosophy of egalitarianism that is generally reflected in the attitudes of West Indian leaders, has been given by R. H. Tawney (1962):

[2] A detailed description and discussion of the selection of the top West Indian leaders along with their names, but not the particular data analysis reported here, are available in Moskos (1967). A summary version will soon appear in Bell (1967). Additional findings from this study are reported in Moskos and Bell (1964a; 1964b; 1964c).

It is to hold that while (man's) natural endowments differ profoundly, it is the mark of a civilized society to aim at eliminating such inequalities as have their source, not in individual difference, but in its own organization, and that individual differences, which are a source of social energy, are more likely to ripen and find expression if social inequalities as far as practicable, are diminished (p. 49).

The measurement of egalitarian attitudes among the West Indian leaders was based on their responses to an open-ended question. Immediately prior to the item in the interview dealing with egalitarian attitudes, the respondent was asked what he considered the best form of government for his territory. Persons who favored political democracy were asked what they considered the essence of democracy. Persons who did not favor political democracy were asked what they considered the best alternative form of government. In either case, if features such as equality of opportunity, the classless society, or related notions were mentioned, the leaders were called "egalitarians." This is a rather stringent test, with the egalitarians being highly egalitarian and the remainder including both highly and mildly inegalitarian attitudes. Thirty-nine percent of the 112 interviewed West Indian leaders were classified as egalitarian, the remaining 61 percent, those who did not explicitly affirm egalitarianism as part and parcel of their social ideology, being termed "inegalitarians."

DIFFERENCES BY TERRITORY

The percentage distribution of egalitarian attitudes among the West Indian leaders, as shown below, differed among the territories.

Territory	Percent Egalitarian	Number of Cases on Which Percent Is Based
British Guiana	55	(13)
Jamaica	50	(24)
Trinidad	41	(22)
Little-Eight	32	(53)

The percentage of egalitarian leaders was highest in British Guiana, where in 1950 a left-wing nationalist movement was formed that has since split into the two current dominant political parties: the Communist-influenced People's Progressive Party and the socialist People's National Congress: In Jamaica, where egalitarian attitudes characterized half the leaders, a viable two-party system has been operating since 1944.[3] Both major parties, the liberal People's National Party and the more conservative Jamaica Labour Party, have each had some time at the helm of government. Political mobilization in Trinidad did not gain real momentum until the formation of the People's National Movement in 1956. The level of political mobilization in the Little-Eight, where the lowest percentage of leaders were egalitarians, seems to resemble that of the larger territories a decade or so ago; only in Barbados have the local political parties advanced beyond being personal vehicles.

Although we are dealing with several different emergent Caribbean nations, among which the incidence of egalitarian attitudes varied, a similar pattern runs through them all with respect to the correlates of egalitarian attitudes among their leaders. From data analyses not presented here, we found that individual correlations of attitudes, activities, and personal background characteristics relating to attitudes toward equality were markedly similar regardless of territory. Thus we treat the West Indies as a whole and group the various territories together in the presentation of the following data.

ELITE DIFFERENTIATION AND EGALITARIAN ATTITUDES

Obviously, some elites are more strategically placed than others to voice and represent economic and social interests and some are more strategically placed than others to make and execute policies designed to bring about economic and social change. Also, the location of structural support for, or against, the spread of economic and social equality is of theoretical interest.

Table 13.1 shows the percentage of West Indian leaders who were egalitarians by selected social characteristics. Starting with the first

[3] As a point of reference, we note that in a 1958 survey of Jamaican elites conducted by Bell, over 70 percent of the respondents were "pro-equalitarian," dividing his scale at the midpoint. This is considerably higher than the 50 percent of the Jamaican leaders in this study having egalitarian attitudes. See Bell (1964, Chapter IV). Bell's earlier study and this one, however, are not strictly comparable. He included middle ranks of leadership as well as upper, whereas the present study is confined to the *top* leaders. There are also differences in the measures used and in procedures of collecting data, for example, a seven-item index of equalitarianism versus an open-ended question and mail questionnaires versus personal interviews. Undoubtedly, the more than 20 percent difference in the two studies is mostly due, if such comparison is valid, to a more stringent test of egalitarianism that was used in the later study, where the leaders had to "volunteer" their egalitarianism.

Table 13.1 *Percentage of West Indian Leaders Who Are Egalitarians by Selected Social Characteristics*

Selected Social Characteristics	Percent Who Are Egalitarians	Number of Cases on Which Percent Is Based
Age		
55 and over	19	(37)
40 to 54	45	(58)
39 and under	65	(17)
Education		
College or higher	49	(37)
Secondary school	30	(57)
Elementary only	50	(18)
Personal wealth		
Wealthy	13	(39)
Not wealthy	53	(73)
Color and ethnicity		
White	18	(39)
Light brown	30	(20)
East Indian or Chinese	25	(12)
Dark brown or black	68	(41)
Institutional sector		
Political or labor	69	(48)
Economic	6	(34)
Mass media	25	(8)
Civil service	37	(8)
Other*	28	(14)

* Includes religious personages, ethnic group leaders, heads of voluntary organizations, free professionals, and educationists.

characteristic given, we can see that egalitarianism decreases with age. Young leaders are more than three times as likely to have egalitarian attitudes than the oldest group of leaders, with the middle-age group falling in between. Perhaps, this merely reflects the increasing "conservatism" that develops with increasing age, or perhaps new and more liberal generations are being added to the age distribution at the bottom, each generation retaining certain characteristic habits of belief and attitude throughout its life. In any event, this correlation between age and egalitarianism may augur well for the continued spread of equality, since new younger leaders have been entering the scene.

Looking at the relationship between attitudes toward equality and amount of formal education, we find egalitarian sentiments most typical of the highest and lowest levels. Leaders with intermediate education levels were the least likely to be egalitarian. Two different factors may account for this U-shaped distribution. On the one hand, the percentage of persons with low educational levels who are egalitarian is evidence of a general finding: greater relative support for equality among West Indian leaders of lower socioeconomic origins (which is corroborated by findings reported below dealing with wealth, color and ethnicity, and institutional sector). On the other hand, the most highly educated leaders, who favored equality relatively more than the middling-educated leaders, often seemed inconsistent with their class interest, as narrowly conceived, and reflected in their attitudes the enlightenment of Western humanitarian philosophy. They had usually been exposed to the latter during their higher education, which, until the establishment of the University College of the West Indies in 1947 in Jamaica, meant an extended stay abroad, most often in the United Kingdom, the United States, or Canada.[4]

Wealth, an important variable in any society, also served to demarcate the West Indian leaders' views toward equality. In this study, a person was termed wealthy if he owned a large home with a permanent household staff and had an income of such an amount and nature that he would probably be able to live close to his current standard of living even if he became incapacitated. Such individuals would be considered wealthy by American standards as well. As reported in Table 13.1, nonwealthy leaders were four times more likely to be egalitarians than wealthy persons.[5]

There was a strong correlation between skin color and attitudes toward equality among the West Indian leaders. Over two thirds of the dark brown or black leaders were egalitarians as compared to 18 percent of the whites. Falling between these two groups, but somewhat closer to the white leaders, were East Indians, Chinese, and persons of light brown complexion. The vast majority of the

[4] For a discussion of the ideological effects of the Jamaican educational system and an analysis of the function of higher education in changing attitudes toward equality in Jamaica, see Duke (1967).

[5] The relatively high number of inegalitarians with a completion of no more than a secondary school level of education may reflect the typical academic pattern of most West Indian economic dominants during the period under consideration. Of the 39 leaders who were termed wealthy in this study: 12 were college graduates; 26 had an educational level of completion of secondary school only; and one had not gone beyond elementary school.

darker-skinned people in the West Indies were low in economic and social status whereas the lighter skinned were generally much more favorably placed in the socioeconomic system.

Because wealth and color are to some extent confounded in the West Indies, it is important to clarify their independent effects on egalitarianism. From a table not shown here, wealth appears to be more important than color. Nonwealthy whites were twice as likely to be egalitarian than were the wealthy nonwhites. The often heard expression in the West Indies that it is "class not color" that underlies differences in many attitudes is supported by this finding.[6]

The final social characteristic presented in Table 13.1 is the institutional sector in which the leaders exercised their national influence. Although some leaders engaged in several spheres of activity, each leader was classified just once according to his primary activity. Egalitarian attitudes were much more frequent among political and labor leaders than any other group and least typical of economic dominants. More egalitarian than the economic dominants, but much less so than the political and labor leaders, were persons involved in the mass media, civil service, and in other areas of activity such as religious personages, ethnic group leaders, heads of voluntary organizations, free professionals, and educationists.

In general, then, egalitarians were characteristically leaders of secular, mass-based organizations that were outgrowths of the modern West Indian awakening, and these were the individuals who held legitimate change most directly in their hands. Contrarily, inegalitarians tended to be leaders who represented the established vested interests of West Indian society. In a study of Warsaw students, Nowak (1960) found attitudes toward equality to be related to perceived self-interest. Similarly, most West Indian economic dominants thought (probably erroneously) that they had most to lose by the spread of economic and social equality. Yet, it must be emphasized that the relationship between the institutional sectors and egalitarianism, as with the other social background variables, was not one to one; there were exceptions to the general pattern.

IMPLICATIONS FOR POLITICAL DEVELOPMENT

Within the new nations, policy questions that were formerly dealt with by imperial officials are now being answered by local leaders who represent new national citizenries and new collective purposes.

[6] Raymond W. Mack (1967) describes the interrelationships of color and class in "Race, Class, and Power in Barbados."

Because it is the transition from colonial to independent status that has posed these policy questions, we have called such questions the "decisions of nationhood." Whether by reasoned planning or by random drifting, some outcome or "decision" with respect to these policy questions must take place (cf. Bell and Oxaal, 1964). The following sections are a modest effort to bring some empirical data to bear on the implications of egalitarian attitudes for a few of the major political, economic, social, and cultural issues concerning the emergent nations under discussion.

Political Independence

One obvious example of a decision of nationhood is the choice of individuals to seek political independence for their home territories. What explains why certain members of a colonial society begin to question the old order and eventually take steps to bring about a dismantlement of an empire, why others look on with alarm at this course of events, and why still others accept the changing order without being personally committed to it? On the basis of both their social judgments and involvements, we classified West Indian leaders into three nationalist types: (1) *true nationalists*—those who favored independence immediately and who worked to bring it about; (2) *acquiescing nationalists*—those who temporized with respect to independence but were not firm supporters of the colonial system; (3) *colonialists*—those who favored the indefinite continuation of the colonial system.

Forty-four of the West Indian leaders were egalitarians. Note from Table 13.2 that all of them were true nationalists; also all of the true nationalists were egalitarians. None of the egalitarians was either an acquiescing nationalist or colonialist. Although there is often some interaction and circularity of causation between some attitudes and others, or perhaps a joint antecedent cause, it is frequently possible to determine the most likely direction of causation. The weight of our knowledge of the modern history of ideas, the recent history of the West Indies, and the personal statements of the West Indian leaders lead us to the conclusion that support of political independence was fostered by an egalitarian ethic and opposition to it by inegalitarian values. Thus, one of the most far-reaching implications of attitudes toward equality was that such attitudes engendered the West Indian nationalist movements. Historically, attaining political independence was one step, and a crucial one, toward obtaining the political power thought necessary by some leaders to transform the British West Indies into new, more egalitarian, societies.

Table 13.2 *Percentage of West Indian Leaders Having Certain Political Attitudes by Egalitarianism*

Political Attitudes	Egalitarian	Inegalitarian
Attitudes toward political independence		
True nationalist	100	0
Acquiescing nationalist	0	41
Colonialist	0	59
Total	100	100
Number of cases	(44)	(68)
Attitudes toward political democracy		
Democrat	44	7
Authoritarian idealist	16	0
Cynical parliamentarian	30	27
Authoritarian	10	66
Total	100	100
Number of cases	(43)	(68)
Attitudes toward global alignments		
Western nations	41	100
Neutralist countries	48	0
Communist countries	11	0
Total	100	100
Number of cases	(44)	(68)

Political Democracy

It was no accident that the arguments invoked to justify claims for political independence in colonial nationalist movements were heavily larded with the rhetoric of the theory of political democracy, in addition to that of equality. Yet, to the dismay of many persons, it has become increasingly clear that the appeals to democracy that were made to justify the demands for independence have done little to insure the establishment and continuation of democratic political systems in many of the new nations. In fact, once the imperial power has withdrawn, the new national leaders and citizenries can raise the question, What form of government should the new nations have? And they have considerable freedom of choice in reaching a decision. Among the several factors relevant to a decision on this issue are the attitudes of the leaders toward equality.

A political typology was constructed based on (1) attitudes toward the suitability of parliamentary democracy for one's home territory (the referent being a representative system with guarantees for the maintenance of civil and minority rights); (2) judgments on the competency of the average West Indian voter, that is, whether a leader was cynical or idealistic with regard to the electorate, an important facet of personal political philosophy.

Democrats were those leaders who thought that parlimentary democracy was very suitable for their home territories *and* that the voters were competent. Those who had qualifications about the parliamentary form or believed it was unsuitable but held favorable attitudes toward the competency of the typical West Indian voter were termed *authoritarian idealists*. Another type, the *cynical parliamentarians*, although favoring a parliamentary system, thought that the average voter was incompetent. *Authoritarians* were those who neither believed in the suitability of the parliamentary form nor thought the typical voter was competent.

For the top West Indian leaders as a whole, the percentage distribution according to these political types was as follows.

Attitudes toward Democracy	Percentage
Democrats	22
Authoritarian idealists	6
Cynical parliamentarians	28
Authoritarians	44
Total	100
Number of cases	(111)

Even though these emergent nations presently have British-type representative systems functioning within them, we must conclude from the above distribution of attitudes that the foundations of democracy may be shaky. However, we know from public opinion surveys that attitudes favorable to democracy are far from unanimous even in the most mature democracies. A breakdown of these data by territory shows that democratic attitudes were most pronounced in Jamaica, where modern democratic political institutions have been in force longer than in other territories (Moskos and Bell, 1964c).

Table 13.2 includes the relationships between egalitarianism and attitudes toward political democracy. In general, egalitarians were more likely to be democrats and less likely to be authoritarians than were the inegalitarians. But the correlation between attitudes toward political democracy and attitudes toward equality is smaller than that discussed earlier between nationalist types and egalitarianism: there is some disagreement, especially among the egalitarians, concerning the most desirable political system. A warning signal may be found in the fact that all of the authoritarian idealists were egalitarians. This group regarded the parliamentary process as it was currently operating as thwarting the egalitarian desires of the masses. That this view may not be entirely unfounded is reflected in the fact that so many (58 percent) of all cynical parliamentarians were inegalitarian in their attitudes.

We predict that the authoritarian idealists represent a type that is more numerous among leaders in many of the new states other than in the Caribbean countries considered here. However, even though they constitute only a small group among West Indian leaders, they are significant in that they tend to be among the *youngest* leaders engaged in political activity, and their numbers may be increasing. Furthermore, still more egalitarians may fill the ranks of the authoritarian idealists (or even those of the out-and-out authoritarians) unless the democratic system in these countries can effectively realize the egalitarian promise of West Indian nationalism, a promise that is part of the same web of basic values as democracy.

We cannot entirely agree with de Tocqueville's dictum that when societies are confronted with the choice of either freedom or equality they "at all times habitually . . . prefer equality to freedom" (de Tocqueville, 1961, p. 190). We do, however, have some support from these data for the inverse: inegalitarians are most likely to be opposed to freedom. Unlike our conclusion that commitment to the value of equality in some sense caused the desire for political independence, we regard attitudes toward equality and political democracy as operating in tandem. Equality and political democracy (or liberty) have a common origin in the movement emanating around the Enlightenment and the subsequent Rights of Man.[7]

Not only is it difficult to relate equality to democracy causally in any unilinear fashion in the modern history of ideas, but also there is no evidence of temporal priority of one or the other of these two

---

[7] See Oxaal (1967). A short version will appear in Bell (1967). Oxaal discusses the intellectual development of key Trinidadian nationalist leaders, and in his larger study he documents the actions they took, after they came to power, to implement the Enlightenment values they had received. James A. Mau (1967), another Fellow in the West Indies Study Program, has collected data in Jamaica showing that egalitarian attitudes and the belief in progress, a central aspect of Enlightenment thought, are in fact positively intercorrelated. A short version of his study will also appear in Bell (1967).

notions in the intellectual development of the West Indian leaders.[8] Rather, the West Indian political awakening parallels the same driving ideals of liberty and equality (and fraternity, or social inclusivism, as we show later) that led to the American and French revolutions. These ideals were codified in such documents as the American Declaration of Independence, the Bill of Rights in the Constitution of the United States, and the French Revolutionary Declaration of the Rights of Man and of the Citizen. They are at the core of the democratic revolution now spreading throughout the world.

Global Alignments

Under colonial rule, peoples' contacts with the outside world, apart from those with the imperial power itself, were indirect and circuitous. But with the successful drive toward nationhood, the question of the most desirable and beneficial international relations could be raised from the point of view of the emergent nation's own welfare. Although there were limitations imposed by economic ties, as well as by bonds of sentiment and culture, to the European power that had dominated them during their colonial years, the new national leaders faced the outside world with considerable freedom of choice to formulate their new nations' foreign policies. Thus, we asked, What should the global alignments of the new nation be?

West Indian leaders were much more likely to recommend that their new nations align with the Western than with the Communist countries, although nearly one fifth preferred so-called neutrality. Specifically, they were asked:

"When (Jamaica) becomes fully independent with which group should (Jamaica) align itself, the Western nations, the Communist countries, or the neutralist countries?" (The name of the territory appropriate to each respondent was inserted in the parentheses.) The percentages choosing each alternative were as follows.

Western nations	77%
Neutralist countries	19
Communist countries	4
Total	100%
Number of cases	(112)

There is some evidence to suggest that between 1958 and 1962 there was a slight shift of opinion away from the West, although

[8] De Tocqueville (1961), on the other hand, holds "the taste and the ideal of freedom" is a "consequence of . . . equality" (p. 192).

neither the data nor the sample of leaders were strictly comparable. In 1958 a mail questionnaire survey of Jamaican leaders showed that 83 percent thought the United States had been morally right more often than the Soviet Union as an actor on the world scene, as compared to 16 percent who thought both were about the same and only one percent who said the Soviet Union was more often right than the United States (Bell, 1960; 1964). These percentages can be compared to the results among the Jamaican leaders in the 1961 to 1962 study: 70 percent preferred alignment with the West, 25 percent preferred neutrality, and 5 percent preferred alignment with the East.

The relationship between attitudes toward equality and attitudes toward global alignments is also given in Table 13.2. It may come as a surprise to the casual reader from the Western democracies, if not to the student of the politics of the new nations, to see that the egalitarian West Indian leaders were much *less* likely to favor alignment with the West than the inegalitarian leaders. In fact, 100 percent of the inegalitarian leaders preferred a Western alignment compared to only 41 percent of the egalitarian leaders. The West Indian leaders most committed to the Western ideal of equality were least likely to favor alignment with the Western nations!

The interrelationships among egalitarianism, attitudes toward political independence, and foreign policy preferences help to explain this finding. The nationalists among the West Indian elites were committed to the ideas of self-determination for their territories and of freedom from the political domination of the United Kingdom. Such commitments carried over into their foreign policy attitudes and led them to prefer the more "independent" posture of neutralism rather than following along after the United States, the United Kingdom, and the other nations of the West, or for that matter after the nations of the Communist world either. To them, neutralism involved the least dilution of their country's newly achieved or soon-hoped-for national sovereignty. At the same time, nationalists' hopes and ambitions were in fact inspired by Western ideals, by the commitment to the Rights of Man and especially by the desire for equality.

At the other extreme, the colonialists among the West Indian elites were inegalitarians. The same combination of factors that produced their anti-independence attitudes also produced their preference for Western alignment. Their fears of what the nationalists would do in the years after independence and their hopes for policies that would not undermine their generally well-established socioeconomic positions were linked alike to their desire for Western alignment, their opposition to the nationalist cause, and their preferences for the conservative or reactionary versions of the Western models of polity, economy, and society. They opposed progressive change; they represented the *status quo;* and they found the basic values of Western civilization, as expressed in the Rights of Man, abominations. According to them, such "abominations," again especially equality, characterized the Communist countries to a much greater extent than the Western nations.

IMPLICATIONS FOR ECONOMIC DEVELOPMENT

A major justification for political independence was that it would bring an end to economic exploitation resulting from colonial imperialism and would permit economic growth and a more equal distribution of economic benefits to the citizenry. Thus, nationhood was viewed not only as a means of achieving equality of opportunity and as being consistent with democratic theory but also as conferring new and proper economic rights on the general population.[9] The drive toward economic development, under the conditions of the underdeveloped new states, required many changes in the old economic system and led, among other things, to another decision of nationhood, How large a role should the government play in the economy?

To document this decision of nationhood, we examine here the relationship between egalitarianism and the economic ideologies of the West Indian leaders, one important aspect of this decision. We classified the leaders into five types according to their views on the proper role of the government in the economy of their territories. The five types follow.

Reactionaries: those who thought the state's role should be about what it was before the rise of the nationalist movements and should not extend beyond providing basic services such as a postal system, roads, police, and fire protection.

Conservatives: those who wanted roughly to maintain the present situation, with the state providing the basic services as well as being partly responsible for welfare schemes for the ill, aged, and unemployed, for public works, and for a general education system but with the reservations that taxation should be less discriminatory against the

---

[9] The economic justification for political independence and especially its implications for the rights and duties of the lower classes have been the subjects of detailed research by Phillips (1963) to appear in shortened version in Bell (1967).

entrepreneur class and that government should be less protective of labor union interests.

Populists: those who lacked long-term economic policies and who were pragmatically concerned with immediate bread-and-butter issues, although accepting a belief in a market economy geared to the demands of labor unions or mass-based political organizations.

Liberals: those who granted greater intervention of the government in the economy but who did not forsee changes beyond the achievement of modern welfare capitalism.

Radicals: those who advocated fundamental changes in the present system so that the state would become the major factor in determining local economic life, with the extreme radicals seeking the abolishment of all private property.

One might expect the egalitarians to be more left in their ideologies, that is, more committed to greater government intervention in the economy than the inegalitarians. This is precisely what the data in Table 13.3 show. Forty-eight percent of the egalitarians were radical

Table 13.3 *Percentage of West Indian Leaders Having Certain Economic Ideologies by Egalitarianism*

Economic Ideologies	Egalitarian	Inegalitarian
Radical	48	0
Liberal	41	10
Populist	11	9
Conservative	0	49
Reactionary	0	32
Total	100	100
Number of cases	(44)	(68)

compared to none of the inegalitarians; 41 percent were liberal compared to 10 percent of the inegalitarians; 11 percent were populist compared to 9 percent; and none of the egalitarians were either conservative or reactionary as compared to 81 percent of the inegalitarians.

This evidence supports the notion that most egalitarians perceived a reordering of the economy as a prerequisite for the attainment of equality of opportunity. It must be noted, however, that egalitarian attitudes were not an exclusive preserve of radical economic ideologists. In fact, slightly over half of all the egalitarians were either liberals or populists. The data reported in Table 13.3 are consistent with findings we have reported elsewhere: if a person was an opponent of the democratic revolution in the West Indies then the chances were that he was also out of step with the nationalist movements whose progressive policies were, in contrast to the rigidly stratified social system that then existed, supportive of political, economic, and social egalitarian principles (Bell, 1964; Moskos, 1967; Moskos and Bell, 1964b).

Like the desire for political independence, we regard a left economic ideology (what we will now loosely refer to as socialist beliefs) as a "dependent" variable, whereas equality has more of an "independent" nature. One reason for viewing socialist attitudes as an effect of egalitarianism was that this was the description given by the West Indian leaders of their personal ideological development. In addition, with regard to its theoretical meaning as well as its role in the history of ideas, socialism concerns instrumentalities dealing with structuring the economy in a way that facilitates the establishment of a certain kind of classless society. In other words, socialism is an economic means to attain more general social consequences, and conceptually it is egalitarianism that leads to a socialist economic ideology, not the other way around. Egalitarians in the colonial circumstance wanted to gain control of their governments by means of political independence and to enlarge the role of government after doing so. Both actions were means of getting the power necessary to transform their societies, the first by taking legitimate governmental power in their hands and the second by expanding that power.

Another implication of equality for economic development can be mentioned here only in passing. The realities of economic growth are such that as new wealth develops it may grow faster in the hands of the few than the many, thus contributing to increased incomes of those groups that already have large incomes, unless government intervenes in the process of distribution. This may result in economic inequalities offsetting some of the relative gains from the spread of a minimum set of economic rights to all members of the society, but it does not offset the absolute gains thereby achieved. In addition, it is by no means agreed among economists that economic inequalities necessarily contribute to economic growth and that economic equalities retard it, although some contend that this is so. In fact, in a discussion of underdeveloped areas Myrdal goes so far as to suggest the opposite:

If we seek to learn from what has actually happened in the richer countries which during the last half-century have proceeded far in the direction of greater equality of opportunities we reach . . . a dynamic theory: that the realisation of more equal opportunities has been needed to spur and sustain economic progress as well as to make good the assumptions of social democracy. A corollary to this is the important fact that in a progressive society—characterized by both redistributional reforms and economic growth as the two types of social change mutually support each other by circular causation—the improvement of the lot of the poor can often be won without substantial sacrifices from those who are better off and is sometimes not only compatible with, but a condition for, the attainment of higher levels in all income brackets, including the higher ones (Myrdal, 1957, p. 121).

IMPLICATIONS FOR SOCIAL AND
CULTURAL DEVELOPMENT

Along with the problems of political modernization, foreign affairs, and economic growth, there are also decisions to be made setting the direction and tempo of social and cultural development in the new states. Our hypothesis is that the distribution of egalitarian attitudes is consequential for this decision-making process. It is tested below by relating attitudes toward equality to a sample of three attitudes toward social and cultural development.

Complementing the ideals of liberty and equality in the triad of the Rights of Man is the desire for fraternity—the reduction of racial, religious, and class distinctions between groups and individuals within a society. With fraternity, as with political democracy, we again are dealing with an associative trait or correlate of egalitarianism rather than one of its effects. To obtain an indicator of fraternalism, we constructed a measure of social inclusivism (or conversely social distance) composed by comparing the attitudes of West Indian leaders toward reducing social barriers *within* their own countries to their attitudes toward increasing their contact with persons *outside* the West Indies.

Leaders who placed highest priority on eliminating internal social barriers were termed "social inclusivists"; conversely, persons who placed secondary emphasis on reducing internal social barriers or who favored the perpetuation of such social distinctions within their societies were designated "social exclusivists." Within the West Indies, of course, as in other colonies, there was a tendency especially among the upper socioeconomic sections to view the imperial power as home

Table 13.4 *Percentage of West Indian Leaders Having Certain Attitudes toward Social and Cultural Development by Egalitarianism*

Attitudes toward Social and Cultural Development	Egalitarian	Inegalitarian
Priority of concern with social inclusiveness		
Greatest need for reducing social barriers at home (inclusivist)	89	13
Greatest need for increasing social contact abroad (exclusivist)	11	87
Total	100	100
Number of cases	(44)	(68)
Teaching of West Indian history (Africa and slavery)		
Favors more emphasis	95	16
Opposes more emphasis	5	84
Total	100	100
Number of cases	(44)	(68)
Desired direction of future cultural development		
Uniquely West Indian	82	31
Basically Anglo-European	18	69
Total	100	100
Number of cases	(44)	(68)

and to prefer contact with "home" rather than with the subordinate groups in the colony.

As shown in Table 13.4, the correlation between favorable attitudes toward equality and social inclusivism is very high. Eighty-nine percent of the egalitarians are social inclusivists compared to only 13 percent of the inegalitarians.

The interviews revealed that the exclusivists were acutely conscious of the institutionalized color and class distinctions of West Indian society and saw the reduction of such distinctions as a peril to their own social status. The inclusivists, on the other hand, thought the realization of the West Indian democratic revolution required an equal access to and equal treatment within public facilities and institutions for all West Indians. In 1961 the nationalist and then premier of Jamaica, Norman W. Manley, addressing a convention of teachers, spoke of this concern.

Let the voice of reason in this country remember that all has not yet been won in Jamaica, let it be understood what we can contribute to the future as a nation that can show the world how black, brown, white, Chinese, Indians—all the races of the world—can dwell together in harmony. . . . We must fight against all traces of discrimination which in fact do exist in this country, but fight always for one purpose—that we will make our contribution to the purpose of God and the purpose of History that created all men equal in the land.

Related to the issue of social inclusivism, with its *leitmotiv* of popular participation in all aspects of the new society, is the question of the cultural development of the West Indies. A popular theme of West Indian fiction and social commentary deals with the question of cultural identity. In recent years this theme has taken the form of a growing consciousness of the unique qualities of the West Indian people. A mood is reflected in this where the proper credentials of nationhood are seen as including an impressive "indigenous" cultural tradition.

Two items in this study measure the leaders' views toward West Indian cultural development. The first concerned attitudes toward teaching the African and slave history of the West Indies in the schools, or as modified in Trinidad and British Guiana for the appropriate respondents, the teaching of the history of the indentured laborers from India. This emphasis on the West Indian past contrasted greatly with the prevailing manner in which history was usually taught in the colonial school system with its almost exclusive concern with the "mother country," the United Kingdom, British cultural contributions, and the world seen through British eyes.[10] Answers were categorized into those favoring or opposing the emphasis of West Indian history.

A second item measuring attitudes toward future cultural development concerned a rather direct question about the leaders' preferences for Anglo-European as opposed to West Indian cultural forms. The answers were simply dichotomized as being primarily West Indian or basically Anglo-European.

Another implication of equality, as indicated in Table 13.4, is shown in the distribution of attitudes toward the teaching of West Indian history and future cultural development. Ninety-five percent of the egalitarians compared to only 16 percent of the inegalitarians favored teaching West Indian history with an emphasis on African origins and slavery, or the Indian origins and indentured labor; and 82 per-

[10] At the time this fieldwork was done, slight corrections in the form of West Indian histories written by West Indians of anticolonial persuasion were beginning to be introduced in a few schools.

cent compared to 31 percent desired a distinctively West Indian future cultural development.

In the wake of the West Indian political independence movements that were engendered by egalitarian beliefs and supported by democratic and social inclusivist principles, our findings indicate there has arisen a new pride in the region's background and local qualities. That is, this new consciousness of West Indian history and culture (what we have called the West Indian Romantic movement), although a consequence of the independence movements, has in turn become another aspect of West Indian nationalism alongside the original Enlightenment (especially egalitarian) values. In brief, the early political nationalism has begun to merge with a later cultural nationalism.

For West Indians, such a cultural nationalism may become an honest and accurate counterbalance to the imperial versions of history and cultural forms with their implicit denigration of the backgrounds of the vast majority of West Indians. But if carried to extreme, it may lapse into another kind of chauvinism or into what Barrington Moore (1958) has termed "nativistic egalitarianism." This could well be a perversion of the doctrine of equality. It might start by denying an out-group's claim to superiority by emphasizing similarities within the in-group and might end with the in-group regarding itself as superior to everyone else and rejecting everything, no matter how intrinsically worthy, that was not "indigenous."

For example, some aspects of incipient West Indian Romanticism stress common racial identity as a source of social cohesion. This emphasis leads to invidious comparisons with nations of predominantly fair-skinned peoples and a heightening of ethnic and racial cleavages between citizens in the emergent Caribbean nations themselves. Nonetheless, we wish to emphasize that although notice must be paid to potentially deleterious strains in the modern West Indian awakening, the major current of West Indian nationalism at the time of this field research was definitely within the humanitarian tradition and strongly motivated by its egalitarian underpinnings.

CONCLUSION

In this chapter we have described and analyzed attitudes of top national leaders toward equality, and we have shown some of the implications for attitudes toward political, economic, social, and cultural change, attitudes that constitute important aspects of the images of the future that are shaping the emerging future in new Caribbean nations or near nations.

Elsewhere, we have shown that there has been a long-term trend toward equality throughout much of West Indian history (*cf.* Bell, 1964; Moskos and Bell, 1965). Thus, the egalitarian-sponsored drive to nationhood represents a continuity with the past. An important process underlying the spread of equality has been the resolution of questions of the legitimacy of particular institutions: certain ideas have led to the questioning of structural arrangements and ideas held by elites have been of particular importance. Thus, the distribution and interrelationships of the attitudes of modern-day West Indian leaders who constitute the new national elites are important indicators of the chances for future structural changes toward more equality and the manner, whether through planned change or violent revolution or static oligarchy, of their accomplishment or retardation.

The over-all level of egalitarianism among West Indian leaders was not overwhelmingly high, but 39 percent, on a rather stringent test, were definitely favorable to the spread of equality. There was variation by country, with the percentage of egalitarians among national leaders being 55 in British Guiana, 50 in Jamaica, 41 in Trinidad, and 32 in the sample of three smaller islands from the Little-Eight.

Some of the variation in egalitarian attitudes was explained by the social differentiation of elites: egalitarians tended to be young; either highly (college or higher) or poorly (elementary only) educated but not in between (secondary school only); dark brown or black in skin color; not wealthy; and leaders of secular and mass-based organizations, specifically political parties or labor unions. But the correlations were not perfect, and there were exceptions to the general pattern, exceptions that the self-interest hypothesis could not explain (as illustrated by the U-shaped correlation with education).

The implications of attitudes toward equality for political, economic, and social development appear to be far-reaching and highly significant. Some of them have been documented in this chapter for these emergent nations as their new national leaders set the course for an independent future. For *political development,* the egalitarian ideal fostered the independence movements as a means to achieve the image of a new egalitarian society, and it tended to be coupled with the ideal of political democracy in doing so. Egalitarianism generally supports democratic values, and even more clearly inegalitarianism supports authoritarian values. Should the inegalitarians be successful in stalling the trend toward equality by manipulation of the democratic process, however, then the egalitarians may be forced to recommend nondemocratic methods, as the authoritarian idealists already do. With respect to foreign affairs, egalitarianism tends to produce neutralist attitudes compared to inegalitarianism that fosters pro-Western attitudes.

For *economic development*, favorable attitudes toward equality result in left economic ideologies whereas unfavorable attitudes toward equality result in conservative or reactionary economic ideologies. The egalitarians generally favor a large role of government in the affairs of the economy for the purpose of reordering the economy for the benefit of the masses of the people. Also, it was suggested that distributional and other reforms could be beneficial to economic growth.

For *social and cultural development*, egalitarianism is linked with the desire to create a socially inclusive society, to break down ascribed social barriers. Furthermore, it produces a drive toward the West Indianization of cultural traditions and the teaching of a new version of social and cultural history in the schools, a history that highlights the ancestors of the lower classes. The latter could be an important corrective to some of the deleterious aspects of cultural domination by the imperial power, but it may contain the danger of being perverted into an exclusivist movement in contradiction to the underlying egalitarian drive.

Finally, through this attitudinal study, we have tried to reconstruct a small piece of social reality by looking through the eyes of elites in these emergent nations. It is, after all, such leaders' perceptions and motivations, their judgments and involvements, that importantly determine for them, as for anyone, the stimulus to which they respond, the goals they try to reach, and the meaning they attach to the actions they decide to take. Leaders, by definition, shape the future more than ordinary men, and therefore shape both the present and the past. Their attitudes toward equality, especially since such attitudes have been the driving force behind much of modern man's history, have obvious and important implications for major aspects of development. This is true not only of the West Indies but also of other nations, both new and old—in fact for humankind as a whole.

REFERENCES

Bell, W., 1960. Images of the United States and the Soviet Union held by Jamaican elite groups. *World Politics*, **12**, 225–248.

Bell, W., 1964. *Jamaican leaders; political attitudes in a new nation.* Berkeley and Los Angeles: Univ. of Cal. Press.

Bell, W. (Ed.), 1967. *The democratic revolution in the West Indies: studies in nationalism, leadership, and the belief in progress.* Cambridge, Mass.: Schenkman.

Bell, W., and Oxaal, I., 1964. *Decisions of nationhood: political and social development in the British Caribbean.* Denver, Col.: Social Science Foundation, Univ. of Denver.

Duke, J. T., 1967. Egalitarianism and future leaders in Jamaica. In Bell, W. (Ed.), *The democratic revolution in the West Indies.* Cambridge, Mass.: Schenkman, 115–139.

Mack, R. W., 1967. Race, class, and power in Barbados. In Bell, W. (Ed.), *The democratic revolution in the West Indies.* Cambridge, Mass.: Schenkman, 140–164.

Manley, N. W., 1961. Address by the Premier to the Jamaican Union of teachers.

Mau, J. A., 1963. Social change and belief in progress: a study of images of the future in Jamaica. Unpublished doctoral dissertation, Univ. of Cal., Los Angeles.

Moore, B., Jr., 1958. *Political power and social theory.* Cambridge, Mass.: Harvard Univ. Press.

Moskos, C. C., Jr., 1967. *The sociology of political independence: A study of nationalist attitudes among West Indian leaders.* Cambridge, Mass.: Schenkman.

Moskos, C. C., Jr., and Bell, W., 1964a. Emergent Caribbean nations face the outside world. *Social Problems, 12,* 24–41.

Moskos, C. C., Jr., and Bell, W., 1964b. West Indian nationalism. *New Society,* No. 69, 16–18.

Moskos, C. C., Jr., and Bell, W., 1964c. Attitudes toward democracy among leaders in four emergent nations. *Brit. J. Sociol., 15,* 317–337.

Mydral, G., 1957. *Economic theory and underdeveloped regions.* London: Gerald Duckworth.

Nowak, S., 1960. Equalitarian attitudes of Warsaw students. *Amer. sociol. Rev., 25,* 219–231.

Oxaal, I., 1967. *Black intellectuals come to power: the rise of Creole nationalism in Trinidad and Tobago.* Cambridge, Mass.: Schenkman.

Phillips, A. P., 1963. The development of a modern labor force in Antigua. Unpublished doctoral dissertation, Univ. of Cal., Los Angeles.

Tawney, R. H., 1962. *Equality.* London: Allen and Unwin.

de Tocqueville, A., 1961. *Democracy in America.* New York: New American Library.

14.   Mass Communication, Attitude Stability, and Change

Joseph T. Klapper

INTRODUCTION

The observed effects of mass communication upon attitude stability and attitude change can be summarized quite briefly. Although the findings themselves are no longer a new story to researchers interested in this specialized area, the story will be rehearsed here as background for what will follow. The rehearsal will be as brief as possible, providing only the most essential minimum of documentation for each of the cited findings. We will then turn to a more interesting topic: the *process* of mass communication effects or, put another way, a partial accounting of why the effects of mass communication are what they are.

OBSERVED EFFECTS

Twenty-odd years of mass communication research have identified some tendencies that are basic and even axiomatic. Perhaps most basic and widely confirmed is the finding that mass communication ordinarily serves as an agent of reinforcement for such attitudes, opinions, and behavioral tendencies as the individual audience members already possess. The term "reinforcement," it must be noted, is not used here in the sense that it is employed in learning theories but rather with less specialized reference to the intensification or support of existing attitudes against the possibly corrosive effects of time and counterinfluences.

A second finding, and a logical correlate of the first, is that mass communication rarely serves as an agent of attitude conversion. Of course, this is not to say that mass communication *never* produces attitude *changes,* but only that conversion in the sense of a reversal of the *direction* of an attitude is a rare effect that occurs under highly specific conditions.

Types of attitude change other than conversion are more common. Thus, the third basic finding is that mass communication often *modifies* existing attitudes of audience members in one direction or the other but to a degree short of nullifying the attitude or of effecting conversion.

The fourth basic finding that needs to be cited here is that mass communication has been found extremely effective in *creating* attitudes or opinions in regard to topics on which the audience member had no previous opinion at all.

Several of these basic findings were documented as early as 1944 by Lazarsfeld, Berelson, and Gaudet (1948) in their now classic study *The People's Choice,* dealing with how the voter made up his mind for whom to vote in the 1940 presidential election, in which Wendell Wilkie opposed Franklin D. Roosevelt. *The People's Choice* reported a panel study involving interviews with a sample of some 600 persons that began *before* the nominating conventions and were repeated at approximately monthly intervals until just after election day. Suitable controls were employed to check the possible influence of the panel procedure itself, which was found to be negligible. The procedure thus permitted a record of the decisions, vacillations, changes, and reported votes of some 600 persons during five months of exposure to campaign propaganda. The final accounting is extremely illuminating.

Fifty-three percent[1] of the respondents reported voting in November for the person for whom they had said they would vote when first interviewed. If mass communication had any effect at all upon these people, the effect was reinforcive. In contrast, some 5 percent of the respondents shifted to the opposition. The rest of the respondents vacillated in the *degree* of their commitment to one candidate, being at times certain that they would vote for him and at times somewhat uncertain but never to the point of declaring for the opposition.

---

[1] These figures deviate slightly from those cited by Lazarsfeld, Berelson, and Gaudet due to different definitions of the terms "reinforcement" and "conversion." The discrepant orders of magnitude occur by either set of definitions.

Among these respondents, then, reinforcement was found to be by far the most common effect, occurring at a rate of roughly ten times that of conversion. Conversion was found to be the least common effect. Changes in *intensity* of attitude, but not *direction* of attitude, made up the bulk of the residue.

Roughly similar findings have emerged from numerous other studies, including a study of the 1948 election pursued by Berelson, Lazarsfeld, and McPhee (1954) as well as studies involving attitudes toward the United Nations (Star and Hughes, 1950), toward the oil industry (Bureau of Applied Social Research, 1954), and toward a wide range of other matters in addition to partisan political opinions.

More refined data in *The People's Choice* related effect to degree of exposure to campaign propaganda. In general, reinforcement was most marked among those who were most exposed, although the exposure variable was closely related in turn to extent of interest in the election. Let it be clear that the term "reinforcement" is not used here where the more simple term "constancy" would do as well. On the contrary, the partisan propaganda served, in all but a handful of cases, to *intensify* respondent convictions, to *buttress* these convictions against opposing propaganda and therefore actively to reinforce existing attitudes. It is important to remember that reinforcement is itself an effect, not an absence of effect.

Further documentation of the relative incidence of reinforcement, conversion, and attitude change short of conversion can be supplied readily, but it is not necessary in the present context. Instead we may turn more profitably to consideration of some of the factors and conditions that are apparently responsible for the relative incidence of these effects.

Although somewhat digressive, it is germane to note at this point that the identification of the factors responsible for the relative incidence of the effects was long delayed by the persistence in mass communication research of what has become known as the "hypodermic model." With rare exceptions, mass communication research up to the late 1950's was designed on the implicit or explicit assumption that the communication was a pure stimulus, like the serum in a hypodermic syringe, which, when injected, would either produce a response or would fail to do so. This simple S-R model was of course duly modified into an S-O-R model, with the audience member as the organism. Although this was a step in the right direction, it can hardly be said that it provided any dramatic breakthroughs. Not until the late 1950's and early 1960's did this model give real ground to the current model. Today's model is at once so simple and obvious in concept and so complex in implementation that it can scarcely be called a model at all. More accurately described, it is a *point of view,* on the basis of which models are designed for specific studies. In brief, this approach no longer conceives the phenomenon under study as a unidirectional affair with one independent variable. Instead, the mass communication situation is viewed as an interactive life experience, in which the audience member and his social milieu affect the nature of the communication that he is exposed to and mediate its effects upon him. The process is regarded as multidirectional, and the independent variables are recognized as numerous. In any given study plan, provision must be made for investigating and controlling these several independent variables.

The process of effect is, in my opinion, almost always a manifestation of one or more of three roads. I have previously formulated these roads and I here draw for their description on my previously published work (Klapper, 1960).

> First, I propose that mass communication *ordinarily* does not serve as a necessary and sufficient cause of audience effects, but rather functions among and through a nexus of mediating factors and influences.
>
> Secondly, I propose that these mediating factors are such that they typically render mass communication a contributory agent, but not the sole cause, in a process of reinforcing the existing conditions. (Regardless of the condition in question—be it the vote intentions of audience members, their tendency toward or away from delinquent behavior, or their general orientation toward life and its problems—and regardless of whether the effect in question be social or individual, the media are more likely to reinforce than to change.)
>
> Thirdly, I propose that on such occasions as mass communication does function in the service of change, one of two conditions is likely to exist. Either:
>
>   (*a*) the mediating factors will be found to be inoperative and the effect of the media will be found to be direct; or
>
>   (*b*) the mediating factors, which normally favor reinforcement, will be found to be themselves impelling toward change.

THE MEDIATING FACTORS

To whatever degree the propositions summarized above are valid, a description of the process of effect will involve identifying the mediating factors and observing them at work. Let us first look at several which are, as it were, resident in the audience member. They are part of the *O* in the now obsolete S-O-R formula. They are also likely to be old friends—familiars long known but perhaps not so widely considered as mediating factors that tend to make mass communications agents of reinforcement.

The most basic of these mediators are audience "predispositions" and their progeny, the *selective processes*. The term "predisposition" is here used in its everyday sense to mean an existing tendency toward or against some view or some mode of behavior. It is now quite firmly established that people's predisposition largely govern the way they *use* mass media. The immediate manifestations of this tendency are known as the selective processes. It has become traditional to talk in terms of three selective processes, namely, *selective exposure, selective retention,* and *selective perception*.

By way of quick review, *selective exposure* refers to the fact that when people have the choice, they are more likely to expose themselves to mass communications that accord with the interests and views that they already have and less likely to select communications not in accord with them. Thus, they expose themselves selectively. For example, both of the presidential election studies previously cited (Berelson *et al.*, 1954; Lazarsfeld *et al.*, 1948) indicated that during a political campaign, partisans chose much more frequently to expose themselves to communications from the party or candidate they favored than from the opposition. Various other studies provide confirmatory findings. For example, Schramm and Carter (1959) found that a "telethon" (a very long television program) broadcast a few years ago on election eve under Republican sponsorship and designed to convert Democratic voters to the support of a Republican candidate played to an audience in which Republicans outnumbered Democrats by two to one. A campaign to impart information about the United Nations and win friends for the organization was found by Star and Hughes (1950) to have reached, almost exclusively, persons who were already well informed about the United Nations and well disposed toward it. Other available examples are legion. The essential point is that selective exposure occurs, and when it occurs, it serves as a sieve admitting communications that have a reinforcement potential and screening or obstructing communications with a conversion potential.

Similar selectivity was observed long ago in reference to *retention* of the contents of communications. Repeatedly, people were observed to recall material with which they were sympathetic far better than they recalled material to which they were not sympathetic. The differential degree of *immediate* recall, furthermore, rapidly intensifies over time: unsympathetic material is not only recalled less well to begin with, but it is also forgotten more rapidly than sympathetic material. An early and now classic demonstration of these tendencies was provided by Levine and Murphy (1943). The phenomena have since been observed often, a relatively recent example being the study by Zimmerman and Bauer (1956). Here, then, is another process that mediates the influence of mass communication: *selective retention*. Again, selectivity functions in a way that increases the likelihood of mass communication serving a reinforcive function and decreases the likelihood of its serving a conversion of even a corrosive function.

The third of the selective processes is commonly known as *selective perception*. The term is somewhat of a misnomer, since it refers in fact to what people make of what they *recall* from what they see of hear. A better term would be "reinforcive interpretation," but whatever the term, it refers to a simple fact that is perennially startling: people tend to misperceive and misinterpret unsympathetic communications material in such a way that it becomes for them a statement in support of their own view. This phenomenon, like the other selective processes, was also documented in a now old and classic study, namely, the Allport-Postman study (1945) of rumor and social transmission. One of the more dramatic of their findings involved a picture of an altercation between a white man and a Negro, in which the white man was holding an open razor. As the picture was described by person after person in a chain, only the first of whom had seen the picture, the razor shifted to the hand of the Negro.

Many later findings echo the earlier ones. Some years ago, for example, a poster was displayed in buses and rapid transit facilities that displayed four men (an Oriental, a Negro, a Jew, and a nondescript Caucasian) above the caption, "It takes all races to make our city run." Persons low in racial prejudice were found to take this poster at its face value. Those with overt prejudice also took it at what they considered its face value: they felt that Negroes and Orientals were necessary to perform menial tasks so that the Caucasians would be free to perform the major functions of the city, wherefore, and indeed, "It takes all races to make our city run." To come even more up to date, an interesting reaction was noted by Katz and Feldman (1962) among viewers of the Kennedy-Nixon debate. Persons who recalled statements with which they disagreed tended to ascribe those statements to the candidate they opposed, regardless of who actually said it. Along the same line, a recent study by Mendelsohn (unpublished) noted that the degree of faith which television viewers placed in computer predictions of election results was determined by whether the computer forecast victory for their candidate or his opponent. In short, then, what has been called "selective perception" also serves, as do selective exposure and selective retention, to mediate the effects of mass communication in a way that increases the likelihood of mass communication serving a reinforcive function and decreases the likelihood of its serving a conversion function.

These three selective processes are, of course, external to the communications. They are imposed *upon* the communication by the beholder. But they modify the communication process by mediating the effect of the communication upon the attitude of the beholder, and they do so, as has been indicated, in such a way as ordinarily to render mass communication an agent of reinforcement rather than an agent of conversion.

Various other mediators serve similar functions, and many of them are clearly social in origin. Two of the most important are (1) groups and group norms, and (2) the process of opinion leadership or personal influence.

There is a long tradition of research that has established the crucial role of the group as a source of individual attitudes and opinions. Such attitudes and opinions have been shown repeatedly to derive not only from basic primary groups, such as the family, but also from quasi-primary groups, such as play and peer groups, and from secondary groups, such as those formed by the mere existence of co-workers, co-memberships in the same union local, and the like.

Such groups are of course the source of many of the opinions, attitudes, and values that are reinforced by mass communication through the agencies of selective exposure, selective retention, and selective perception. These group-engendered attitudes derive, in fact, from group norms, and the group continues to serve as an anchoring point in holding the individual to the group opinion, thus directing the selective processes through which the individual reacts to mass communication. An excellent illustration of the end results of this process is seen in the political homogeneity of groups, the degree of which correlates with how primary the group is. For example, *The People's Choice* revealed that at the end of the election campaign of 1940, absolute homogeneity reigned in 96 percent of the families of respondents who voted. (Of 413 such persons, only 17 reported that any member of his or her family voted differently than he did. In 396 cases, the family managed to resolve all differences it may have had during the campaign.) Less overwhelming, but nevertheless marked, homogeneity was observed among co-workers and among members of formal organizations.

Groups also serve in their own right to further mediate the effects of communication, and it would seem that they usually do so in the direction of reinforcement. Both formal and informal group discussion intensifies selective exposure by making group members aware of sympathetic communications, as well as by serving as a secondary arena for transmission of the contents of such communication. Studies by the USIA, for example, have revealed that East Europeans who listen to western broadcasts regularly make each other aware of programs to come and advise each other of the content of the programs they may have missed. At times the process becomes circular: the media advise groups of events, such as teach-ins or rallies, which will enunciate positions that the group favors. At the very least, the media thus serve to assure the group that their position is supported, and at the most the media stimulate the group to direct or indirect participation in the event itself. Media dissemination of communications at the event have a waiting audience before they are actually broadcast or published.

The group and the communication also serve to redefine group norms and to bring drifters back to orthodoxy. McKeachie (1954) has demonstrated, for example, that group discussion of controversial communications will lead members to attitude changes that can best be described as a return from the periphery to the center of sanctioned opinions—a kind of canceling out of the minor attitude changes short of conversion which were mentioned earlier.

This reinforcive increment that groups and communications mutually bestow upon each other has long been exploited by skillful campaigners who may or may not be wholly aware of the scientific bases of the symbiosis and also by skilled propagandists, who are probably well aware of it. Thus, group attendance on specific mass communications and group discussion thereof have typically been a compulsory component of so-called educational campaigns following both rightist and leftist revolutions, and also of campaigns pursued by such apolitical figures as Billy Graham.

This discussion cannot, of course, review all the ways in which groups and group norms may, can, and do serve to mediate the effects of mass communication. We will rest content with having indicated that they do so and with pointing out one other extremely important way in which they do, namely, by serving as an arena for individual face-to-face personal influence.

The term "personal influence" is here used to refer to a phenomenon that has been called a variety of names, including "opinion leadership," "influentialism," "initiation," and "the two-step flow" of communication. The concept, like others cited earlier, was first noted by Lazarsfeld, Berelson, and Gaudet in *The People's Choice*. It has been further investigated and refined, exaggerated, and modified by perhaps 50 different studies and evaluation papers, including those by Lazarsfeld, *et al.*, 1948; Katz and Lazarsfeld, 1955; Merton, 1949; Katz, 1957; Coleman, Katz, and Menzel, 1966; Rogers, 1962 and perhaps 30 other investigators particularly in the areas of rural and industrial sociology and market research.

The bare bones of the concept of personal influence lie in the fact that in reference to decisions in various areas of attitude and behavior, people have been found to be influenced by *specific* other individuals as strongly or more strongly than they have been influenced by mass communication. These others have variously been called opinion leaders, gatekeepers, influentials, initiators, and tastemakers. They are not, however, characteristically political leaders or teachers or preachers or elites. What are the chief demographic characteristics of opinion leaders? Interestingly enough, they cannot be characterized as a whole, apart from those who heed their words. Their chief characteristic is that they can influence the attitudes and opinions of a few people like themselves, typically from one to five others. Even within that sphere, their leadership seldom extends beyond a limited range of topics. For example, the opinion leader heeded on political matters is likely to carry little weight in reference to ladies' fashions or the arts. The influence of the opinion leader is typically exerted in informal face-to-face discourse and may or may not be purposive.

To date, this process of personal influence has been studied in reference to voting; to views on public issues; everyday fashion and marketing decisions, including the choice of what movie to see; the manner in which physicians adopt new drugs; the purchase of new products and, perhaps more thoroughly studied than anything else, the adoption or refusal to adopt new agricultural techniques. In virtually all of these spheres, the exercise of opinion leadership, or of personal influence, has been found to be as critical or more critical than the influence of mass communications.

But in fact, where opinion leadership exists, it has been found typically much involved with mass communication. To begin with, the opinion leader is typically more exposed to appropriate mass communications than are his followers: the political opinion leader reads and sees more mass communication regarding political issues than do his followers. The fashion leader, the what-movie-should-we-see leader, and the agricultural opinion leader variously read more fashion magazines, movie magazines, and farm magazines than do their followers. And either they pass on this information, or they do not pass it on. In this sense they function as "gatekeepers," and it is in this connection that the term "two-step flow" developed. The opinion leader may also direct followers to mass communication to document or promote his opinion, or, vice versa, he may serve to interpret to his followers what mass communication on a given topic *really* means. In short, then, where opinion leadership exists, it mediates the effects of mass communication.

Now what is the direction of this mediation? Clearly, the opinion leader can be an agent in attitude change. In fact, documentation of the existence and characteristics of opinion leaders was closely associated with research on innovation and change. Thus, influence in changing vote intentions, fashions, or effecting adoption of new techniques was seen as a primary function of opinion leaders.

I have suspected for some years that this was an error or rather a research oversight reflecting too narrow a focus. Thus, I noted in 1960 that another finding had been overlooked in the search for change agents: the opinion leader is also typically an embodiment of group norms. His very success as an opinion leader lay in the fact that his advice paid off: it provided the followers satisfaction in terms of the shared values of the informal groups to which both leader and follower belonged. I felt then, and I still feel, that under these circumstances, the weight of opinion leadership is probably conservative. There is at least one interesting and supporting datum: the influence of opinion leaders in regard to changes in voting intention as observed by Berelson, Lazarsfeld, and Gaudet was most prominent on persons whose opinions had deviated away from the group, and its effect was to bring them back within the fold of group opinion.

What is clearly needed is research on opinion leadership that seeks out the phenomenon in instances of *decision-making*, rather than only in instances of change. I suspect that such research would find opinion leaders working in the direction of stabilizing group norms and reinforcing member attitudes more often than in the direction of changing them. If this is so, then opinion leadership, or personal influence, is one more of the factors that may affect the communication process in the direction of reinforcing existing attitudes.

Thus, personal influence, groups and group norms, and the selective processes all serve as mediators, which tend to render mass communication an agent of reinforcement. It is of more than passing interest that most of these mediators are social in function and that all are largely social in origin.

CONVERSION

This discussion has been at some pains to document the view that mass communication very frequently reinforces the views of its audiences and very rarely *converts* those audiences. But this is not to say that mass communication never serves a conversion function. It is rather to say that mass communication rarely serves such a function and that it seems to do so only under quite specific conditions. Conditions favoring such an effect exist when the mediating factors break down or, when in atypical situations, they reverse their direction of mediation.

The former situation is represented, for example, in studies seeking to assess the effects of Voice of America broadcasts to European satellite countries (International Research Associates, 1953). One finding was that those who defected from these countries had, in many instances, lived for years under Stalinistic communism with comparative contentment, either not listening to the Voice of America or remaining unaffected by its broadcasts. The sudden responsiveness of such persons to the broadcasts is bewildering at first sight: apparently, the communications not only made them intensely anticommunist but warm and informed proponents of Western views as well, all within a short time. More intensive study showed that most of these sudden converts had defected for reasons with little directly political bearing. There were, for example, young men facing the draft. There were factory managers who had been demoted for failure to meet their production quotas. For a variety of such reasons, life at home suddenly presented an unattractive future. To avoid this glum outlook, they began searching for something better. When this search began, the Voice of America offered convenient alternatives and thence became an effective *agent* of conversion. More generally when the person was predisposed to change, the voice of America offered alternatives to implement a change. A somewhat similar sequence is suggested by findings on the effect of United Nations information campaigns upon Communist troops participating in the Korean conflict (Schramm and Riley, 1951).

Two points bear emphasis in reference to these instances of conversion. First, the convertees were, in a sense, predisposed to change, and in that sense conversion was a kind of implementive reinforcement. Secondly, the predisposing forces were, like the reinforcive mediators, social in origin. In these cited instances, the social conditions that had nutured reinforcement collapsed, and a different set of social supports was made evident by the media and adopted by the media audience.

But if the commoner effects of mass communication are usually mediated by factors that are social in origin, there is at least one medium capability which is apparently due to the occasional *absence* of these social factors. Specifically, the media have been observed to be quite potent in creating opinions about issues or matters on which the audience has no views at all or lacks any other sources of information. The phenomenon has been demonstrated by social scientists and is observable in naturalistic conditions. Thus, for example, Annis and Meier (1934) found more than thirty years ago that only a few "editorials," written for the experiment, were adequate to create in American students either positive or negative attitudes about the prime minister of Australia. Hovland and his colleagues (1953) noted attitude changes among students after single communications about such topics as the likelihood of the Soviet Union developing an atomic submarine. The capability of the media, or laboratory approximations of the media, in these instances is not hard to explain: a point of view is presented in reference to which the audience member has no information and no defensive (or sympathetic) predispositions. The selective processes are largely inoperative. Groups to which the audience member belongs have no norms on the subject, and opinion leaders are devoid of opinion. The mediating factors, in short, are perforce inoperative, and the communication's message comes through unscreened.

Although the specific topics cited above do not seem very likely to have been particularly salient to their audiences, it cannot be assumed that the mass communication's ability to create opinions and attitudes where none existed before is, therefore, of mere academic interest. Views may thus be born—as, for example, in reference to Soviet atomic capabilities—that will later become socially important predispositions. Furthermore, and perhaps more importantly, such effects can and do occur among children who are at the time without pertinent attitudes simply because the topic is not *as yet* salient in their lives. Thus, Himmelweit, Oppenheim, and Vince (1958) found that British children without other sources of information acquired from television concepts about the characteristics of social classes *other than their own* and about the characteristics of foreign lands and foreign peoples. Views so acquired can be presumed to become susceptible to defense and reinforcement by all the regular mediators and may accordingly be well entrenched by the time the topic in question *becomes* salient to the child.

Considerations such as these lend some urgency to the need felt by communication researchers to learn more of the long-term effects of mass communication. Current interest in longitudinal studies and in studies embracing methods derived from functional theory (Klapper, 1963) are manifestations of attempts to conquer the methodological hurdles of establishing cause and effect relationships over observation periods extending decades rather than weeks. In a world of newly developing countries and newly emerging philosophies, the need for knowledge of the long-term effects of mass communication seems too obvious to belabor.

REFERENCES

Allport, G., and Postman, L. G., 1945. The basic psychology of rumor. *Trans. N. Y. Acad. Sci.,* 8, Series II, 61–81.

Annis, A. D., and Meier, N. C., 1934. The induction of opinion through suggestions by means of planted content. *J. soc. Psychol.,* 5, 65–81.

Berelson, B., Lazarsfeld, P. F., and McPhee, W. N., 1954. *Voting: a study of opinion formation in a presidential campaign.* Chicago: The Univ. of Chicago Press.

Bureau of Applied Social Research, 1954. *The effects of Oil Progress Week, 1952: a summary of a supplemental report.* New York: Bureau of Appl. soc. Res., Columbia Univ.

Coleman, J., Katz, E., and Menzel, H., 1966. *Medical innovations: a diffusion study.* Indianapolis: Bobbs-Merrill.

Himmelweit, Hilde T., Oppenheim, A. N., and Vince, Pamela, 1958. *Television and the child.* London and New York: Oxford Univ. Press.

Hovland, C. I., Janis, I. L., and Kelley, H. H., 1953. *Communication and persuasion.* New Haven: Yale Univ. Press.

International Research Associates, Inc., 1953. Media of communication and the free world as seen by Czechoslovak, Hungarian and Polish refugees: a report prepared for the Division of Radio Program Evaluation of the Department of State.

Katz, E., 1957. The two-step flow of communication: an up-to-date report on an hypothesis. *Publ. Opin. Quart.,* 21, 61–78.

Katz, E., and Feldman, J. J., 1962. The debates in light of research: a survey of surveys. In S. Kraus (Ed.), *The great debates.* Bloomington: Indiana Univ. Press, pp. 173–223.

Katz, E., and Lazarsfeld, P. F., 1955. *Personal influence: the part played by people in the flow of mass communications.* Glencoe, Ill.: The Free Press.

Klapper, J. T., 1960. *The effects of mass communication.* New York: The Free Press.

Klapper, J. T., 1963. Mass communication research: an old road resurveyed. *Publ. Opin. Quart.*, **27**, 515–527.

Lazarsfeld, P. F., Berelson, B., and Gaudet, Hazel, 1948. *The people's choice.* New York: Columbia Univ. Press.

Levine, J. M., and Murphy, G., 1943. The learning and forgetting of controversial material. *J. abnorm. soc. Psychol.*, **38**, 507–517.

McKeachie, W. J., 1954. Individual conformity to attitudes of classroom groups. *J. abnorm. soc. Psychol.*, **49**, 282–289.

Mendelsohn, H. Unpublished

Merton, R. K., 1949. Patterns of influence: a study of interpersonal influence and of communications behavior in a local community. In P. F. Lazarsfeld and F. N. Stanton (Eds.), *Communications research, 1948–1949.* New York: Harper, pp. 180–219.

Rogers, E. M., 1962. *Diffusion of innovations.* New York: The Free Press.

Schramm, W., and Carter, R. F., 1959. Effectiveness of a political telethon. *Publ. Opin. Quart.*, **23**, 121–126.

Schramm, W., and Riley, J. W., Jr., 1951. Communication in the Sovietized state as demonstrated in Korea. *Amer. Sociol. Rev.*, **16**, 757–766.

Star, Shirley A., and Hughes, Helen McG., 1950. Report of an educational campaign: The Cincinnati plan for the United Nations. *Amer. J. Sociol.*, **55**, 389–400.

Zimmerman, Claire, and Bauer, R. A., 1956. The effect of an audience upon what is remembered. *Publ. Opin. Quart.*, **20**, 238–248.

Author Index